Universal Principles
of Design

ROCKPORT

Universal Principles
of Design

William Lidwell
Kritina Holden
Jill Butler

GLOUCESTER MASSACHUSETTS

ROCKPORT
PUBLISHERS

The Art Institute Of Houston
Resource Center
1900 Yorktown
Houston Texas 77056

100 Ways to Enhance Usability,
Influence Perception, Increase Appeal, Make Better
Design Decisions, and Teach through Design

First published in the United States
of America by:

Rockport Publishers, Inc.
33 Commercial Street
Gloucester, Massachusetts 01930-5089
Telephone: (978) 282-9590
Fax: (978) 283-2742
www.rockpub.com

Library of Congress
Cataloging-in-Publication Data
Lidwell, William.
    Universal principles of design :
    a cross-disciplinary reference /
William Lidwell, Kritina Holden, and
Jill Butler.
        p.   cm.
    ISBN 1-59253-007-9 (paper over board)
    1. Design-Dictionaries. I. Holden, Kritina. II.
        Butler, Jill. III. Title.
    NK1165.L53 2003
    745.4'03—dc21   2003009384
                                  CIP

ISBN 1-59253-007-9

10 9 8 7 6 5 4 3 2 1

Design: Collaborated, Inc.
        James Evelock
        Tony Leone

Printed in China

For our dads...

John C. Butler
Larry W. Lidwell

Contents

Alphabetical

Contents

Categorical

Introduction

Not long ago, designers were eclectic generalists. They studied art, science, and religion in order to understand the basic workings of nature, and then applied what they learned to solve the problems of the day. Over time, the quantity and complexity of accumulated knowledge led to increased specialization among designers, and breadth of knowledge was increasingly traded for depth of knowledge. This trend continues today. As designers become more specialized, awareness of advances and discoveries in other areas of specialization diminishes. This is inevitable and unfortunate, since much can be learned from progress in other design disciplines.

Convenient access to cross-disciplinary design knowledge has not previously been available. A designer interested in learning about other areas of specialization would have to study texts from many different design disciplines. Determining which texts in each discipline are worthy of study would be the first challenge, deciphering the specialized terminology of the texts the second, and enduring the depth of detail the third. The effort is significant, and rarely expended beyond brief excursions into unfamiliar areas to research specific problems. The goal of this book is to assist designers with these challenges, and reduce the effort required to learn about the key principles of design across disciplines.

The concepts in this book, broadly referred to as "principles," consist of laws, guidelines, human biases, and general design considerations. The principles were selected from a variety of design disciplines based on several factors, including utility, degree of misuse or misunderstanding, and strength of supporting evidence. The selection of 100 concepts should not be interpreted to mean that there are only 100 relevant principles of design—there are obviously many more.

The book is organized alphabetically so that principles can be easily and quickly referenced by name. For those interested in addressing a specific problem of design, the principles have also been indexed by questions commonly confronting designers (see previous page). Each principle is presented in a two-page format. The left-hand page contains a succinct definition, a full description of the principle, examples of its use, and guidelines for use. Side notes appear to the right of the text, and provide elaborations and references. The right-hand page contains visual examples and related graphics to support a deeper understanding of the principle.

Sound design is not only within the reach of a small set of uniquely talented individuals, but can be achieved by virtually all designers. The use of well-established design principles increases the probability that a design will be successful. Use *Universal Principles of Design* as a resource to increase your cross-disciplinary knowledge and understanding of design, promote brainstorming and idea generation for design problems, and refresh your memory of design principles that are infrequently applied. Finally, use it as a means of checking the quality of your design process and product. A paraphrase of William Strunk's famous admonition makes the point nicely:

The best designers sometimes disregard the principles of design. When they do so, however, there is usually some compensating merit attained at the cost of the violation. Unless you are certain of doing as well, it is best to abide by the principles.

William Lidwell
Kritina Holden
Jill Butler

80/20 Rule

A high percentage of effects in any large system are caused by a low percentage of variables.[1]

The 80/20 rule asserts that approximately 80 percent of the effects generated by any large system are caused by 20 percent of the variables in that system. The 80/20 rule is observed in all large systems, including those in economics, management, user interface design, quality control, and engineering, to name a few. The specific percentages are not important, as measures of actual systems indicate that the proportion of critical variables varies between 10 percent and 30 percent. The universality of the 80/20 rule suggests a link to normally distributed systems, which limits its application to variables that are influenced by many small and unrelated effects—e.g., systems that are used by large numbers of people in a variety of ways. A few examples of the 80/20 rule include:[2]

80 percent of a product's usage involves *20* percent of its features.
80 percent of a town's traffic is on *20* percent of its roads.
80 percent of a company's revenue comes from *20* percent of its products.
80 percent of innovation comes from *20* percent of the people.
80 percent of progress comes from *20* percent of the effort.
80 percent of errors are caused by *20* percent of the components.

The 80/20 rule is useful for focusing resources and, in turn, realizing greater efficiencies in design. For example, if the critical 20 percent of a product's features are used 80 percent of the time, design and testing resources should focus primarily on those features. The remaining 80 percent of the features should be reevaluated to verify their value in the design. Similarly, when redesigning systems to make them more efficient, focusing on aspects of the system beyond the critical 20 percent quickly yields diminishing returns; improvements beyond the critical 20 percent will result in less substantial gains that are often offset by the introduction of errors or new problems into the system.

All elements in a design are not created equal. Use the 80/20 rule to assess the value of elements, target areas of redesign and optimization, and focus resources in an efficient manner. Noncritical functions that are part of the less-important 80 percent should be minimized or removed altogether from the design. When time and resources are limited, resist efforts to correct and optimize designs beyond the critical 20 percent, as such efforts yield diminishing returns. Generally, limit the application of the 80/20 rule to variables in a system that are influenced by many small and unrelated effects.

See also Cost-Benefit, Form Follows Function, Highlighting, and Normal Distribution.

[1] Also known as *Pareto's Principle*, *Juran's Principle*, and *Vital Few and Trivial Many Rule*.

[2] The first recognition of the 80/20 rule is attributed to Vilfredo Pareto, an Italian economist who observed that 20 percent of the Italian people possessed 80 percent of the wealth. The seminal work on the 80/20 rule is *Quality Control Handbook* by Joseph M. Juran (Ed.), McGraw-Hill, 1951.

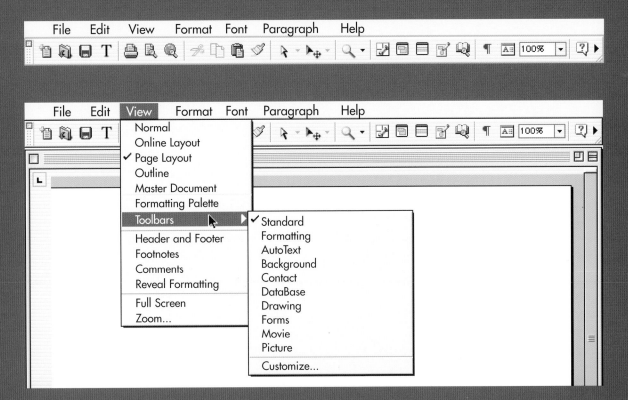

Graphical user interfaces conceal most of their functions in drop-down menus (bottom image). This reduces the complexity of the display, but also makes frequently used functions more difficult to access. Identifying the critical 20 percent of the functions and making them readily available in toolbars solves the problem (top image).

Accessibility

Objects and environments should be designed to be usable, without modification, by as many people as possible.[1]

The principle of accessibility asserts that designs should be usable by people of diverse abilities, without special adaptation or modification. Historically, accessibility in design focused on accommodating people with disabilities. As knowledge and experience of accessible design increased, it became increasingly clear that many required "accommodations" could be designed to benefit everyone. There are four characteristics of accessible designs: perceptibility, operability, simplicity, and forgiveness.[2]

Perceptibility is achieved when everyone can perceive the design, regardless of sensory abilities. Basic guidelines for improving perceptibility are: present information using redundant coding methods (e.g., textual, iconic, and tactile); provide compatibility with assistive sensory technologies (e.g., ALT tags for images on the Internet); and position controls and information so that seated and standing users can perceive them.

Operability is achieved when everyone can use the design, regardless of physical abilities. Basic guidelines for improving operability are: minimize repetitive actions and the need for sustained physical effort; facilitate use of controls through good affordances and constraints; provide compatibility with assistive physical technologies (e.g., wheelchair access); and position controls and information so that seated and standing users can access them.

Simplicity is achieved when everyone can easily understand and use the design, regardless of experience, literacy, or concentration level. Basic guidelines for improving simplicity are: remove unnecessary complexity; clearly and consistently code and label controls and modes of operation; use progressive disclosure to present only relevant information and controls; provide clear prompting and feedback for all actions; and ensure that reading levels accommodate a wide range of literacy.

Forgiveness is achieved when designs minimize the occurrence and consequences of errors. Basic guidelines for improving forgiveness are: use good affordances and constraints (e.g., controls that can only be used the correct way) to prevent errors from occurring; use confirmations and warnings to reduce the occurrence of errors; and include reversible actions and safety nets to minimize the consequence of errors (e.g., the ability to undo an action).

See also Affordance, Forgiveness, Legibility, Normal Distribution, and Readability.

[1] Also known as *barrier-free design* and *universal design*.

[2] The four characteristics of accessible designs are derived from *W3C Web Content Accessibility Guidelines 1. 0*, 1999; *ADA Accessibility Guidelines for Buildings and Facilities*, 1998; and *Accessible Environments: Toward Universal Design* by Ronald L. Mace, Graeme J. Hardie, and Jaine P. Place, The Center for Universal Design, North Carolina State University, 1996.

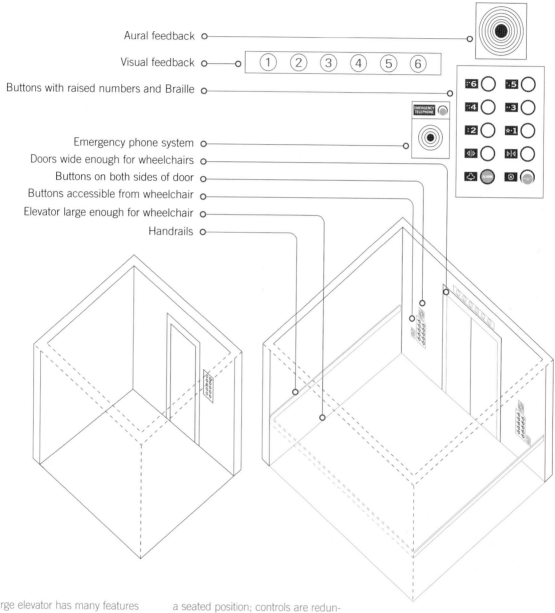

Aural feedback

Visual feedback ①②③④⑤⑥

Buttons with raised numbers and Braille

Emergency phone system

Doors wide enough for wheelchairs

Buttons on both sides of door

Buttons accessible from wheelchair

Elevator large enough for wheelchair

Handrails

The large elevator has many features that make it more accessible than the small elevator: wide doors permit easy access; handrails help people maintain a standing position; two sets of controls are easily accessible from a seated position; controls are redundantly coded with numbers, icons, and Braille; feedback is provided visually and aurally; and an emergency phone system offers access to special assistance.

Advance Organizer

An instructional technique that helps people understand new information in terms of what they already know.

Advance organizers are brief chunks of information—spoken, written, or illustrated—presented prior to new material to help facilitate learning and understanding. They are distinct from overviews and summaries in that they are presented on a more abstract level than the rest of the information—they present the "big picture" prior to the details. Since the technique depends on a defined entry point, it is generally applied to linear presentations (e.g., traditional classroom instruction), and does not work as well in nonlinear, exploratory learning contexts (e.g., free-play simulation).[1]

There are two kinds of advance organizers: expository and comparative. The decision to use or another depends on whether the information is new to people or similar to material they already know. Expository advance organizers are useful when audiences have little or no knowledge similar to the information being taught. For example, prior to presenting information on how to control a forklift to an audience that knows nothing about them, an advance expository organizer would first briefly describe the equipment and its function.[2]

Comparative advance organizers are useful when audiences have existing knowledge similar to the information being presented. For example, in teaching experienced forklift operators about how to control a new type of forklift, an advance comparative organizer would compare and contrast features and operations between the familiar forklift and the new forklift.

The technique's effectiveness has been difficult to validate, but it does appear to have measurable benefits. Use advance organizers in learning situations that begin with an introduction and present information in a linear sequence. When presenting novel information, use expository advance organizers. When presenting information that is similar to what people know, use comparative advance organizers.[3]

See also Inverted Pyramid and Wayfinding.

[1] The seminal work on advance organizers is *The Psychology of Meaningful Verbal Learning*, Grune and Stratton, 1963; and *Educational Psychology: A Cognitive View* (2nd ed.), Holt Reinhart, 1978, both by David P. Ausubel. See also, "In Defense of Advanced Organizers: A Reply to the Critics" by David P. Ausubel, *Review of Educational Research*, vol. 48 (2), p. 251–257.

[2] An overview or summary, by contrast, would just present the key points on how to control a forklift.

[3] See, for example, "Twenty Years of Research on Advance Organizers: Assimilation Theory is Still the Best Predictor of Effects" by Richard E. Mayer, *Instructional Science*, 1979, vol. 8, p. 133–167.

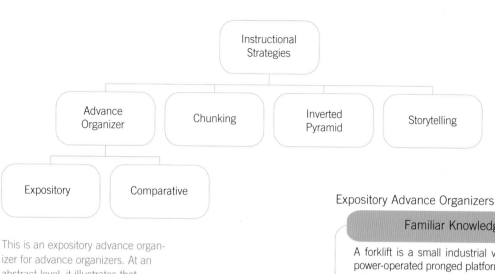

This is an expository advance organizer for advance organizers. At an abstract level, it illustrates that advance organizers are a kind of instructional strategy (like chunking, inverted pyramid, and storytelling) and that there are two types.

An expository advance organizer defines a forklift using familiar concepts (e.g., vehicle) prior to presenting specific information about forklift operation.

Expository Advance Organizers

Familiar Knowledge

A forklift is a small industrial vehicle with a power-operated pronged platform that can be raised and lowered for insertion under a load to be lifted and moved.

New Information

To operate a forklift safely, the operator should know:
1. How a forklift works
2. How to inspect a forklift
3. How to operate a forklift

How a forklift works

How to inspect a forklift

How to operate a forklift

Comparitive Advance Organizers

Familiar Knowledge	New Information
Acme Forklift 1300A	Acme Forklift 2300A
Acme Forklift 1300A Rated Capacity	Acme Forklift 2300A Rated Capacity
Acme Forklift 1300A Load Center	Acme Forklift 2300A Load Center
Acme Forklift 1300A Special Intructions	Acme Forklift 1300A Special Instructions

A comparative advance organizer leverages familiarity with the 1300A model forklift to introduce the 2300A model.

Aesthetic-Usability Effect

Aesthetic designs are perceived as easier to use than less-aesthetic designs.[1]

The aesthetic-usability effect describes a phenomenon in which people perceive more-aesthetic designs as easier to use than less-aesthetic designs—whether they are or not. The effect has been observed in several experiments, and has significant implications regarding the acceptance, use, and performance of a design.[2]

Aesthetic designs look easier to use and have a higher probability of being used, whether or not they actually are easier to use. More usable but less-aesthetic designs may suffer a lack of acceptance that renders issues of usability moot. These perceptions bias subsequent interactions and are resistant to change. For example, in a study of how people use computers, researchers found that early impressions influenced long-term attitudes about their quality and use. A similar phenomenon is well documented with regard to human attractiveness—first impressions of people influence attitude formation and measurably affect how people are perceived and treated.[3]

Aesthetics play an important role in the way a design is used. Aesthetic designs are more effective at fostering positive attitudes than unaesthetic designs, and make people more tolerant of design problems. For example, it is common for people to name and develop feelings toward designs that have fostered positive attitudes (e.g., naming a car), and rare for people to do the same with designs that have fostered negative attitudes. Such personal and positive relationships with a design evoke feelings of affection, loyalty, and patience—all significant factors in the long-term usability and overall success of a design. These positive relationships have implications for how effectively people interact with designs. Positive relationships with a design result in an interaction that helps catalyze creative thinking and problem solving. Negative relationships result in an interaction that narrows thinking and stifles creativity. This is especially important in stressful environments, since stress increases fatigue and reduces cognitive performance.[4]

Always aspire to create aesthetic designs. Aesthetic designs are perceived as easier to use, are more readily accepted and used over time, and promote creative thinking and problem solving. Aesthetic designs also foster positive relationships with people, making them more tolerant of problems with a design.

See also Attractiveness Bias, Form Follows Function, Golden Ratio, Law of Prägnanz, Ockham's Razor, and Rule of Thirds.

[1] Note that the authors use the term *aesthetic-usability effect* for convenient reference. It does not appear in the seminal work or subsequent research.

[2] The seminal work on the aesthetic-usability effect is "Apparent Usability vs. Inherent Usability: Experimental Analysis on the Determinants of the Apparent Usability" by Masaaki Kurosu and Kaori Kashimura, *CHI '95 Conference Companion*, 1995, p. 292–293.

[3] "Forming Impressions of Personality" by Solomon E. Asch, *Journal of Abnormal and Social Psychology*, 1946, vol. 41, 258–290.

[4] "Emotion & Design: Attractive Things Work Better" by Donald Norman, www.jnd.org, 2002.

Nokia was one of the first companies to realize that adoption of cellular phones required more than basic communication features. Cellular phones need to be recharged frequently, carried around, and often suffer from signal loss or interference; they are not trouble-free devices. Aesthetic elements like color covers and customizable rings are more than ornaments; the aesthetic elements create a positive relationship with users that, in turn, make such troubles more tolerable and the devices more successful.

While VCR's around the world continue flashing *12:00* because users cannot figure out the poorly designed time and recording controls, TiVo is setting a new bar for recording convenience and usability. TiVo's intelligent and automated recording features, simple navigation through attractive on-screen menus, and pleasant and distinct auditory feedback are changing the way people record and watch their favorite programs.

Affordance

A property in which the physical characteristics of an object or environment influence its function.

Objects and environments are better suited for some functions than others. Round wheels are better suited than square wheels for rolling; therefore, round wheels are said to better afford rolling. Stairs are better suited than fences for climbing; therefore, stairs are said to better afford climbing. This is not to say that square wheels cannot be rolled or fences climbed, rather that the physical characteristics of round wheels and fences influence the way they function and are likely to be used.[1]

When the affordance of an object or environment corresponds with its intended function, the design will perform more efficiently and will be easier to use. Conversely, when the affordance of an object or environment conflicts with its intended function, the design will perform less efficiently and be more difficult to use. For example, a door with a handle affords pulling. Sometimes, doors with handles are designed to open only by pushing—the affordance of the handle conflicts with the door's function. Replace the handle with a flat plate, and it now affords pushing—the affordance of the flat plate corresponds to the way in which the door can be used. The design is improved.

Images of common physical objects and environments can enhance the usability of a design. For example, a drawing of a three-dimensional button on a computer screen leverages our knowledge of the physical characteristics of buttons and, therefore, appears to afford pressing. The popular "desktop" metaphor used by computer operating systems is based on this idea—images of common items like trash cans and folders leverage our knowledge of how those items function in the real world and, thus, suggest their function in the software environment.[2]

Whenever possible, you should design objects and environments to afford their intended function, and negatively afford improper use. For example, stackable chairs should only stack one way. Mimic familiar objects and environments in abstract contexts (e.g., software interfaces) to imply the way in which new systems can be used. When affordances are successfully employed in a design, it will seem inconceivable that the design could function or be used otherwise.

See also Constraint, Mapping, Mimicry, and Wayfinding.

[1] The seminal work on affordances is "The Theory of Affordances" by James Gibson, in *Perceiving, Acting, and Knowing* by R. E. Shaw & J. Bransford (Eds), Lawrence Erlbaum Associates, 1977; and *The Ecological Approach to Visual Perception* by James Gibson, Houghton Mifflin, 1979. A popular treatment of affordances can be found in *The Design of Everyday Things* by Donald Norman, Doubleday, 1990.

[2] Note that the term *affordance* refers to the properties of a physical object or environment only. When images of physical objects or environments are used (e.g., image of a button), the images, themselves, do not afford anything. The knowledge of button affordances exists in the mind of the perceiver based on experience with physical buttons—it is not a property of the image. Therefore, the affordance is said to be *perceived*. See, for example, "Affordances and Design" by Donald Norman, www.jnd.org.

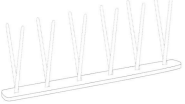

OXO is well known for the handle designs of their products; shape, color, and texture combine to create irresistible gripping affordances.

Outdoor lighting structures often afford landing and perching for birds. Where birds perch, birds poop. This anti-perch fixture is designed to attach to such structures and reduce the perching affordance.

With opposing male and female surfaces and featureless sides, Legos naturally afford plugging into one another.

Door affordances frequently conflict, as shown in the door on the left. The "push" affordance of the door is knowable only because of the sign, which conflicts with the powerful "pull" affordance of the handle. By replacing the handle with a flat plate, the conflict is eliminated and the sign is superfluous.

The recessed footplates and handlebar orientation of the Segway Human Transporter afford one mounting position for the user—the correct one.

Alignment

The placement of elements such that edges line up along common rows or columns, or their bodies along a common center.

Elements in a design should be aligned with one or more other elements. This creates a sense of unity and cohesion, which contributes to the design's overall aesthetic and perceived stability. Alignment can also be a powerful means of leading a person through a design. For example, the rows and columns of a grid or table make explicit the relatedness of elements sharing those rows and columns, and lead the eyes left-right and top-bottom accordingly. Edges of the design medium (e.g., edge of a page or screen) and the natural positions on the design medium (e.g., centerlines) should also be considered alignment elements.

In paragraph text, left-aligned and right-aligned text blocks provide more powerful alignment cues than do center-aligned text blocks. The invisible column created by left-aligned and right-aligned text blocks presents a clear, visual cue against which other elements of the design can be aligned. Center-aligned text blocks, conversely, provide more visually ambiguous alignment cues, and can be difficult to connect with other elements. Justified text provides more alignment cues than unjustified text, and should be used in complex compositions with many elements.

Although alignment is generally defined in terms of rows and columns, more complex forms of alignment exist. In aligning elements along diagonals, for example, the relative angles between the invisible alignment paths should be 30 degrees or greater; separation of less than 30 degrees is too subtle and difficult to detect.[1] In spiral or circular alignments, it may be necessary to augment or highlight the alignment paths so that the alignment is perceptible; otherwise the elements can appear disparate, and the design disordered. As with all such principles of this type, there are exceptions (e.g., the misalignment of elements to attract attention or create tension). However, these exceptions are rare, and alignment should be considered the general rule.

For most designs, align elements into rows and columns or along a centerline. When elements are not arranged in a row/column format, consider highlighting the alignment paths. Use left- or right-justified text to create the best alignment cues, and consider justified text for complex compositions.

See also Aesthetic-Usability Effect and Good Continuation.

[1] See, for example, *Elements of Graph Design* by Stephen M. Kosslyn, W. H. Freeman and Company, 1994, p. 172.

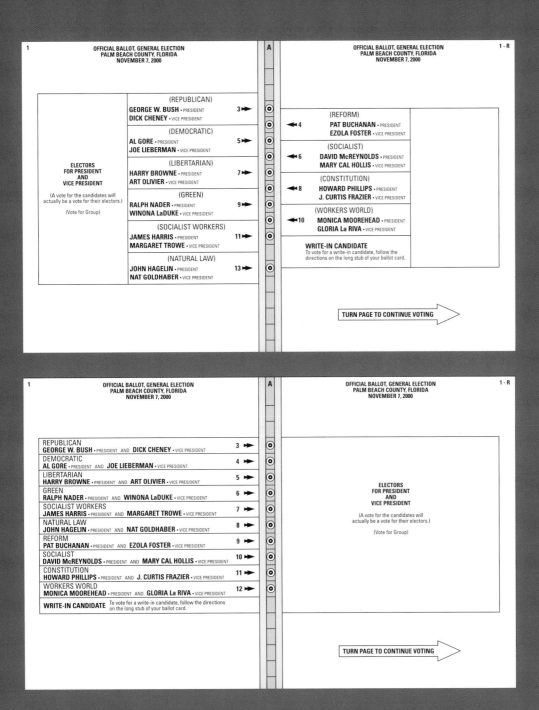

The design of the "butterfly ballot" of Palm Beach County, Florida, may have decided the presidential election of 2000. Although there are several problems with the design of the butterfly ballot, most confusion likely resulted from the misalignment of the row and punch-hole lines. This conclusion is supported by the improbable number of votes for Patrick Buchanan in Palm Beach County, as well as the number of double votes that occurred for candidates that were adjacent on the ballot. A simple adjustment to the ballot design would have dramatically reduced the error rate.

Archetypes

Universal patterns of theme and form resulting from innate biases or dispositions.

Archetypes are found in the themes of myths (e.g., death and rebirth), characters in literature (e.g., hero and villain), and imagery in dreams (e.g., eyes and teeth). They are believed to be a product of unconscious biases and dispositions that have been "hardwired" in the brain over the course of human evolution. Since these innate biases and dispositions are unconscious, their existence is inferred when common patterns emerge in many cultures over long periods. Identifying and aligning appropriate archetypes with a design will increase its probability of success.[1]

Harley-Davidson aligns its product design and branding with the outlaw archetype, emphasizing freedom and living outside the rules of society. Products have a certain look and feel (e.g., black and chrome motorcycles with a loud, distinctive sound) and marketing images emphasize rugged looking people in black leather. Nike (named after the Greek goddess of victory), by contrast, aligns its brand with the Hero archetype, using heroic sports figures to promote its product. Michael Jordan, Tiger Woods, and Lance Armstrong are all shown wearing Nike products while typically striking a heroic pose. This does not mean that a picture of Michael Jordan on a Harley wouldn't help sell motorcycles, or that a picture of a group of outlaws wearing Nike leather jackets wouldn't help sell sportswear. It does mean that the probability of success would be lower because the archetypes do not align with the design.[2]

In storytelling, archetypal themes are all too familiar. For example, one archetypal plot—the Hero's Journey—can be summarized as follows: a prospective hero is called to an adventure that he or she refuses; a meeting with a mentor occurs and the hero meets the call; the hero experiences various trials, often including the defeat or death of the mentor by an ultimate enemy; the hero must overcome self-doubt and confront the ultimate enemy; the hero defeats the ultimate enemy and returns home to great celebration. This archetypal theme has been successfully employed by filmmakers like George Lucas and George Miller, and is also evident in the works of Steven Spielberg, John Boorman, Francis Coppola, and a number of Disney animated films.[3]

Consider archetypal themes and forms in all aspects of a design—from form and function to name and brand. Since archetypes influence perception on an unconscious and primarily affective level, they are especially useful when traditional modes of communication (e.g., language) cannot be used. Note that reactions to specific archetypes may vary across cultures and, therefore, should be tested on target populations prior to use.

See also Affordance, Mimicry, and Threat Detection.

[1] The seminal work on archetypes is "The Archetypes and the Collective Unconscious" by Carl G. Jung, in the *Collected Works of C. G. Jung,* Vol. 9 Part 1 (translated by R. F. C. Hull), Princeton University Press, 1981.

[2] See *The Hero and the Outlaw: Building Extraordinary Brands through the Power of Archetypes* by Margaret Mark and Carol S. Pearson, McGraw-Hill Trade, 2001.

[3] The seminal work on archetypes in storytelling is *The Hero with a Thousand Faces* by Joseph Campbell, Princeton University Press, 1960.

These are proposed designs for a marker system to warn future generations of the presence of a nuclear-waste disposal site. The design specification required the markers to stand for the life of the radioactive hazard (10,000 years), clearly warn people to stay away from the area, and assume that future civilizations will not be knowledgeable of radioactive hazards or speak any language known today. The designs address this seemingly impossible specification through the brilliant application of archetypal theme and form—parched earth, snakelike earthworks, and claws and thorns—to warn future humans of the radioactive hazards on an affective, instinctive level.

Attractiveness Bias

A tendency to see attractive people as more intelligent, competent, moral, and sociable than unattractive people.[1]

Attractive people are generally perceived more positively than unattractive people. They receive more attention from the opposite sex, receive more affection from their mothers, receive more leniency from judges and juries, and receive more votes from the electorate than do unattractive people. All other variables being equal, attractive people are preferred in hiring decisions, and will make more money doing the same work than unattractive people. The attractiveness bias is a function of both biological and environmental factors.[2]

Biologically speaking, people are attractive when they exude health and fertility. Good biological measures for health and fertility are average and symmetrical facial features, and a waist-to-hip ratio in the ideal range (0.70 for women, 0.90 for men). An absence of these features is thought to be an indicator of malnutrition, disease, or bad genes; none of which are preferable attributes for a potential mate. Biological factors of attraction are innate and true across cultures. For example, in studies presenting images of attractive and unattractive people to babies (two-months-old and six-months-old), the babies looked longer at the attractive people regardless of their gender, age, or race.[3]

Environmentally speaking, men are attracted to women when they exaggerate socially acknowledged features of sexuality (e.g., lipstick to exaggerate lips); and women are attracted to men when they appear to possess wealth and power (e.g., expensive automobiles). For example, in studies presenting images of attractive and unattractive people to men and women, along with descriptions of their occupations, women preferred unattractive men with high-paying occupations equally to attractive men with medium-paying occupations. However, men never preferred unattractive women regardless of their financial status. Environmental factors of attraction vary considerably across cultures.[4]

Consider the attractiveness bias in design contexts involving images of people, such as marketing and advertising. When the presentation of attractive women is a key element of a design, use renderings or images of women with waist-to-hip ratios of approximately 0.70, accented by culturally appropriate augmentations of sexual features. When the presentation of attractive men is a key element of a design, use renderings or images of men with waist-to-hip ratios of approximately 0.90, and visible indicators of wealth or status (e.g., expensive clothing).

See also Baby-Face Bias, Most Average Facial Appearance Effect, and Waist-to-Hip Ratio.

[1] Also known as *look-ism*.

[2] The seminal work on the attractiveness bias is "What Is Beautiful Is Good" by Karen Dion, Ellen Berscheid, and Elaine Walster, *Journal of Personality and Social Psychology*, 1972, vol. 24(3), p. 285–290. A nice contemporary review of the attractiveness bias research is "Maxims or Myths of Beauty? A Meta-analytic and Theoretical Review" by Judith H. Langlois, et al., *Psychological Bulletin*, 2000, vol. 126(3), p. 390–423.

[3] See, for example, "Baby Beautiful: Adult Attributions of Infant Competence as a Function of Infant Attractiveness" by Cookie W. Stephan and Judith H. Langlois, *Child Development*, 1984, vol. 55, p. 576–585.

[4] *Survival of the Prettiest: The Science of Beauty* by Nancy Etcoff, Anchor Books, 2000.

The first presidential debate between Richard Nixon and Robert Kennedy (1960) is a classic demonstration of the attractiveness bias. Nixon was ill and running a fever. He wore light colors and no makeup, further whitening his already pale complexion and contrasting his five-o'clock shadow. Kennedy wore dark colors, makeup, and practiced his delivery in a studio prior to the debate. People who listened to the debate by radio believed Nixon to be the winner. However, people who watched the debate on TV came to a very different conclusion.

Baby-Face Bias

A tendency to see people and things with baby-faced features as more naïve, helpless, and honest than those with mature features.

People and things with round features, large eyes, small noses, high foreheads, short chins, and relatively lighter skin and hair are perceived as babylike and, as a result, as having babylike personality attributes: naiveté, helplessness, honesty, and innocence. The bias is found across all age ranges, cultures, and many mammalian species.[1]

The degree to which people are influenced by the baby-face bias is evident in how babies are treated by adults. For example, babies with weak baby-face features receive less positive attention from adults and are rated as less likable, less attractive, and less fun to be with than babies with strong baby-face features. Large, round heads and eyes appear to be the strongest of the facial cues contributing to this bias. For example, premature babies often lack these key baby-face features (e.g., their eyes are closed, and their heads are less round) and are rated by adults as less desirable to care for or be around. A potentially related phenomenon is the rate of child abuse for premature babies, which is approximately 300 percent greater than for normal-term babies.[2]

Baby-faced adults are subject to a similar biased. However, unlike with children, there are liabilities to being a baby-faced adult. Baby-faced adults appearing in commercials are effective when their role involves innocence and honesty, such as a personal testimonial for a product, but ineffective when their role involves speaking authoritatively about a topic, such as a doctor asserting the benefit of a product. Baby-faced adults are perceived as simple and naïve, and have difficulty being taken seriously in situations where expertise or confrontation is required. In legal proceedings, baby-faced adults are more likely to be found innocent when the alleged crime involves an intentional act, but are more likely to be found guilty when the alleged crime involves a negligent act. It is apparently more believable that a baby-faced person would do wrong accidentally than purposefully. Interestingly, when a baby-faced defendant pleads guilty, they receive harsher sentences than mature-faced defendants—it seems the contrast between the expectation of innocence and the conclusion of guilt evokes a harsher reaction than when the expectation and the conclusion align.

Consider the baby-face bias in the design of characters or products when facial attributes are prominent (e.g., cartoon characters for children). Characters of this type can be made more appealing by exaggerating the various neonatal features (e.g., larger, rounder eyes). In marketing and advertising, use mature-faced people when conveying expertise and authority; use baby-faced people when conveying testimonial information and submissiveness.

See also Attractiveness Bias, Mimicry, and Savanna Preference.

[1] The seminal work on the baby-face bias is "Ganzheit und Teil in der tierischen und menschlichen Gemeinschaft" [Part and Parcel in Animal and Human Societies] by Konrad Lorenz, *Studium Generale*, 1950, vol. 3(9).

[2] See *Reading Faces: Window to the Soul* by Leslie A. Zebraowitz, Westview Press, 1998. There are many other factors that could account for this statistic. For example, the level of care and frequency of crying in premature babies is significantly higher than for normal-term babies, which could contribute to the stress of the caregiver.

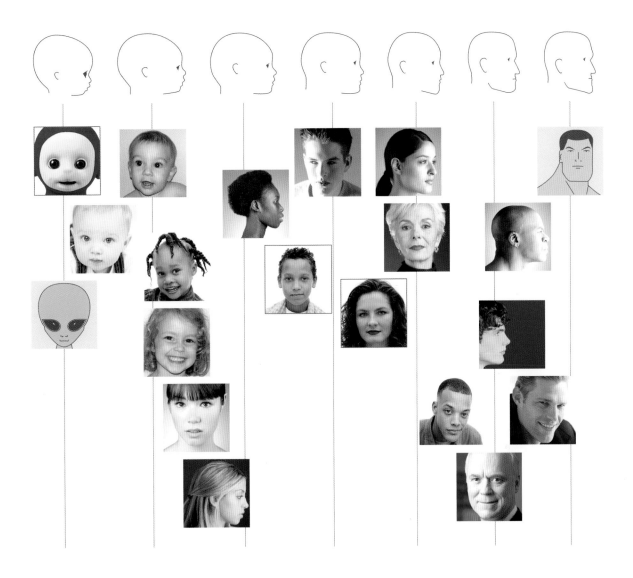

Baby-face characteristics include round features, large eyes, small noses, high foreheads, and short chins. Superneonatal and super-mature features are usually only found in cartoon characters and mythic creatures. Baby-face features correlate with perceptions of helplessness and innocence, whereas mature features correlate with perceptions of knowledge and authority.

Chunking

A technique of combining many units of information into a limited number of units or chunks, so that the information is easier to process and remember.

The term *chunk* refers to a unit of information in short-term memory—a string of letters, a word, or a series of numbers. The technique of chunking seeks to accommodate short-term memory limits by formatting information into a small number of units. The maximum number of chunks that can be efficiently processed by short-term memory is four, plus or minus one. For example, most people can remember a list of five words for 30 seconds, but few can remember a list of ten words for 30 seconds. By breaking the list of ten words into multiple, smaller chunks (e.g., two groups of three words, and one group of four words), recall performance is essentially equivalent to the single list of five words.[1]

Chunking is often applied as a general technique to simplify designs. This is a potential misapplication of the principle. The limits specified by this principle deal specifically with tasks involving memory. For example, it is unnecessary and counterproductive to restrict the number of dictionary entries on a page to four or five. Reference-related tasks consist primarily of scanning for a particular item; chunking in this case would dramatically increase the scan time and effort, and yield no benefits.

Chunk information when people are required to recall and retain information, or when information is used for problem solving. Do not chunk information that is to be searched or scanned. In environments where noise or stress can interfere with concentration, consider chunking critical display information in anticipation of diminished short-term memory capacity. Use the contemporary estimate of 4 ± 1 chunks when applying this technique.[2]

See also Errors, Mnemonic Device, Performance Load, and Signal-to-Noise Ratio.

[1] The seminal work on short-term memory limits is "The Magical Number Seven, Plus or Minus Two: Some Limits on Our Capacity for Processing Information" by George Miller, *The Psychological Review*, 1956, vol. 63, p. 81–97. As made evident by the title of Miller's paper, his original estimate for short-term memory capacity was 7 ± 2 chunks.

[2] A readable contemporary reference is *Human Memory: Theory and Practice* by Alan Baddeley, Allyn & Bacon, 1997. Regarding short-term memory limits, see, for example, "The Magical Number Four in Short-Term Memory: A Reconsideration of Mental Storage Capacity" by Nelson Cowan, *Behavioral and Brain Sciences*, 2001, vol. 24, p. 87–114.

This e-learning course by EduNeering makes excellent use of chunking. Note that the number of content topics (left gray panel) observes the appropriate limits, as do the information chunks on the topics themselves. Overview and Challenge are not counted because they contain organizing information and quizzes only.

EDU**NEERING**
Sound

Overview
▶ Sound
Loss
Conservation Program
Protection
High Noise Areas
Challenge

Comments
Exit

What creates sound?

the vibration of matter
(usually air)

travels in waves   travels through all materials

travels outward in all directions

Characteristics

The two main characteristics of sound are amplitude and frequency.

Amplitude is the strength of a vibration (or height of a sound wave) and is measured in decibels (dB). For every one-decibel increase, there is roughly a 20 to 30% increase in perceived loudness. The human ear can detect a human voice starting at around 5 dB, and sounds at 135 dB can cause pain. Hearing protection is recommended when you are exposed to sounds of 85 dB or greater.

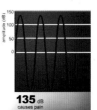

135 dB
causes pain

Frequency is the number of sound waves in a given amount of time and is measured in hertz (Hz). One hertz equals one sound wave per second. The human ear is best adapted to hear middle-frequency sounds, about 20 to 20,000 Hz.

High-frequency sound waves make high-pitched sounds, while low-frequency sound waves make low-pitched sounds. Middle-frequency sounds in the human hearing range seem louder than sounds of higher or lower pitch.

3 Hz
three sound waves per second

Relating amplitude and frequency

To learn more about the relationship between amplitude and frequency, experiment with the settings below. Press the play button to see and hear the results.

EXPLORE

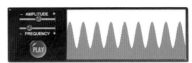

AMPLITUDE +
FREQUENCY +
PLAY

How much have you learned?

Practice your knowledge by completing the activity below.

L E A R N I N G

CLICK TO START

A C T I V I T Y

List 1
angry
hoarse
snuggle
search
fatigue
stutter
scorch
warning
teenager
anxious

List 2
thrunced
rooped
croodle
poosk
quanked
maffle
brizzle
gardyloo
haspenald
cark

Familiar words are easier to remember and chunk together than unfamiliar words. Of the two lists, list 1 is easier to recall.

292635732   7045556791
292-63-5732   (704) 555-6791

Large strings of numbers are difficult to recall. Chunking large strings of numbers into multiple, smaller strings can help. Most people can remember their Social Security number and frequently called phone numbers.

Classical Conditioning

A technique used to associate a stimulus with an unconscious physical or emotional response.

Classical conditioning was the first type of learning to be studied by behavioral psychologists. Lab workers discovered the technique when they noticed that dogs in the laboratory began salivating as soon as they entered the room. Because the lab workers feed the dogs, their presence (neutral stimulus) had become associated with food (trigger stimulus), and, therefore, elicited the same response as the food itself (salivation). Similar behaviors are seen in fish when they surface at the sight of an approaching person, or in cats when they come running at the sound of a can opener.[1]

Classical conditioning is commonly used in animal training (e.g., associating chemical traces of TNT with sugar water to train bees to detect bombs), behavior modification in people (e.g., associating smoking with aversive images or tastes), and marketing and advertising (i.e., associating products or services with attractive images or feelings). For example, television and magazine advertising firms use classical conditioning frequently to associate products and services with specific thoughts and feelings. Images of attractive people stimulate reward centers in the brain, and condition positive associations with products, services, and behaviors. Conversely, disturbing images of extreme violence or injury stimulate pain centers in the brain, and condition negative associations with products, services, and behaviors. Human emotions condition quickly and easily in this way, particularly when the association is negative. In a classic experiment, a young child was exposed to a white rat accompanied by a loud noise. The child not only grew to fear the white rat (which he did not fear previously), but other furry things as well (e.g., fur coats). Many phobias are caused by this type of association. For example, many children become anxious when visiting the dentist because previous experiences have been painful—dentists often give children treats in an attempt to reverse this association.[2]

Use classical conditioning to influence the appeal of a design or influence specific kinds of behaviors. Repeated pairings of a design with a trigger stimulus will condition an association over time. Examples of positive trigger stimuli include anything that causes pleasure or evokes a positive emotional response—a picture of food, the sound of a drink being poured, images of attractive people. Examples of negative trigger stimuli include anything that causes pain or evokes a negative emotional response—physical pain of a vaccination, an embarrassing experience, or images of extreme pain and violence.

See also Exposure Effect, Operant Conditioning, and Shaping.

[1] The seminal work in classical conditioning is *Conditioned Reflexes: An Investigation of the Physiological Activity of the Cerebral Cortex* by Ivan Pavlov, 1927 (translated and edited by G. V. Anrep, Dover Publications, 1984).

[2] See "Conditioned Emotional Reactions" by John B. Watson and Rosalie Rayner, *Journal of Experimental Psychology*, 1920, vol. 3(1), p. 1–14; and "Reward Value of Attractiveness and Gaze" by Knut K. W. Kampe, Chris D. Frith, Raymond J. Dolan, and Uta Frith, *Nature*, 2001, v. 413, p. 589.

Not everyone who gets hit by a drunk driver dies.

Jacqueline Saburido was 20 years old when the car she was riding in was hit by a drunk driver. Today, at 23, she is still working to put her life back together.

Learn more at www.TexasDWI.org

DON'T DRINK & DRIVE

◻▦ **Save a Life**
Texas Department of Transportation

Texas Department of Public Safety • Texas Alcoholic Beverage Commission • Texans Standing Tall • Partnership for a Drug-Free Texas • Texas Commission on Alcohol and Drug Abuse
© 2002 Texas Department of Transportation

The power of this campaign against drunk driving is matched only by the courage of Jacqueline Saburido, who allows us to share in her life after being hit by a drunk driver. The emotional reaction evoked by seeing the seriousness of Jacqueline's injuries is associated with the behavior that caused them. If this campaign does not give people pause before drinking and driving, nothing will.

Closure

A tendency to perceive a set of individual elements as a single, recognizable pattern, rather than multiple, individual elements.

The principle of closure is one of a number of principles referred to as Gestalt *principles of perception*. It states that whenever possible, people tend to perceive a set of individual elements as a single, recognizable pattern, rather than multiple, individual elements. The tendency to perceive a single pattern is so strong that people will close gaps and fill in missing information to complete the pattern if necessary. For example, when individual line segments are positioned along a circular path, they are first perceived holistically as a circle, and then as comprising multiple, independent elements. The tendency to perceive information in this way is automatic and subconscious; it is likely a function of an innate preference for simplicity over complexity, and pattern over randomness.[1]

Closure is strongest when elements approximate simple, recognizable patterns, such as geometric forms, and are located near one another. When simple, recognizable patterns are not easily perceived, designers can create closure through transitional elements (e.g., subtle visual cues that help direct the eye to find the pattern). Generally, if the energy required to find or form a pattern is greater than the energy required to perceive the elements individually, closure will not occur.

The principle of closure enables designers to reduce complexity by reducing the number of elements needed to organize and communicate information. For example, a logo design that is composed of recognizable elements does not need to complete many of its lines and contours to be clear and effective. Reducing the number of lines in the logo not only reduces its complexity, but it makes the logo more interesting to look at—viewers subconsciously participate in the completion of its design. Many forms of storytelling leverage closure in a similar way. For example, in comic books, discrete scenes in time are presented to readers, who then supply what happens in between. The storyline is a unique combination of information provided by the storyteller, and information provided by the reader.[2]

Use closure to reduce the complexity and increase the interestingness of designs. When designs involve simple and recognizable patterns, consider removing or minimizing the elements in the design that can be supplied by viewers. When designs involve more complex patterns, consider the use of transitional elements to assist viewers in finding or forming the pattern.

See also Good Continuation, Law of Prägnanz, and Proximity.

[1] The seminal work on closure is "Untersuchungen zür Lehre von der Gestalt, II" [Laws of Organization in Perceptual Forms] by Max Wertheimer, *Psychologische Forschung*, 1923, vol. 4, p. 301–350, reprinted in *A Source Book of Gestalt Psychology* by Willis D. Ellis (ed.), Routledge & Kegan Paul, 1999, p. 71–88.

[2] See, for example, *Understanding Comics: The Invisible Art* by Scott McCloud, Kitchen Sink Press, 1993.

The elements are perceived holistically as a single pattern first (circle), and then as individual elements.

PENGUIN ICE

Elements in text and graphics can be minimized to allow viewers to participate in the completion of the pattern. The result is a more interesting design.

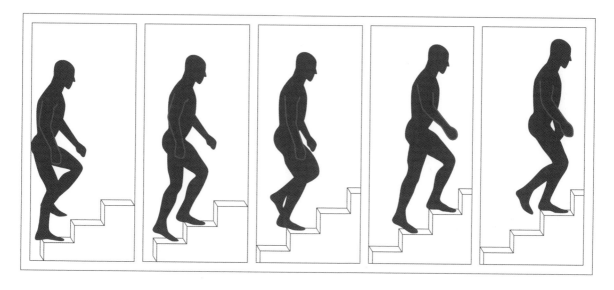

Series images are understood as representing motion because people supply the information in between the images.

Cognitive Dissonance

A tendency to seek consistency among attitudes, thoughts, and beliefs.

People strive to have consistency among their attitudes, thoughts, and beliefs. Cognitive dissonance is the state of mental discomfort that occurs when a person's attitudes, thoughts, or beliefs (i.e., cognitions) conflict. If two cognitions agree with one another, there is *consonance*, and a state of comfort results. If two cognitions disagree with one another, there is *dissonance*, and a state of discomfort results.[1]

People alleviate cognitive dissonance in one of three ways: by reducing the importance of dissonant cognitions, adding consonant cognitions, or removing or changing dissonant cognitions. For example, advertising campaigns that urge people to *show how much you care* by buying diamonds seek to create cognitive dissonance in consumers—i.e., dissonance between the love that people have for others, and the pressure to prove that love by buying diamonds. In order to alleviate the dissonance, people can reduce the importance of the dissonant cognition (e.g., a diamond is, after all, just a bunch of pressed carbon), add consonant cognitions (e.g., recognize that the advertising campaign is trying to manipulate them using cognitive dissonance), or remove or change dissonant cognitions (e.g., show how much you care by doing something else or, of course, buying the diamonds).

When a situation involves incentives, it is interesting to note that incentives of different sizes yield different results. When incentives for an unpleasant task are small, people reduce dissonance by changing the dissonant cognition (e.g., "it is okay to perform this task because I like it"). When incentives for an unpleasant task are large, people reduce dissonance by adding a consonant cognition (e.g., "it is okay to perform this task because I am paid well"). When incentives are small, people are inclined to change the way the way they feel about what they are doing to alleviate dissonance. When incentives increase, people retain their original beliefs and alleviate dissonance by justifying their participation with their compensation. A small incentive is usually required to get a person to consider an unpleasant thought or engage in an unpleasant activity. Any incentive beyond this small incentive reduces, not increases, the probability of changing attitudes and beliefs—this critical point is known as *the point of minimum justification*.[2]

Consider cognitive dissonance in the design of advertising and marketing campaigns, or any other context where influence and persuasion is key. Use consonant and dissonant information when attempting to change beliefs. Engage people to invest their time, attention, and participation to create dissonant cognitions, and then provide simple and immediate mechanisms to alleviate the dissonance. When using compensation to reinforce change, use the minimal compensation possible to achieve change.

See also Consistency, Cost-Benefit, and Hierarchy of Needs.

[1] The seminal work on cognitive dissonance is *A Theory of Cognitive Dissonance* by Leon Festinger, Row, Perterson & Company, 1957. A comprehensive review of the theory is *Cognitive Dissonance: Progress on a Pivotal Theory in Social Psychology* edited by Eddie Harmon-Jones and Judson Mills, American Psychological Association, 1999.

[2] See, for example, "Cognitive Consequences of Forced Compliance" by Leon Festinger and James Carlsmith, *Journal of Abnormal and Social Psychology*, 1959, vol. 58, p. 203–210.

The *point of minimum justification* represents the optimal level of incentive required to change behavior and attitude. Incentives exceeding this level will continue to change behavior, but will fail to change attitude.

Perhaps the most successful use of cognitive dissonance in the history of advertising is the AOL free-hours campaign delivered on CD-ROM. The incentive to try AOL is provided in the form of a free trial period. People who try the service go through a set-up process, where they define unique e-mail addresses, screen names, and passwords, investing time and energy to get it all to work. The greater the time and energy invested during this trial period, the greater the cognitive dissonance at the time of expiration. Since the compensation to engage in this activity was minimal, the way most people alleviate the dissonance is to have positive feelings about the service—which leads to paid subscriptions.

Color

Color is used in design to attract attention, group elements, indicate meaning, and enhance aesthetics.

Color can make designs more visually interesting and aesthetic, and can reinforce the organization and meaning of elements in a design. If applied improperly, colors can seriously harm the form and function of a design. The following guidelines address common issues regarding the use of color.[1]

Number of Colors
Use color conservatively. Limit the palette to what the eye can process at one glance (about five colors depending on the complexity of the design). Do not use color as the only means to impart information since a significant portion of the population has limited color vision.

Color Combinations
Achieve aesthetic color combinations by using adjacent colors on the color wheel (analogous), opposing colors on the color wheel (complementary), colors at the corners of a symmetrical polygon circumscribed in the color wheel (triadic and quadratic), or color combinations found in nature. Use warmer colors for foreground elements, and cooler colors for background elements. Light gray is a safe color to use for grouping elements without competing with other colors.

Saturation
Use saturated colors (pure hues) when attracting attention is the priority. Use desaturated colors when performance and efficiency are the priority. Generally, desaturated, bright colors are perceived as friendly and professional; desaturated, dark colors are perceived as serious and professional; and saturated colors are perceived as more exciting and dynamic. Exercise caution when combining saturated colors, as they can visually interfere with one another and increase eye fatigue.

Symbolism
There is no substantive evidence supporting general effects of color on emotion or mood. Similarly, there is no universal symbolism for different colors—different cultures attach different meanings to colors. Therefore, verify the meaning of colors and color combinations for a particular target audience prior to use.[2]

See also Expectation Effect, Highlighting, Interference Effects, Similarity, and Uniform Connectedness.

[1] A nice treatment of color theory is *Interaction of Color* by Josef Albers, Yale University Press, 1963. For a more applied treatment, see *The Art of Color: The Subjective Experience and Objective Rationale of Color* by Johannes Itten, John Wiley & Sons, 1997; and *Human-Computer Interaction* by Jenny Preece, et al., Addison Wesley, 1994.

[2] It is reasonable to assume that dark colors will make people sleepy, light colors will make people lively, and irritating colors will make people irritated. Otherwise, the only observable influence of color on behavior is its ability to lead people to repaint walls unnecessarily. For those determined to try to calm drunks and win football games through the application of color, see *The Power of Color* by Morton Walker, Avery Publishing, 1991.

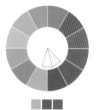 

Analogous   Example from Nature

Analogous color combinations use colors that are next to each other on the color wheel.

Triadic   Example from Nature

Triadic color combinations use colors at the corners of an equilateral triangle circumscribed in the color wheel.

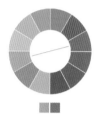 

Complementary   Example from Nature

Complementary color combinations use two colors that are directly across from each other on the color wheel.

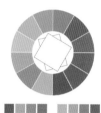

Quadratic   Example from Nature

Quadratic color combinations use colors at that corners of a square or rectangle circumscribed in the color wheel.

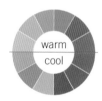

Hues from yellow to red-violet on the color wheel are warm. Hues from violet to green-yellow are cool.

Saturation refers to the amount of gray added to a hue. As saturation increases, the amount of gray decreases. Brightness refers to the amount of white added to a hue— as brightness increases, the amount of white increases.

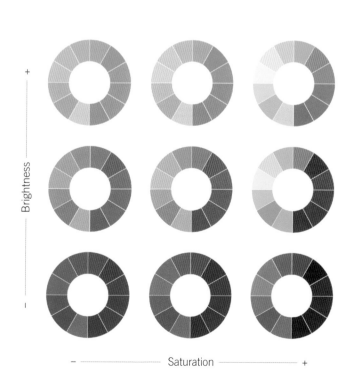

Common Fate

Elements that move in the same direction are perceived to be more related than elements that move in different directions or are stationary.

The principle of common fate is one of a number of principles referred to as *Gestalt principles of perception*. It asserts that elements that move together in a common direction are perceived as a single group or chunk, and are interpreted as being more related than elements that move at different times or in different directions. For example, a row of randomly arranged *X*s and *O*s that is stationary is naturally grouped by similarity, *X*s with *X*s, and *O*s with *O*s. However, if certain elements in the row move in one direction, and other elements move in the opposite direction, elements are grouped by their common motion and direction.[1]

Perceived relatedness is strongest when the motion of elements occurs at the same time and velocity, and in the same direction. As any of these factors vary, the elements are decreasingly related. One exception is when the motion exhibits an obvious pattern or rhythm (e.g., wave patterns), in which case the elements are seen as related. Although common fate relationships usually refer to moving elements, they are also observed with static objects that flicker (i.e., elements that alternate between brighter and darker states). For flickering elements, perceived relatedness is strongest when the elements flicker at the same time, frequency, and intensity, or when a recognizable pattern or rhythm is formed.[2]

Common fate relationships influence whether elements are perceived as figure or ground elements. When certain elements are in motion and others are stationary, the moving objects will be perceived as figure elements, and stationary ones will be perceived as ground elements. When elements within a region move together with the bounding edge of the region, the elements and the region will be perceived as the figure. When elements within a region move together, but the bounding edge of the region remains stationary or moves opposite to the elements, the elements within the region will be perceived as the ground.[3]

Consider common fate as a grouping strategy when displaying information with moving or flickering elements. Related elements should move at the same time, velocity, and direction, or flicker at the same time, frequency, and intensity. It is possible to group elements when these variables are dissimilar, but only if the motion or flicker forms a recognizable pattern. When moving elements within bounded regions, move the edges of the region in the same direction as the elements to achieve a figure relationship or in the opposite direction as the elements to achieve a ground relationship.

See also Figure-Ground Relationship and Similarity.

[1] The seminal work on common fate is "Untersuchungen zür Lehre von der Gestalt, II" [Laws of Organization in Perceptual Forms] by Max Wertheimer, *Psychologische Forschung*, 1923, vol. 4, p. 301–350, reprinted in *A Source Book of Gestalt Psychology* by Willis D. Ellis (ed.), Routledge & Kegan Paul, 1999, p. 71v88.

[2] See, for example, "Generalized Common Fate: Grouping by Common Luminance Changes" by Allison B. Sekuler and Patrick J. Bennett, *Psychological Science*, 2001, Vol. 12(6), p. 437–444.

[3] "Common Fate as a Determinant of Figure-Ground Organization" by Joseph Lloyd Brooks, Stanford-Berkeley Talk, 2000, Stanford University, May 16, 2000.

OXOOXOXXXOO

OXOOXOXXXOO

The *X*s and *O*s group by smilarity- when stationary, such as *X*s with *X*s, *O*s with *O*s. However, when a mix of the *X*s and *O*s move up and down in a common fashion, they are grouped primarily by common fate.

Radar tracking displays use common fate to group tracked aircraft with key information about their identities and headings.

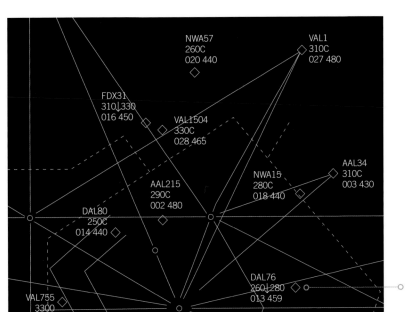

NWA57
260C
020 440

VAL1
310C
027 480

FDX31
310↓330
016 450

VAL1504
330C
028 465

AAL34
310C
003 430

NWA15
280C
018 440

AAL215
290C
002 480

DAL80
250C
014 440

DAL76
260↓280
013 459

This object is being tracked by radar. The object and its label are visually grouped because they are moving at the same speed and in the same direction.

VAL755
3300
031 459

AAL427
200↓263
004 440

USA442
200↓231
037 440

USA990
200↓225
038 440

Comparison

A method of illustrating relationships and patterns in
system behaviors by representing two or more system
variables in a controlled way.

People understand the way the world works by identifying relationships and patterns in or between systems. One of the most powerful methods of identifying and
understanding these relationships is to represent information in controlled ways so
that comparisons can be made. Key techniques for making valid comparisons are
apples to apples, single contexts, and benchmarks.[1]

Apples to Apples

Comparison data should be presented using common measures and common
units. For example, when comparing crime rates of different countries, it is necessary to account for differences in variables such as population, types of laws, and
level of law enforcement. Otherwise, conclusions based on the comparison will be
unreliable. Common methods of ensuring apples-to-apples comparisons include
clearly disclosing details of how variables were measured, making corrections to
the data as necessary to eliminate confounding variables, and representing the
variables using the same graphical and numerical standards.

Single Context

Comparison data should be presented in a single context, so that subtle differences and patterns in the data are detectable. For example, the ability to detect
patterns across multiple graphs is lower if the graphs are located on separate
pages versus the same page. Common methods of representing information in
single contexts include the use of a small number of displays that combine many
variables (versus many separate displays), and multiple small views of system
states (known as *small multiples*) in a single display (versus multiple displays).

Benchmarks

Claims about evidence or phenomena should be accompanied by benchmark
variables so that clear and substantive comparisons can be made. For example,
claims about the seriousness of the size of U.S. debt are meaningful only when
accompanied by benchmark information about U.S. gross national product (GNP);
a debt can appear serious when depicted as a quantity, but irrelevant when presented as a percentage of GNP. Common types of benchmark data include past
performance data, competitor data, or data from well-accepted industry standards.

Use comparisons to convincingly illustrate patterns and relationships. Ensure that
compared variables are apples to apples by measuring and representing variables
in common ways, correcting for confounds in the data as necessary. Use multivariate displays and small multiples to present comparisons in single contexts when
possible. Use benchmarks to anchor comparisons and provide a point of reference from which to evaluate the data.

See also Garbage In–Garbage Out, Layering, and Signal-to-Noise Ratio.

[1] See, for example, *Visual Explanations*,
Graphics Press, 1998; and *Envisioning
Information*, Graphics Press, 1990 both by
Edward R. Tufte.

This is a modified version of Florence Nightingale's famous *Coxcomb graphs*. The graphs are composed of twelve wedges, each representing a month. Additionally, each wedge has three layers representing three different causes of death. A quick review of the graphs reveals that the real threat to British troops was not the Russians, but cholera, dysentery, and typhus. The graphs also convincingly illustrate the impact of improved hygienic practices at military camps and hospitals, which were aggressively implemented beginning in March 1855. The graphs make apples-to-apples comparisons, representing the same variable (death rates) the same way (area of the wedge).

The graphs are multivariate, integrating a number of key variables so that patterns and relationships in the data can be studied within one context. Deaths resulting from war wounds serve as a compelling benchmark to illustrate the significance of disease, as does the earlier graph for the later graph. The graphs have been corrected based on original data published in Nightingale's *Notes on Matters Affecting the Health, Efficiency and Hospital Administration of the British Army*, 1858.

Diagram of the Causes of Mortality in the Army in the East

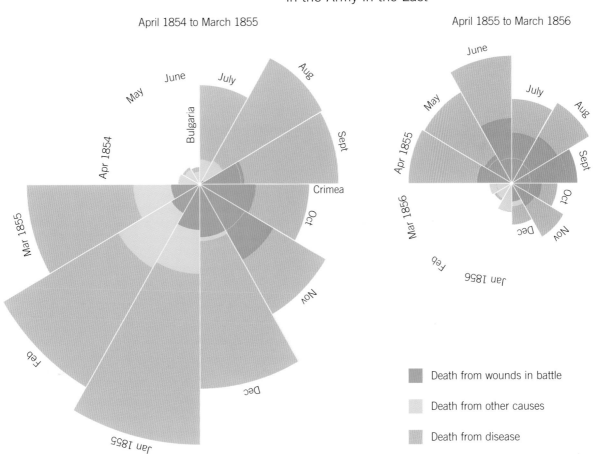

April 1854 to March 1855

April 1855 to March 1856

Death from wounds in battle

Death from other causes

Death from disease

Confirmation

A technique for preventing unintended actions by requiring verification of the actions before they are performed.[1]

Confirmation is a technique used for critical actions, inputs, or commands. It provides a means for verifying that an action or input is intentional and correct before it is performed. Confirmations are primarily used to prevent a class of errors called *slips*, which are unintended actions. Confirmations slow task performance, and should be reserved for use with critical or irreversible operations only. When the consequences of an action are not serious, or when actions are completely and easily reversible, confirmations are not needed. There are two basic confirmation techniques: dialog and two-step operation.[2]

Confirmation using a dialog involves establishing a verbal interaction with the person using the system. It is most commonly represented as a dialog box on a software display (e.g., "Are you sure you want to delete all files?"). In this method, dialog boxes directly ask the user if the action was intended and if they would like to proceed. Confirmations should be used sparingly, or people will learn to ignore them and become frustrated at the frequent interruption. Dialog messages should be concise but detailed enough to accurately convey the implications of the action. The message should end with one question that is structured to be answered *Yes* or *No*, or with an action verb that conveys the action to be performed (the use of *OK* and *Cancel* should be avoided for confirmations). For less critical confirmations that act more as reminders, an option to disable the confirmation should be provided.

Confirmation using a two-step operation involves a preliminary step that must occur prior to the actual command or input. This is most often used with hardware controls, and is often referred to as an *arm/fire* operation—first you arm the component, and then you fire (execute) it. For example, a switch cover might have to be lifted in order to activate a switch, two people might have to turn two unique keys in order to launch a nuclear weapon, or a control handle in a spacecraft might have to be rotated and then pushed down in order to be activated. The purpose of the two-step operation is to prevent accidental activation of a critical control. If the operation works only when the two-step sequence has been completed, it is unlikely that the operation will occur accidentally. Two-step operations are commonly used for critical operations in aircraft, nuclear power plants, and other environments involving dangerous operations.

Use confirmations to minimize errors in the performance of critical or irreversible operations. Avoid overusing confirmations to ensure that they are unexpected and uncommon; otherwise, they may be ignored. Use a two-step operation for hardware confirmations, and a dialog box for software confirmations. Permit less critical confirmations to be disabled after an initial confirmation.

See also Constraint, Errors, Forgiveness, and Garbage In–Garbage Out.

[1] Also known as *verification principle* and *forcing function*.

[2] See, for example, *The Design of Everyday Things* by Donald Norman, Doubleday, 1990; and *To Err Is Human: Building a Safer Health System* edited by Linda T. Kohn, Janet M. Corrigan, and Molla S. Donaldson, National Academy Press, 2000.

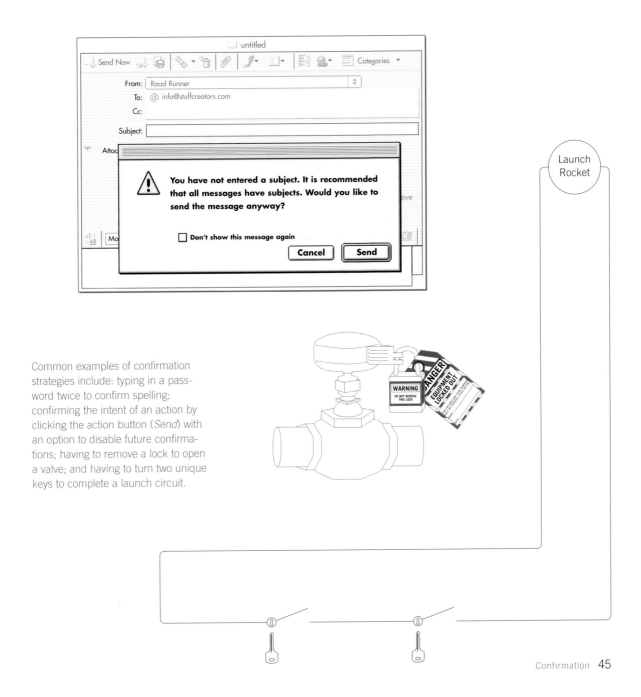

Common examples of confirmation strategies include: typing in a password twice to confirm spelling; confirming the intent of an action by clicking the action button (*Send*) with an option to disable future confirmations; having to remove a lock to open a valve; and having to turn two unique keys to complete a launch circuit.

Consistency

The usability of a system is improved when similar parts are expressed in similar ways.

According to the principle of consistency, systems are more usable and learnable when similar parts are expressed in similar ways. Consistency enables people to efficiently transfer knowledge to new contexts, learn new things quickly, and focus attention on the relevant aspects of a task. There are four kinds of consistency: aesthetic, functional, internal, and external.[1]

Aesthetic consistency refers to consistency of style and appearance (e.g., a company logo that uses a consistent font, color, and graphic). Aesthetic consistency enhances recognition, communicates membership, and sets emotional expectations. For example, Mercedes-Benz vehicles are instantly recognizable because the company consistently features its logo prominently on the hood or grill of its vehicles. The logo has become associated with quality and prestige, and informs people how they should feel about the vehicle—i.e., respected and admired.

Functional consistency refers to consistency of meaning and action (e.g., a traffic light that shows a yellow light before going to red). Functional consistency improves usability and learnability by enabling people to leverage existing knowledge about how the design functions. For example, videocassette recorder control symbols, such as for rewind, play, forward, are now used on devices ranging from slide projectors to MP3 music players. The consistent use of these symbols on new devices enables people to leverage existing knowledge about how the controls function, which makes the new devices easier to use and learn.

Internal consistency refers to consistency with other elements in the system (e.g., signs within a park are consistent with one another). Internal consistency cultivates trust with people; it is an indicator that a system has been designed, and not cobbled together. Within any logical grouping elements should be aesthetically and functionally consistent with one another.

External consistency refers to consistency with other elements in the environment (e.g., emergency alarms are consistent across different systems in a control room). External consistency extends the benefits of internal consistency across multiple, independent systems. It is more difficult to achieve because different systems rarely observe common design standards.

Consider aesthetic and functional consistency in all aspects of design. Use aesthetic consistency to establish unique identities that can be easily recognized. Use functional consistency to simplify usability and ease of learning. Ensure that systems are always internally consistent, and externally consistent to the greatest degree possible. When common design standards exist, observe them.

See also Modularity, Recognition Over Recall, and Similarity.

[1] Use consistent approaches when possible, but do not compromise clarity or usability for consistency. In the words of Emerson, "A foolish consistency is the hobgoblin of little minds ..."

Restaurant chains frequently use consistency to provide customers with the same experience across many locations. For example, Bob Evans uses the same logo, typefaces, color schemes, menus, staff uniforms, interior design, and architecture across its restaurants. This consistency improves brand recognition, reduces costs, and establishes a relationship with customers that extends beyond any single restaurant.

Constancy

The tendency to perceive objects as unchanging, despite changes in sensory input.[1]

People tend to perceive objects as constant and unchanging, despite changes in perspective, lighting, color, or size. For example, a person viewed at a distance produces a smaller image on the retina than that same person up close, but the perception of the size of the person is constant. The ability to perceive objects as having constant properties despite variations in how they are perceived eliminates the need to reinterpret those objects when they are perceived under different conditions. This indicates that perception involves more than simply receiving sensory inputs; rather, it is a process of continuously reconciling sensory inputs with memories about the properties of things in the world. A few examples of constancy include: [2]

Size Constancy—The size of objects is perceived to be constant, even though a change in distance makes objects appear smaller or larger (e.g., a city skyline at a great distance appears small, but the perception of the size of the buildings remains constant).

Brightness Constancy—The brightness of objects is perceived to be constant, even though changes in illumination make the objects appear brighter or darker (e.g., a white shirt appears gray in a dark room, but the perception of the color of the shirt remains constant).

Shape Constancy—The shape of objects is perceived to be constant, even though changes in perspective make the objects appear to have different shapes (e.g., a wheel from the side appears circular, at an angle it appears elliptical, and from the front it appears rectangular, but the perception of the shape of the wheel remains constant).

Loudness Constancy—The loudness of a sound is perceived to be constant, even though a change in distance makes the sound seem softer or louder (e.g., music playing on a radio seems to get softer as you walk away from it, but the perception of the volume of the radio remains constant).

All senses exhibit constancy to some extent. Consider the tendency when designing high-fidelity renderings, simulations, or models of objects and environments. For example, changes in properties like distance, perspective, and illumination should change appropriately for the type of interaction. Use recognizable objects and distance cues to provide size and shape references for unfamiliar objects. Consider illumination levels and background colors in environments when making decisions about color and brightness levels; lighting and color variations in the environment can trick the senses and alter the perception of color.

See also Color, Highlighting, Interference Effects, and Orientation Sensitivity.

[1] Also known as *perceptual constancy*.

[2] Seminal works on constancy include "Brightness Constancy and the Nature of Achromatic Colors" by Hans Wallach, *Journal of Experimental Psychology*, 1948, vol. 38, p. 310–324; and "Determinants of Apparent Visual Size With Distance Variant" by A. F. Holway and Edwin G. Boring, *American Journal of Psychology*, 1941, vol. 54, p. 21–37. A nice review of the various forms of constancy is found in *Sensation and Perception* by Margaret W. Matlin and Hugh J. Foley, 4th ed., Allyn & Bacon, 1997.

Despite their apparent differences, the pair of circles within the grid blocks are the same color and brightness—a fact easily revealed by covering the areas surrounding the circles.

The perceived differences are caused by correction errors made by the visual processing system, which tries to maintain constancy by offsetting color and brightness variations across different background conditions.

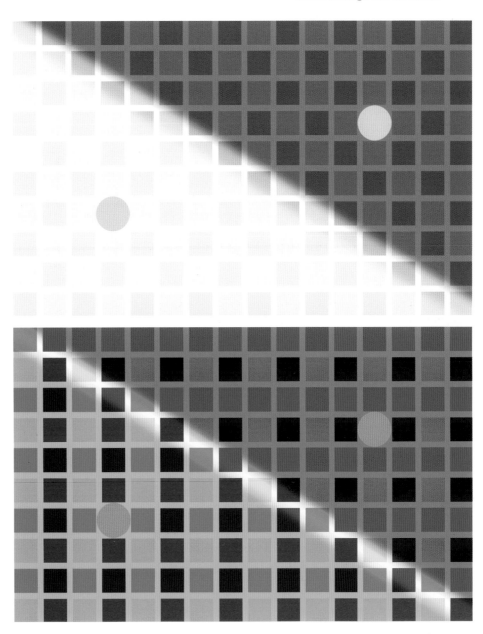

Constraint

A method of limiting the actions that can be performed on
a system.

Constraints limit the possible actions that can be performed on a system. For
example, dimming or hiding options that are not available at a particular time
effectively constrains the options that can be selected. Proper application of *constraints* in this fashion makes designs easier to use and dramatically reduces the
probability of error during interaction. There are two basic kinds of constraints:
physical constraints and psychological constraints.[1]

Physical constraints limit the range of possible actions by redirecting physical
motion in specific ways. The three kinds of physical constraints are paths, axes,
and barriers. Paths convert applied forces into linear or curvilinear motion using
channels or grooves (e.g., scroll bar in software user interfaces). Axes convert
applied forces into rotary motion, effectively providing a control surface of infinite
length in a small space (e.g., a trackball). Barriers absorb or deflect applied forces,
thereby halting, slowing, or redirecting the forces around the barrier (e.g., boundaries of a computer screen). Physical constraints are useful for reducing the
sensitivity of controls to unwanted inputs, and denying certain kinds of inputs
altogether. Paths are useful in situations where the control variable range is relatively small and bounded. Axes are useful in situations where control real estate is
limited, or the control variables are very large or unbounded. Barriers are useful
for denying errant or undesired actions.

Psychological constraints limit the range of possible actions by leveraging the way
people perceive and think about the world. The three kinds of psychological constraints are symbols, conventions, and mappings. Symbols influence behavior by
communicating meaning through language, such as the text and icon on a warning sign. Conventions influence behavior based on learned traditions and practices, such as "red means *stop*, green means *go*." Mappings influence behavior
based on the perceived relationships between elements. For example, light
switches that are close to a set of lights are perceived to be more related than
switches that are far away. Symbols are useful for labeling, explaining, and warning
using visual, aural, and tactile representation—all three if the message is critical.
Conventions indicate common methods of understanding and interacting, and are
useful for making systems consistent and easy to use. Mappings are useful for
implying what actions are possible based on the visibility, location, and appearance of controls.[2]

Use constraints in design to simplify usability and minimize errors. Use physical
constraints to reduce the sensitivity of controls, minimize unintentional inputs,
and prevent or slow dangerous actions. Use psychological constraints to improve
the clarity and intuitiveness of a design.

See also Affordance, Archetypes, Control, Errors, Forgiveness, and Mapping.

[1] The seminal work on psychological constraints
is *The Design of Everyday Things* by Donald
Norman, Doubleday, 1990.

[2] Note that Norman uses the terms *semantic
constraints*, *cultural constraints*, and *logical
constraints*.

Physical Constraints

Paths

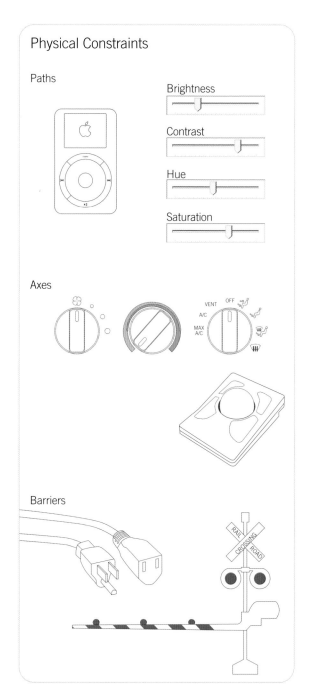

Brightness

Contrast

Hue

Saturation

Axes

VENT   OFF
A/C
MAX
A/C

Barriers

RAIL ROAD CROSSING

Psychological Constraints

Symbols

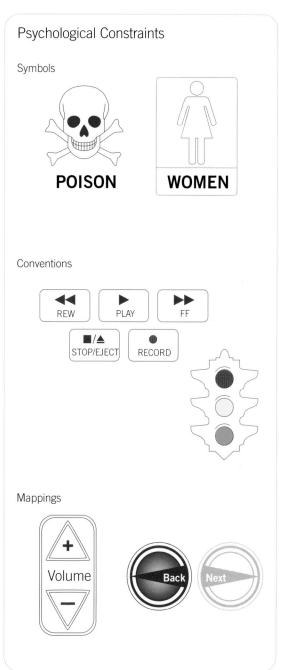

POISON   WOMEN

Conventions

REW   PLAY   FF

STOP/EJECT   RECORD

Mappings

+
Volume
−

Back   Next

Control

The level of control provided by a system should be related to the proficiency and experience levels of the people using the system.

People should be able to exercise control over what a system does, but the level of control should be related to their proficiency and experience using the system. Beginners do best with a reduced amount of control, while experts do best with greater control. A simple example is when children learn to ride a bicycle. Initially, training wheels are helpful in reducing the difficulty of riding by reducing the level of control (e.g., eliminating the need to balance while riding). This allows the child to safely develop basic riding skills with minimal risk of accident or injury. Once the basic skills are mastered, the training wheels get in the way, and hinder performance. As expertise increases, so too does the need for greater control.[1]

A system can accommodate these varying needs by offering multiple ways to perform a task. For example, novice users of word processors typically save their documents by accessing the *File* menu and selecting *Save*, whereas more proficient users typically save their documents using a keyboard shortcut. Both methods achieve the same outcome, but one favors simplicity and structure, while the other favors efficiency and flexibility. This tradeoff is standard when allocating system control. Beginners benefit from structured interactions with minimal choices, typically supported by prompts, constraints, and ready access to help. Experts benefit from less structured interactions that provide more direct access to functions, bypassing the support devices of beginners. Since accommodating multiple methods increases the complexity of the system, the number of methods for any given task should be limited to two—one for *beginners*, and one for *experts*.

The need to provide expert shortcuts is limited to systems that are used frequently enough for people to develop expertise. For example, the design of museum kiosks and ATMs should assume that all users are first-time users, and not try to accommodate varying levels of expertise. When systems are used frequently enough for people to develop expertise, it is often useful to provide simple ways to customize the system design. This represents the highest level of control a design can provide. It enables the appearance and configuration of a system to be aligned with personal preferences and level of expertise, and enables the efficiency of use to be fine-tuned according to individual needs over time.

Consider the allocation of control in the design of complex systems. When possible, use a method that is equally simple and efficient for beginners and experts. Otherwise, provide methods specialized for beginners and experts. Conceal expert methods to the extent possible to minimize complexity for beginners. When systems are complex and frequently used, consider designs that can be customized to conform to individual preference and levels of expertise.

See also Constraint, Flexibility-Usability Tradeoff, and Hierarchy of Needs.

[1] See, for example, *The Psychology of Human-Computer Interaction* by Stuart K. Card, Thomas P. Moran, and Allen Newell, Lawrence Erlbaum Associates, 1983; and *The Humane Interface: New Directions for Designing Interactive Systems* by Jef Raskin, Addison-Wesley 2000.

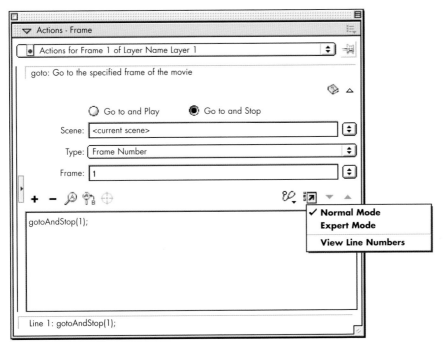

One method of accommodating variations in proficiency is to provide different methods of interaction for beginners and experts. For example, Macromedia Flash supports novice and expert developers by providing different user modes when writing scripts. Selecting the *Expert Mode* permits unconstrained command entry into the editor field. Selecting *Normal Mode* permits constrained entry only, requiring commands to be entered into specialized fields so that they can be immediately checked for correctness.

Convergence

A process in which similar characteristics evolve independently in multiple systems.

Natural or human-made systems that best approximate optimal strategies afforded by the environment tend to be successful, while systems exhibiting lesser approximations tend to become extinct. This process results in the convergence of form and function over time. The degree of convergence in an environment indicates its stability and receptivity to different kinds of innovation.

In nature, for example, the features of certain early dinosaurs—use of surface area for thermoregulation, and scales as an outer skin—evolved over millions of years to become the birds we see today. The genesis of flight for birds is different from that of other flying organisms such as bats and butterflies, but the set of adaptations for flight in all organisms has converged to just gliding and flapping. In human-created designs, this process can happen more quickly. For example, the design of virtually all automobiles today includes elements such as a four-wheel chassis, steering wheel, and an internal combustion engine—a convergence of form and function in decades versus millions of years.[1]

In both cases, the high degree of convergence indicates a stable environment— one that has not changed much over time—and designs that closely approximate the optimal strategies afforded by that environment. The result is a rate of evolution that is slow and incremental, tending toward refinements on existing convergent themes. Contrast this with the life-forms during the Cambrian period (570 million years ago) and dot-com companies of the 1990s; both periods of great diversity and experimentation of system form and function. This low degree of convergence indicates a volatile environment—one that is still changing—with few or no stable optimal strategies around which system designs can converge. The result is a rapid and disruptive rate of evolution, often resulting in new and innovative approaches that depart from previous designs.[2]

Consider the level of stability and convergence in an environment prior to design. Stable environments with convergent system designs are receptive to minor innovations and refinements but resist radical departures from established designs. Unstable environments with no convergent system designs are receptive to major innovations and experimentation, but offer little guidance as to which designs may or may not be successful. Focus on variations of convergent designs in stable environments, and explore analogies with other environments and systems for guidance when designing for new or unstable environments.[3]

See also Iteration and Mimicry.

[1] See, for example, *Cats' Paws and Catapults: Mechanical Worlds of Nature and People* by Steven Vogel, W. W. Norton & Company, 2000.

[2] For opposing perspectives on convergence in evolution, see *Wonderful Life: The Burgess Shale and the Nature of History* by Stephen Jay Gould, W. W. Norton & Company, 1990; and *The Crucible of Creation: The Burgess Shale and the Rise of Animals* by Simon Conway Morris, Oxford University Press, 1998.

[3] Alternatively, environments can be modified. For example, stable environments can be destabilized to promote innovation—e.g., a shift from managed markets to free markets.

Environmental and system analogies
often reveal new design possibilities.
The set of strategies for flight has
converged to just gliding and flapping
but expands to include buoyancy
and jet propulsion when flight is
reconsidered as movement through a
fluid. In this case, the degree of convergence still indicates environments
that have been stable for some time.
New flying systems that do not use
one or more of these strategies are
unlikely to compete successfully in
similar environments.

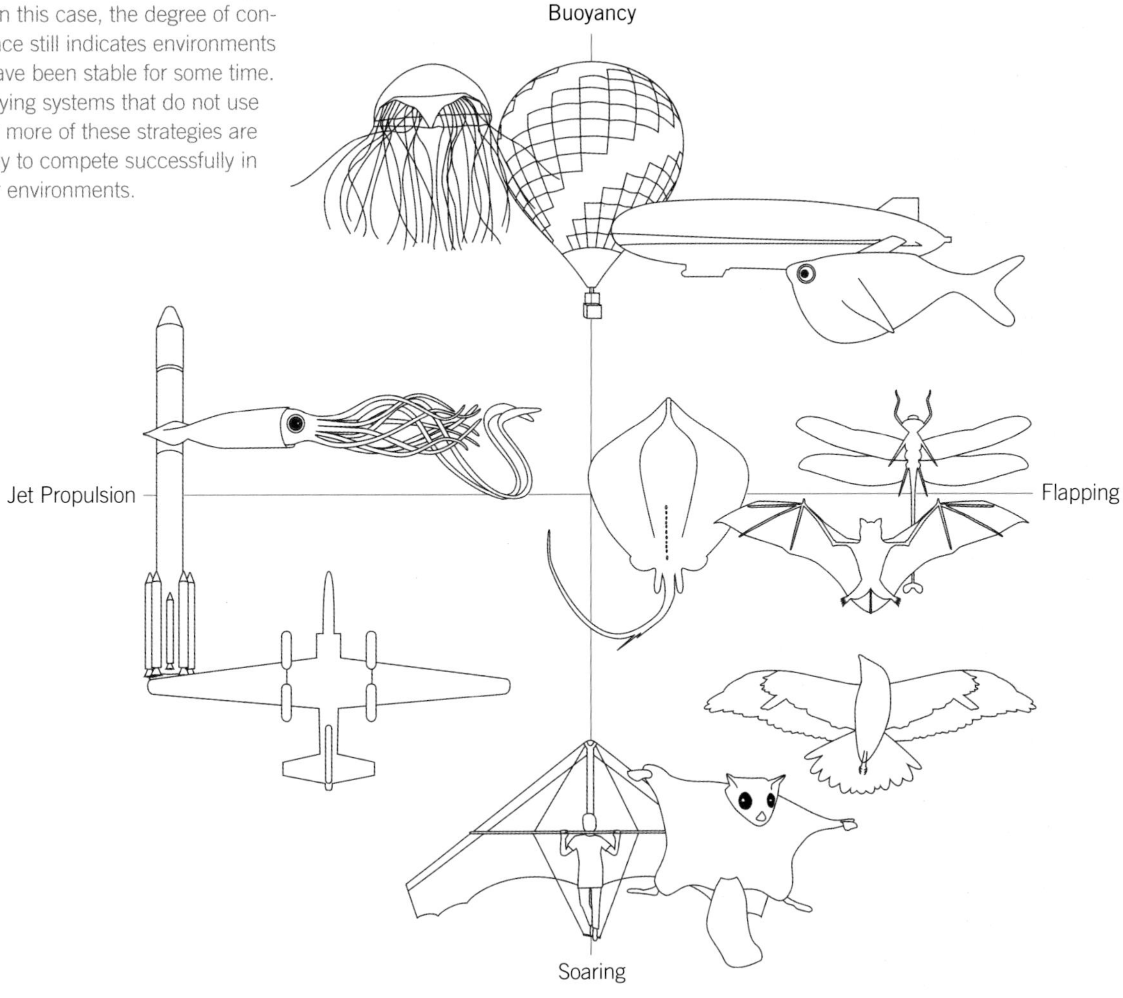

Buoyancy

Jet Propulsion

Flapping

Soaring

Cost-Benefit

An activity will be pursued only if its benefits are equal to or greater than the costs.

From a design perspective, the cost-benefit principle is typically used to assess the financial return associated with new features and elements. The cost-benefit principle can also be applied to determine design quality from a user perspective. If the costs associated with interacting with a design outweigh the benefits, the design is poor. If the benefits outweigh the costs, the design is good. For example, walking some distance to see a museum exhibit constitutes a cost. The level of interest in the exhibit constitutes a benefit. Thus, if the level of interest outweighs the cost of the walk, the exhibit design is good.

The quality of every design aspect can be measured using the cost-benefit principle. How much reading is too much to get the point of a message? How many steps are too many to set the time and date of a video recorder? How long is too long for a person to wait for a Web page to download? The answer to all of these questions is that it depends on the benefits of the interaction. For example, the often-cited maximum acceptable download time for pages on the Internet is ten seconds. However, the acceptability of download time is a function of the benefits provided by the downloaded page. A high-benefit page can more than compensate for the cost of a download taking longer than ten seconds. Conversely, a low-benefit page cannot compensate the cost of any download time. Reducing interaction costs does improve the quality of the design, but to simply design within cost limits without consideration of the interaction benefits misses the point of design altogether—i.e., to provide benefit.

A common mistake regarding application of the cost-benefit principle is to presume which aspects of a system will be perceived as costs, and which will be perceived as benefits. For example, new design features or elements that excite designers are often never used or even noticed by people who interact with the design. In many cases, such features and elements increase the design's interaction costs by adding complexity to the system. In order to avoid this, observe people interacting with the design or similar designs in the actual target environment. Focus groups and usability tests are valuable in assessing the cost-benefits of a design during development, when natural observation is not possible.

Consider the cost-benefit principle in all aspects of design. Do not make design decisions based on cost parameters alone without due consideration of the benefits realized from interactions. Verify cost-benefit perceptions of target populations through careful observations, focus groups, and usability tests.

See also 80/20 Rule, Aesthetic-Usability Effect, and Expectation Effect.

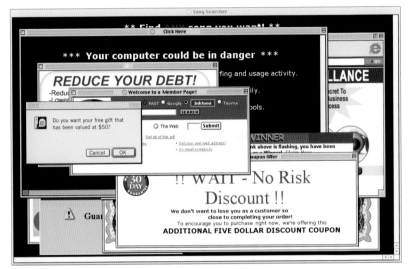

From a user perspective, Internet advertising via pop-up windows is all cost and no benefit. If the advertisements were properly designed to minimize cost and maximize benefit, people would be more likely to pay attention and form positive associations.

These banner advertisements demonstrate one method of improving the cost-benefit of Internet advertising: creative interactivity. Whether shooting viruses, playing slots, or engaging in word play, these advertisements use entertainment to compensate people for their time and attention.

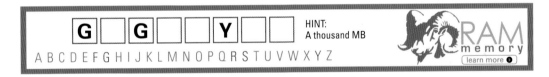

Defensible Space

A space that has territorial markers, opportunities for surveillance, and clear indications of activity and ownership.

Defensible spaces are used to deter crime. A defensible space is an area such as a neighborhood, house, park, or office that has features that convey ownership and afford easy and frequent surveillance. These features allow residents to establish control over their private and community property, and ultimately deter criminal activity. There are three key features of defensible spaces: territoriality, surveillance, and symbolic barriers.[1]

Territoriality is the establishment of clearly defined spaces of ownership. Common territorial features include community markers and gates to cultivate a community identity and mark the collective territory of residents; visible boundaries such as walls, hedges, and fences to create private yards; and privatization of public services so that residents must take greater personal responsibility and ownership (e.g., private trash cans instead of public dumpsters). These territorial elements explicitly assign custodial responsibility of a space to residents, and communicate to outsiders that the space is owned and protected.

Surveillance is the monitoring of the environment during normal daily activities. Common surveillance features include external lighting; windows and doors that open directly to the outside of first-floor dwellings; mailboxes located in open and well-trafficked areas; and well-maintained courtyards, playgrounds, and walkways that increase pedestrian activity and casual surveillance. These features make it more difficult for people to engage in unnoticed activities.

Symbolic barriers are objects placed in the environment to create the perception that a person's space is cared for and worthy of defense. Common symbolic barriers include picnic tables, swings, flowers, and lawn furniture—any symbol that conveys that the owner of the property is actively involved in using and maintaining the property. Note that when items that are atypical for a community are displayed, it can sometimes symbolize affluence and act as a lure rather than a barrier. Therefore, the appropriateness of various kinds of symbolic barriers must be considered within the context of a particular community.[2]

Incorporate defensible space features in the design of residences, offices, industrial facilities, and communities to deter crime. Clearly mark territories to indicate ownership and responsibility; increase opportunities for surveillance and reduce environmental elements that allow concealment; reduce unassigned open spaces and services; and use typical symbolic barriers to indicate activity and use.

See also Control, Prospect-Refuge, Visibility, and Wayfinding.

[1] The seminal works on defensible space are *Defensible Space: People and Design in the Violent City*, Macmillan, 1972; and *Creating Defensible Space*, U.S. Department of Housing and Urban Development, 1996, both by Oscar Newman.

[2] "Territorial Cues and Defensible Space Theory: The Burglar's Point of View" by Julie E. MacDonald and Robert Gifford, *Journal of Environmental Psychology*, 1989, vol. 9, p. 193–205.

Before

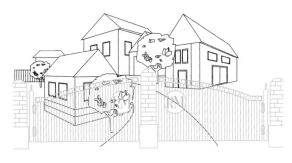

Territoriality

Elements that indicate ownership and improve surveillance enhance the defensibility of a space. In this case, the addition of community markers and gating indicates a territory that is owned by the community; improved lighting and public benches increase opportunities for casual surveillance; and local fences, doormats, shrubbery, and other symbolic barriers clearly convey that the space is owned and maintained.

Surveillance

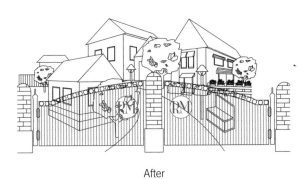

After

Symbolic Barriers

Depth of Processing

A phenomenon of memory in which information that is analyzed deeply is better recalled than information that is analyzed superficially.[1]

Thinking hard about information improves the likelihood that the information will be recalled at a later time. For example, consider two tasks that involve interacting with and recalling the same information. In the first task, a group of people is asked to locate a keyword in a list and circle it. In the second task, another group of people is asked to locate a keyword in a list, circle it, and then define it. After a brief time, both groups are asked to recall the keywords from the tasks. The group that performed the second task will have better recall of the keywords because they had to analyze the keywords at a deeper level than the group in the first task; they had to think harder about the information.[2]

This phenomenon of memory results from the two ways in which information is processed, known as *maintenance rehearsal* and *elaborative rehearsal*. Maintenance rehearsal simply repeats the same kind of analysis that has already been carried out. For example, people often use maintenance rehearsal when they repeat a phone number back to themselves to help them remember; no additional analysis is performed on the phone number. Elaborative rehearsal involves a deeper, more meaningful analysis of the information. For example, people engage in elaborative rehearsal when they read a text passage and then have to answer questions about the meaning of the passage; additional analysis as to word and sentence meaning require additional thought. Generally, elaborative rehearsal results in recall performance that is two to three times better than maintenance rehearsal.[3]

The key determining factors as to how *deeply* information is processed are the distinctiveness of the information, the relevance of the information, and the degree to which the information is elaborated. Distinctiveness refers to the uniqueness of the information relative to surrounding information and previous experience. Relevance refers to the degree to which the information is perceived to be important. The degree of elaboration refers to how much thought is required to interpret and understand the information. Generally, deep processing of information that involves these factors will result in the best possible recall and retention of information.[4]

Consider depth of processing in design contexts where recall and retention of information is important. Use unique presentation and interesting activities to engage people to deeply process information. Use case studies, examples, and other devices to make information relevant to an audience. Note that deep processing requires more concentration and effort than mere exposure (e.g., classroom lecture), and therefore frequent periods of rest should be incorporated into the presentation and tasks.

See also Advance Organizer, Mnemonic Device, Picture Superiority Effect, and von Restorff Effect.

[1] Also known as *levels-of-processing approach*.

[2] The seminal work on depth of processing is "Levels of Processing: A Framework for Memory Research" by Fergus I. M. Craik and Robert S. Lockhart, *Journal of Verbal Learning and Verbal Behavior*, 1972, vol. 11, p. 671–684.

[3] See, for example, "Depth of Processing and the Retention of Words in Episodic Memory" by Fergus I. M. Craik and Endel Tulving, *Journal of Experimental Psychology: General*, 1975, vol. 104, p. 268–294.

[4] See, for example, "The Self as a Mnemonic Device: The Role of Internal Cues" by Francis S. Bellezza, *Journal of Personality and Social Psychology*, 1984, vol. 47, p. 506–516.

Level of Processing

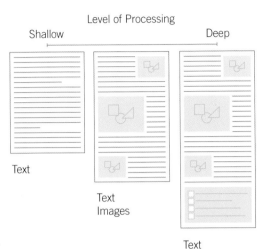

Shallow ——————————————— Deep

Text

**Text
Images**

**Text
Images
Questions**

The more deeply learners process information, the better they learn. Depth of processing is improved through the use of multiple presentation media and learning activities that engage learners in elaborative rehearsal—as in this e-learning course by EduNeering.

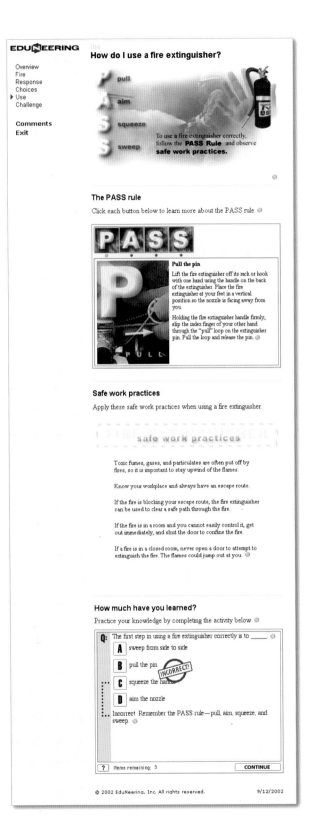

Development Cycle

Successful products typically follow four stages of creation: requirements, design, development, and testing.

All products progress sequentially through basic stages of creation. Understanding and using effective practices for each stage allows designers to maximize a product's probability of success. There are four basic stages of creation for all products: requirements, design, development, and testing.[1]

Requirements
In formal processes, requirements are gathered through market research, customer feedback, focus groups, and usability testing. Informally, design requirements are often derived from direct knowledge or experience. Design requirements are best obtained through controlled interactions between designers and members of the target audience, and not simply by asking people what they want or like—often they do not know, or cannot clearly articulate their needs.

Design
This stage is where design requirements are translated into a form that yields a set of specifications. The goal is to meet the design requirements, though an implicit goal is to do so in a unique fashion. Excellent design is usually accomplished through careful research of existing or analogous solutions, active brainstorming of many diverse participants, ample use of prototyping, and many iterations of trying, testing, and tuning concepts. A design that is appreciably the same at the beginning and end of this stage is probably not much of a design.

Development
The development stage is where design specifications are transformed into an actual product. The goal of development is to precisely meet the design specifications. Two basic quality control strategies are used to accomplish this: reduce variability in the materials, creations of parts, and assembly of parts; and verify that specifications are being maintained throughout the development process.

Testing
The testing stage is where the product is tested to ensure that it meets design requirements and specifications, and will be accepted by the target audience. Testing at this stage generally focuses on the quality of modules and their integration, real-world performance (real contexts, real users), and ease and reliability of installation.

Gather requirements through controlled interactions with target audiences, rather than simple feedback or speculation by team members. Use research, brainstorming, prototyping, and iterative design to achieve optimal designs. Minimize variability in products and processes to improve quality. Test all aspects of the design to the degree possible.

See also Hierarchy of Needs, Iteration, Life Cycle, Prototyping, and Scaling Fallacy.

[1] A nice treatment of contemporary product development issues and strategies is found in *Products in Half the Time: New Rules, New Tools* by Preston G. Smith and Donald G. Reinertsen, John Wiley & Sons, 2nd ed., 1997; and *Managing the Design Factory: The Product Developer's Toolkit* by Donald G. Reinertsen, Free Press, 1997.

Linear

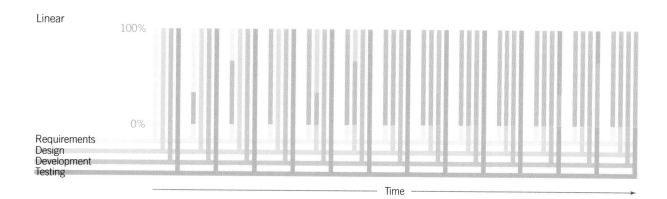

100%

0%

Requirements
Design
Development
Testing

Time

Iterative

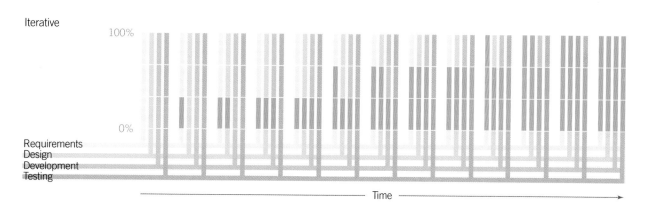

100%

0%

Requirements
Design
Development
Testing

Time

Although progress through the development cycle is sequential, it can be linear or iterative. The linear model (also known as the *waterfall model*) proceeds through the development cycle once, completing each stage before proceeding to the next. The iterative model (also known as the *spiral model*) proceeds through the development cycle multiple times, completing an increasing percentage of each stage with each iteration. The linear model is preferred when requirements and specifications are exact and unchanging, and the cost of iteration is prohibitive. In all other cases, the iterative model is preferred.

Entry Point

A point of physical or attentional entry into a design.

People do judge books by their covers, Internet sites by their first pages, and buildings by their lobbies. This initial impression of a system or environment greatly influences subsequent perceptions and attitudes, which then affects the quality of subsequent interactions. This impression is largely formed at the entry point to a system or environment. For example, entering many Internet sites entails going through a slow-loading splash screen, followed by a slow-loading main page, followed by several pop-up windows with advertisements—all this to enter a site that may or may not have the information the person was looking for. Such errors in entry point design annoy visitors who make it through, or deter visitors altogether. Either way, it does not promote additional interaction. The key elements of good entry point design are minimal barriers, points of prospect, and progressive lures.[1]

Minimal Barriers

Barriers should not encumber entry points. Examples of barriers to entry are highly trafficked parking lots, noisy displays with many unnecessary elements, sales-people standing at the doors of retail stores, or anything that impedes people from getting to and moving through an entry point. Barriers can be aesthetic as well as functional in nature. For example, a poorly maintained building front or landscape is an aesthetic barrier to entry.

Points of Prospect

Entry points should allow people to become oriented and clearly survey available options. Points of prospect include store entrances that provide a clear view of store layout and aisle signs, or Internet pages that provide good orientation cues and navigation options. Points of prospect should provide sufficient time and space for a person to review options with minimal distraction or disruption—i.e., people should not feel hurried or crowded by their surroundings or other people.

Progressive Lures

Lures should be used to attract and pull people through the entry point. Progressive lures can be compelling headlines from the front page of a newspaper, greeters at restaurants, or the display of popular products or destinations (e.g., restrooms) just beyond the entry point of a store. Progressive lures get people to incrementally approach, enter, and move through the entry point.

Maximize the effectiveness of the entry point in a design by reducing barriers, establishing clear points of prospect, and using progressive lures. Provide suffi-cient time and space for people to review opportunities for interaction at the entry point. Consider progressive lures like highlighting, entry point greeters, and popular offerings visibly located beyond the entry point to get people to enter and progress through.

See also Immersion, Prospect-Refuge, and Wayfinding.

[1] See, for example, *Why We Buy: The Science of Shopping* by Paco Underhill, Touchstone Books, 2000; *Hotel Design, Planning, and Development* by Walter A. Rutes, Richard H. Penner, Lawrence Adams, W. W. Norton & Company, 2001; and "The Stanford-Poynter Eyetracking Study" by Marion Lewenstein, Greg Edwards, Deborah Tatar, and Andrew DeVigal, http://www.poynterextra.org.

The redesign of the *Wall Street Journal* creates a clear entry point to each edition by highlighting the region of the page containing news summaries. The summaries also act as a point of prospect, allowing readers to quickly scan for stories of interest with no competing visual barriers. Page references on select summaries act as progressive lures, leading readers to the full articles in different sections of the paper.

Apple Computer retail stores maintain the high standards of design excellence for which Apple is known. The stores appear more like museums than retail shops, creating tempting visual spectacles that are hard to pass by.

Apple Retail Store
Level 1

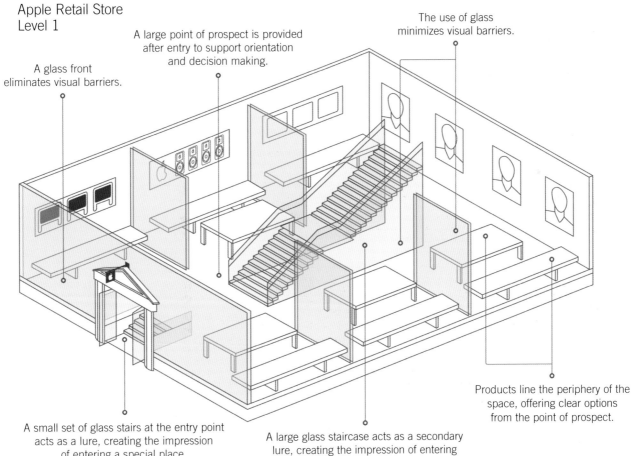

A large point of prospect is provided after entry to support orientation and decision making.

The use of glass minimizes visual barriers.

A glass front eliminates visual barriers.

A small set of glass stairs at the entry point acts as a lure, creating the impression of entering a special place.

A large glass staircase acts as a secondary lure, creating the impression of entering another special space.

Products line the periphery of the space, offering clear options from the point of prospect.

Errors

An action or omission of action yielding an unintended result.

Most accidents are caused by what is referred to as *human error*, yet most accidents are actually due to design errors rather than errors of human operation. An understanding of the causes of errors suggests specific design strategies that can greatly reduce their frequency and severity. There are two basic types of errors: slips and mistakes.[1]

Slips are sometimes referred to as *errors of action* or *errors of execution*, and occur when an action is not what was intended. For example, a slip occurs when a person dials a frequently dialed phone number when intending to dial a different number. Slips are the result of automatic, unconscious processes, and frequently result from a change of routine or an interruption of an action. For example, a person forgets their place in a procedure when interrupted by a phone call.[2]

Minimize slips by providing clear feedback on actions. Make error messages clear, and include the consequences of the error, as well as corrective actions, if possible. Position controls to prevent accidental activation of functions that may have detrimental consequences. When this is not possible, use confirmations to interrupt the flow and verify the action. Consider the use of affordances and constraints to influence actions.

Mistakes are sometimes referred to as *errors of intention* or *errors of planning*, and occur when an intention is inappropriate. For example, a mistake occurs when a nurse interprets an alarm incorrectly and then administers the incorrect medicine. Mistakes are caused by conscious mental processes, and frequently result from stress or decision-making biases. For example, a person is biased to select only from visible options.

Minimize mistakes by increasing situational awareness and reducing environmental noise. Make key indicators and controls visible within one eyespan whenever possible. Reduce stress and cognitive load by minimizing the auditory and visual noise. Provide just enough feedback to accomplish warnings and other functions, and no more. Consider the use of confirmations that require multiple steps to verify the intention of highly critical tasks. Train on error recovery and troubleshooting, emphasizing communication with other team members.

Finally, always incorporate the principle of forgiveness into a design. Forgiveness refers to the use of design elements to reduce the frequency and severity of errors when they occur, enhancing the design's safety and usability.

See also Affordance, Confirmation, Constraint, and Forgiveness.

[1] The seminal work on errors is "Categorization of Action Slips" by Donald A. Norman, *Psychological Review*, 1981, vol. 88, p. 1–15; and *Absent Minded? The Psychology of Mental Lapses and Everyday Errors* by James Reason and Klara Mycielska, Prentice-Hall, 1982.

[2] Note that there are many different error taxonomies. A nice review and discussion regarding the various taxonomies is found in *Human Error* by James Reason, Cambridge University Press, 1990. A very readable and interesting treatment of human error is *Set Phasers on Stun and Other True Tales of Design, Technology, and Human Error* by Steven Casey, Aegean Publishing Company, 1998.

Two Types of Slips

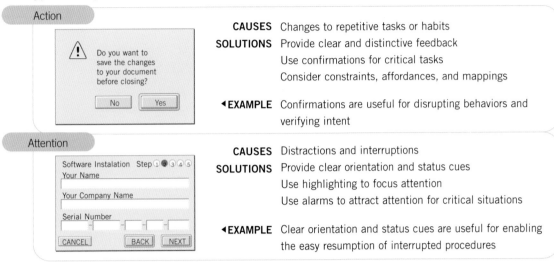

Action

CAUSES Changes to repetitive tasks or habits

SOLUTIONS Provide clear and distinctive feedback

Use confirmations for critical tasks

Consider constraints, affordances, and mappings

◄**EXAMPLE** Confirmations are useful for disrupting behaviors and verifying intent

Attention

CAUSES Distractions and interruptions

SOLUTIONS Provide clear orientation and status cues

Use highlighting to focus attention

Use alarms to attract attention for critical situations

◄**EXAMPLE** Clear orientation and status cues are useful for enabling the easy resumption of interrupted procedures

Three Types of Mistakes

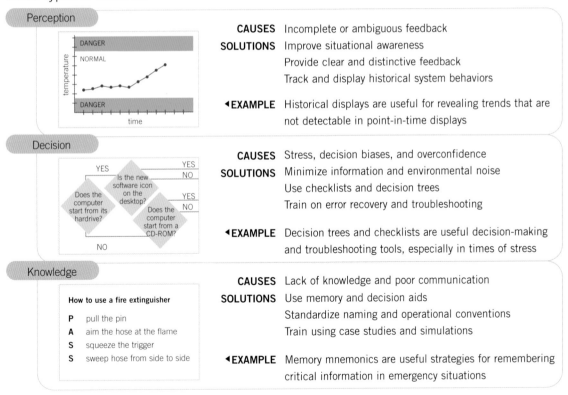

Perception

CAUSES Incomplete or ambiguous feedback

SOLUTIONS Improve situational awareness

Provide clear and distinctive feedback

Track and display historical system behaviors

◄**EXAMPLE** Historical displays are useful for revealing trends that are not detectable in point-in-time displays

Decision

CAUSES Stress, decision biases, and overconfidence

SOLUTIONS Minimize information and environmental noise

Use checklists and decision trees

Train on error recovery and troubleshooting

◄**EXAMPLE** Decision trees and checklists are useful decision-making and troubleshooting tools, especially in times of stress

Knowledge

CAUSES Lack of knowledge and poor communication

SOLUTIONS Use memory and decision aids

Standardize naming and operational conventions

Train using case studies and simulations

◄**EXAMPLE** Memory mnemonics are useful strategies for remembering critical information in emergency situations

Expectation Effect

A phenomenon in which perception and behavior changes as a result of personal expectations or the expectations of others.

The expectation effect refers to ways in which expectations affect perception and behavior. Generally, when people are aware of a probable or desired outcome, their perceptions and behavior are affected in some way. A few examples of this phenomenon include.[1]

Halo Effect—Employers rate the performance of certain employees more highly than others based on their overall positive impression of those employees.

Hawthorne Effect—Employees are more productive based on their belief that changes made to the environment will increase productivity.

Pygmalion Effect—Students perform better or worse based on the expectations of their teacher.

Placebo Effect—Patients experience treatment effects based on their belief that a treatment will work.

Rosenthal Effect—Teachers treat students differently based on their expectations of how students will perform.

Demand Characteristics—Participants in an experiment or interview provide responses and act in ways that they believe are expected by the experimenter or interviewer.

The expectation effect demonstrates that expectations can greatly influence perceptions and behavior. For example, tell a large group of people that a new product will change their lives, and a significant number will find their lives changed—the belief is simply a device that helps create the change. Once a person believes something will happen, the belief alone creates that possibility. Unfortunately, this can have a negative impact on the ability to accurately measure a design's success. Since designers are naturally biased toward their designs, they often unintentionally influence test subjects through words or actions, or may omit certain results in order to corroborate their expectations. Test subjects often respond by seeking to meet the expectations communicated to them.

Consider the expectation effect when introducing and promoting a design. When trying to persuade, set expectations in a credible fashion for the target audience rather than letting them form their own unbiased conclusions. When evaluating a design, use proper test procedures to avoid biases resulting from the expectation effect.

See also Exposure Effect, Framing, and Uncertainty Principle.

[1] Seminal works on the expectation effect include *The Human Problems of an Industrial Civilization* by Elton Mayo, Macmillan, 1933; "The Effect of Experimenter Bias on the Performance of the Albino Rat" by Robert Rosenthal and Kermit Fode, *Behavioral Science*, 1963, vol. 8, p. 115–118; "Teachers' Expectancies: Determinants of Pupils' IQ Gains" by Robert Rosenthal and Lenore Jacobson, *Psychological Reports*, vol. 19, p. 115–118. For a nice review of the placebo effect, see *The Placebo Effect: An Interdisciplinary Exploration* edited by Anne Harrington, Harvard University Press, 1999.

The expectation effect can influence perception and behavior, but the changes are temporary. For example, the marker along the time axis indicates the point at which an expectation was set. A change in performance may be observed as a result (e.g., increased productivity) but usually reverts back to baseline.

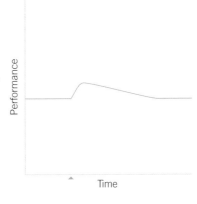

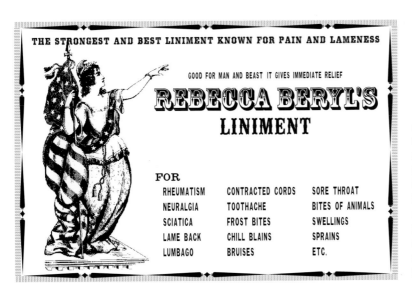

THE STRONGEST AND BEST LINIMENT KNOWN FOR PAIN AND LAMENESS

GOOD FOR MAN AND BEAST IT GIVES IMMEDIATE RELIEF

REBECCA BERYL'S LINIMENT

FOR

RHEUMATISM	CONTRACTED CORDS	SORE THROAT
NEURALGIA	TOOTHACHE	BITES OF ANIMALS
SCIATICA	FROST BITES	SWELLINGS
LAME BACK	CHILL BLAINS	SPRAINS
LUMBAGO	BRUISES	ETC.

A credible presentation will generate an expectation effect in about 30 percent of any given audience. Keeping the claims and outcomes vague often helps—a believing person is biased to interpret ambiguous effects in accordance with their expectations. This technique was used to sell snake oil solutions, and is still widely used to sell astrology, psychic predictions, and things such as fad diets.

SAGITTARIUS

November 23–December 21
It's a favorable time for real estate, investments, and moneymaking opportunities to be successful. Romance could develop through social activities or short trips. Don't expect new acquaintances to be completely honest about themselves. Your lucky day this week will be Sunday.

Exposure Effect

Repeated exposure to stimuli for which people have neutral feelings will increase the likeability of the stimuli.[1]

The exposure effect occurs when stimuli are repeatedly presented and, as a result, are increasingly well liked and accepted. For example, the more a song or slogan is repeated, the more popular it is likely to become; a phenomenon exploited by both radio and television networks. The exposure effect applies only to stimuli that are perceived as neutral or positive. Repeated exposures to an offending stimulus may actually amplify the negative perception, rather than remedy it. The exposure effect is observed with music, paintings, drawings, images, people, and advertisements.[2]

The strongest exposure effects are seen with photographs, meaningful words, names, and simple shapes; the smallest effects are seen with icons, people, and auditory stimuli. The exposure effect gradually weakens as the number of presentations increases—probably due to boredom. Complex and interesting stimuli tend to amplify the effect, whereas simple and boring stimuli tend to weaken it. Interestingly, the longer a stimulus is exposed, the weaker the exposure effect. The strongest effect is achieved when exposures are so brief or subtle that they are subliminal (not consciously processed), or when they are separated by a delay.[3]

Familiarity plays a primary role in aesthetic appeal and acceptance; people like things more when frequently exposed to them. For example, the initial resistance by many people to the Vietnam Veterans Memorial was primarily caused by a lack of familiarity with its minimalist, abstract design. Similar resistance was experienced by Pablo Picasso with his Cubist works, Gustave Eiffel with the Eiffel Tower, Frank Lloyd Wright with the Guggenheim Museum, and many others whose works are today widely accepted as brilliant and beautiful. As the level of exposure to these works increased with time, familiarity with the works also increased and resulted in greater acceptance and popularity.

Use the exposure effect to strengthen advertising and marketing campaigns, enhance the perceived credibility and aesthetic of designs, and generally improve the way people think and feel about a message or product. Keep the exposures brief, and separate them with periods of delay. The exposure effect will be strongest for the first ten exposures; therefore, focus resources on early presentations for maximum benefit. Expect and prepare for resistance to a design if it is significantly different from the norm.

See also Aesthetic-Usability Effect, Classical Conditioning, Cognitive Dissonance, and Framing.

[1] Also known as *mere exposure effect, repetition-validity effect, frequency-validity effect, truth effect,* and *repetition effect.*

[2] The seminal application of the exposure effect was in early 20th-century propaganda—see, for example, *Adolf Hitler: A Chilling Tale of Propaganda* by Max Arthur and Joseph Goebbels, Trident Press International, 1999. The seminal empirical work on the exposure effect is "Attitudinal Effects of Mere Exposure" by Robert Zajonc, *Journal of Personality and Social Psychology Monographs*, vol. 9(2), p. 1–27.

[3] See, for example, "Exposure and Affect: Overview and Meta-Analysis of Research, 1968–1987" by Robert F. Bornstein, *Psychological Bulletin*, 1989, vol. (106), p. 265–289.

СОВЕТСКАЯ ВЛАСТЬ
В МИЛЛИОН РАЗ ДЕМОКРАТИЧНЕЕ
САМОЙ ДЕМОКРАТИЧЕСКОЙ
БУРЖУАЗНОЙ РЕСПУБЛИКИ

The exposure effect has always been a primary tool of propagandists. Ubiquitous positive depictions, such as these of Vladimir Lenin, are commonly used to increase the likeability and support of political leaders. Similar techniques are used in marketing, advertising, and electoral campaigns.

Face-ism Ratio

The ratio of face to body in an image that influences the way the person in the image is perceived.[1]

Images depicting a person with a high face-ism ratio—the face takes up most of the image—focus attention on the person's intellectual and personality attributes. Images depicting a person in a low face-ism ratio—the body takes up most of the image—focus attention on the physical and sensual attributes of the person. The face-ism ratio is calculated by dividing the distance from the top of the head to the bottom of the chin (head height) by the distance from the top of the head to the lowest visible part of the body (total visible height). An image without a face would have a face-ism ratio of 0.00, and an image with only a face would have a face-ism ratio of 1.00. Irrespective of gender, people rate individuals in high face-ism images as being more intelligent, dominant, and ambitious than individuals in low face-ism images.

The term *face-ism* originated from research on gender bias in the media. It was found that images of men in magazines, movies, and other media have significantly higher face-ism ratios than images of women. This appears true across most cultures, and is thought to reflect gender-stereotypical beliefs regarding the characteristics of men and women. While there is little consensus as to why this is the case, it is likely the result of unconscious processes resulting from a mix of biological and cultural factors. In one experiment, for example, male and female college students were randomly assigned a task to draw either a man or a woman. The students were told they would be evaluated on their drawing skills, and were given no additional instructions. Both genders drew men with prominent and detailed faces, and drew women with full bodies and minimally detailed faces.[2]

Consider face-ism in the representation of people in photographs and drawings. When the design objective requires more thoughtful interpretations or associations, use images with high face-ism ratios. When the design objective requires more ornamental interpretations or associations, use images with low-face-ism ratios. Note that the interpretations of the images will be the same irrespective of the subject's or viewer's gender.

See also Attractiveness Bias, Baby-Face Bias, Classical Conditioning, Framing, and Waist-to-Hip Ratio.

[1] The term *face-ism* is used by some researchers to refer to the tendency of the media to represent men in high face-ism images, and women in low face-ism images—also referred to as *body-ism*.

[2] The seminal work on face-ism is "Face-ism" by Dane Archer, Debra D. Kimes, and Michael Barrios, *Psychology Today*, 1978, p. 65–66; and "Face-ism: 5 Studies of Sex-Differences in Facial Prominence" by Dane Archer, Bonita Iritani, Debra D. Kimes, and Michael Barrios, *Journal of Personality and Social Psychology*, 1983, vol. 45, p. 725–735.

Face-ism Ratio = .96

Face-ism Ratio = .55

Face-ism Ratio = .37

The effect of face-ism is evident in these photographs. The high face-ism photograph emphasizes more cerebral or personality-related attributes like intelligence and ambition. The lower face-ism photographs emphasize more physical attributes like sensuality and physical attractiveness.

Factor of Safety

The use of more elements than is thought to be necessary to offset the effects of unknown variables and prevent system failure.[1]

Design requires dealing with unknowns. No matter how knowledgeable the designer and how thoroughly researched the design specification, basic assumptions about unknowns of one kind or another are inevitable in every design process. Factors of safety are used to offset the potential effects of these unknowns. This is achieved by adding materials and components to the system in order to make the design exceed the specification that is believed to be necessary to meet the design requirements. For example, designing an Internet service that can support one thousand users is straightforward. However, to account for unanticipated uses of the service (e.g., downloading large files), the design specification can be multiplied by a safety factor (e.g., three). In this case, a safety factor of three would mean that the service would be rated to support one thousand users, but actually designed to support three times that many, or three thousand users.

The size of the safety factor corresponds directly to the level of ignorance of the design parameters. The greater the ignorance, the greater the safety factor. For example, structures that are well understood and made of materials of consistent quality, such as steel and concrete structures, typically use a safety factor ranging from two to four. Structures that are well understood and made of materials of varying quality, such as wood, may use a safety factor ranging from four to eight. When ignorance is combined with materials of varying quality, the safety factor can get quite large. For example, the designers of the Great Pyramid at Giza unknowingly applied a safety factor of over twenty.[2]

Increasing the safety factor in a design translates into the addition of elements (e.g., materials). More elements means more cost. New designs must typically have large factors of safety because the number of unknowns is great. If a design performs reliably over time, confidence that the unknowns in the system have been managed combines with the pressure to reduce costs, and typically leads to a "tuning" process to reduce elements and lower the safety factor. Unfortunately, this process usually continues until an accident or failure occurs, at which point cost considerations become secondary and safety factors are again increased.[3]

Use safety factors to minimize the probability of failure in a design. Apply them in proportion to the ignorance of the design parameters and the severity of the consequences of failure. Reduce safety factors with caution, especially when specifications extend beyond design precedents. Observe the rated capacity of a system when making decisions that stress system limits, and not the designed capacity (capacity including factors of safety), except in cases of emergency.

See also Errors, Modularity, Structural Forms, and Weakest Link.

[1] Also known as *factor of ignorance*.

[2] Note that different elements within a system can observe different factors of safety. For example, a wing on an aircraft may apply a factor of safety that is much greater than the factor of safety applied to less critical elements.

[3] See, for example, *To Engineer Is Human: The Role of Failure in Successful Design*, Macmillan, 1985; and *Design Paradigms: Case Histories of Error and Judgment in Engineering*, Cambridge University Press, 1994, both by Henry Petroski.

The O-ring design of the space shuttle *Challenger*'s solid rocket booster was designed to have a safety factor of three. However, low temperatures contributed to the erosion of O-rings in past launches and, consequently, to the erosion of this safety factor; at low temperatures, the safety factor was well below three. On the morning of January 28, 1986, the temperature at the launch pad was 36 degrees F (2.2 degrees C)—the lowest launch temperature to date. Despite the objections of several engineers, the decision to proceed with the launch was based largely on the belief that the safety factor was sufficient to offset any low-temperature risks. Catastrophic failure occurred shortly after launch.

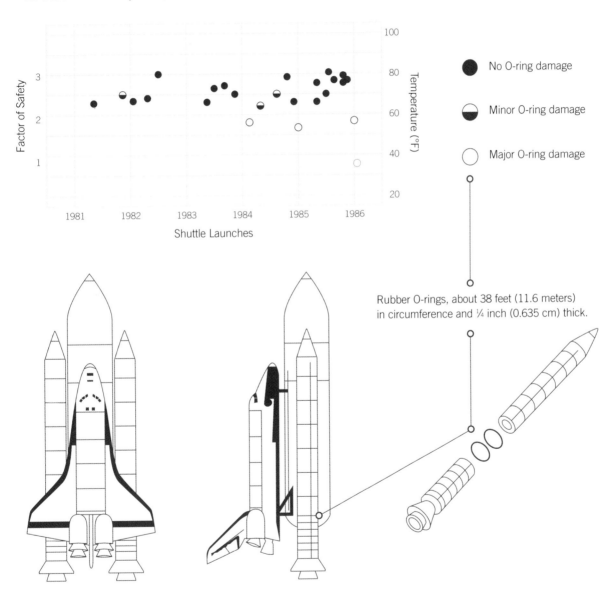

Rubber O-rings, about 38 feet (11.6 meters) in circumference and ¼ inch (0.635 cm) thick.

Feedback Loop

A relationship between variables in a system where the consequences of an event feed back into the system as input, modifying the event in the future.

Every action creates an equal and opposite reaction. When reactions loop back to affect themselves, a feedback loop is created. All real-world systems are compose of many such interacting feedback loops—animals, machines, businesses, and ecosystems, to name a few. There are two types of feedback loops: positive and negative. Positive feedback amplifies system output, resulting in growth or decline. Negative feedback dampens output, stabilizing the system around an equilibrium point.[1]

Positive feedback loops are effective for creating change, but generally result in negative consequences if not moderated by negative feedback loops. For example, in response to head and neck injuries in football in the 1950s, designers created plastic football helmets with internal padding to replace leather helmets. The helmets provided more protection, but induced players to take increasingly greater risks when tackling. More head and neck injuries occurred than before. By concentrating on the problem in isolation (e.g., not considering changes in player behavior) designers inadvertently created a positive feedback loop in which players used their head and neck in increasingly risky ways. This resulted in more injuries, which resulted in additional redesigns that made the helmet shells harder and more padded, and so on.[2]

Negative feedback loops are effective for resisting change. For example, the Segway Human Transporter uses negative feedback loops to maintain equilibrium. As a rider leans forward or backward, the Segway accelerates or decelerates to keep the system in equilibrium. To achieve this smoothly, the Segway makes one hundred adjustments every second. Given the high adjustment rate, the oscillations around the point of equilibrium are so small as to not be detectable. However, if fewer adjustments were made per second, the oscillations would increase in size and the ride would become increasingly jerky.

A key lesson of feedback loops is that things are connected—changing one variable in a system will affect other variables in that system and other systems. This is important because it means that designers must not only consider particular elements of a design, but also their relation to the design as a whole and the greater environment. Consider positive feedback loops to perturb systems to change, but include negative feedback loops to prevent runaway behaviors that lead to system failure. Consider negative feedback loops to stabilize systems, but be cautious in that too much negative feedback in a system can lead to stagnation.[3]

See also Convergence, Errors, and Shaping.

[1] In terms of practical application, the seminal works on systems and feedback loops include *Industrial Dynamics*, MIT Press, 1961; *Urban Dynamics*, MIT Press, 1969; and *World Dynamics*, MIT Press, 1970, by Jay W. Forrester.

[2] See, for example, *Why Things Bite Back: Technology and the Revenge of Unintended Consequences* by Edward Tenner, Vintage Books, 1997.

[3] See, for example, *Macroscope: A New World Scientific System* by Joel De Rosnay, translated by Robert Edwards, Harper & Row Publishers, 1979.

Positive Feedback Loop

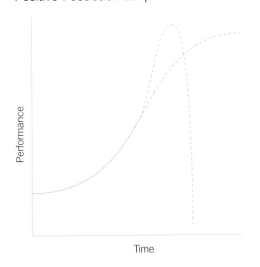

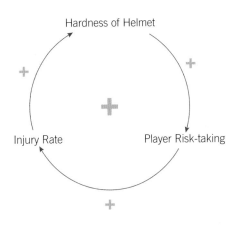

The design history of the football helmet is a classic example of positive feedback. Positive feedback loops will eventually collapse, or taper to an S-shaped curve if limited by some other factor, such as new rules penalizing the use of helmets in tackling.

Negative Feedback Loop

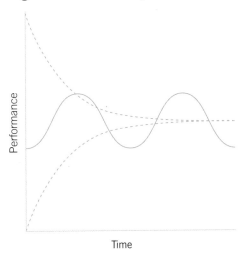

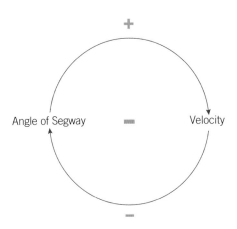

Negative feedback loops are used to stabilize systems—in this case, to balance the Segway and its rider. Negative feedback loops are applied similarly in thermostatic systems and fly-by-wire controls in aircraft. Negative feedback loops assume a goal state, or oscillate around a goal state if there are delays between the variables in the loop.

Fibonacci Sequence

A sequence of numbers in which each number is the sum of the preceding two.

A Fibonacci sequence is a sequence of numbers in which each number is the sum of the two preceding numbers (e.g., 1, 1, 2, 3, 5, 8, 13). Patterns exhibiting the sequence are commonly found in natural forms, such as the petals of flowers, spirals of galaxies, and bones in the human hand. The ubiquity of the sequence in nature has led many to conclude that patterns based on the Fibonacci sequence are intrinsically aesthetic and, therefore, worthy of consideration in design.[1]

Fibonacci patterns are found in many classic works, including classic poetry, art, music, and architecture. For example, it has been argued that Virgil used Fibonacci sequences to structure the poetry in the *Aeneid*. Fibonacci sequences are found in the musical compositions of Mozart's sonatas and Beethoven's Fifth Symphony. Le Corbusier meshed key measures of the human body and Fibonacci sequences to develop the *Modulor*, a classic system of architectural proportions and measurements to aid designers in achieving practical and harmonious designs.[2]

Fibonacci sequences are generally used in concert with the golden ratio, a principle to which it is closely related. For example, the division of any two adjacent numbers in a Fibonacci sequence yields an approximation of the golden ratio. Approximations are rough for early numbers in the sequence but increasingly accurate as the sequence progresses. As with the golden ratio, debate continues as to the aesthetic value of Fibonacci patterns. Are such patterns considered aesthetic because people find them to be more aesthetic or because people have been taught to believe they are aesthetic? Research on the aesthetics of the golden ratio tends to favor the former, but little empirical research exists on the aesthetics of *non-golden* Fibonacci patterns.[3]

The Fibonacci sequence continues to be one of the most influential patterns in mathematics and design. Consider Fibonacci sequences when developing interesting compositions, geometric patterns, and organic motifs and contexts, especially when they involve rhythms and harmonies among multiple elements. Do not contrive designs to incorporate Fibonacci sequences, but also do not forego opportunities to explore Fibonacci relationships when other aspects of the design are not compromised.

See also Aesthetic-Usability Effect, Golden Ratio, and Most Average Facial Appearance Effect.

[1] The seminal work on the Fibonacci sequence is *Liber Abaci* [Book of the Abacus] by Leonardo of Pisa, 1202. Contemporary seminal works include *The Geometry of Art and Life* by Matila Ghyka, Dover Publications, 1978 [1946]; *Elements of Dynamic Symmetry* by Jay Hambidge, Dover Publications, 1978 [1920].

[2] See, for example, *Structural Patterns and Proportions in Virgil's Aeneid* by George Eckel Duckworth, University of Michigan Press, 1962; and "Did Mozart Use the Golden Section?" by Mike May, *American Scientist*, March-April 1996; and *Le Modulor* by Le Corbusier, Birkhauser, 2000 [1948].

[3] "All That Glitters: A Review of Psychological Research on the Aesthetics of the Golden Section" by Christopher D. Green, *Perception*, 1995, vol. 24, p. 937–968.

Le Corbusier derived two Fibonacci
sequences based on key features
of the human form to create the
Modulor. The sequences purportedly
represent a set of ideal measurements
to aid designers in achieving practical
and harmonious proportions in design.
Golden ratios were calculated by dividing each number in the sequence by
its preceding number (indicated by
horizontal lines).

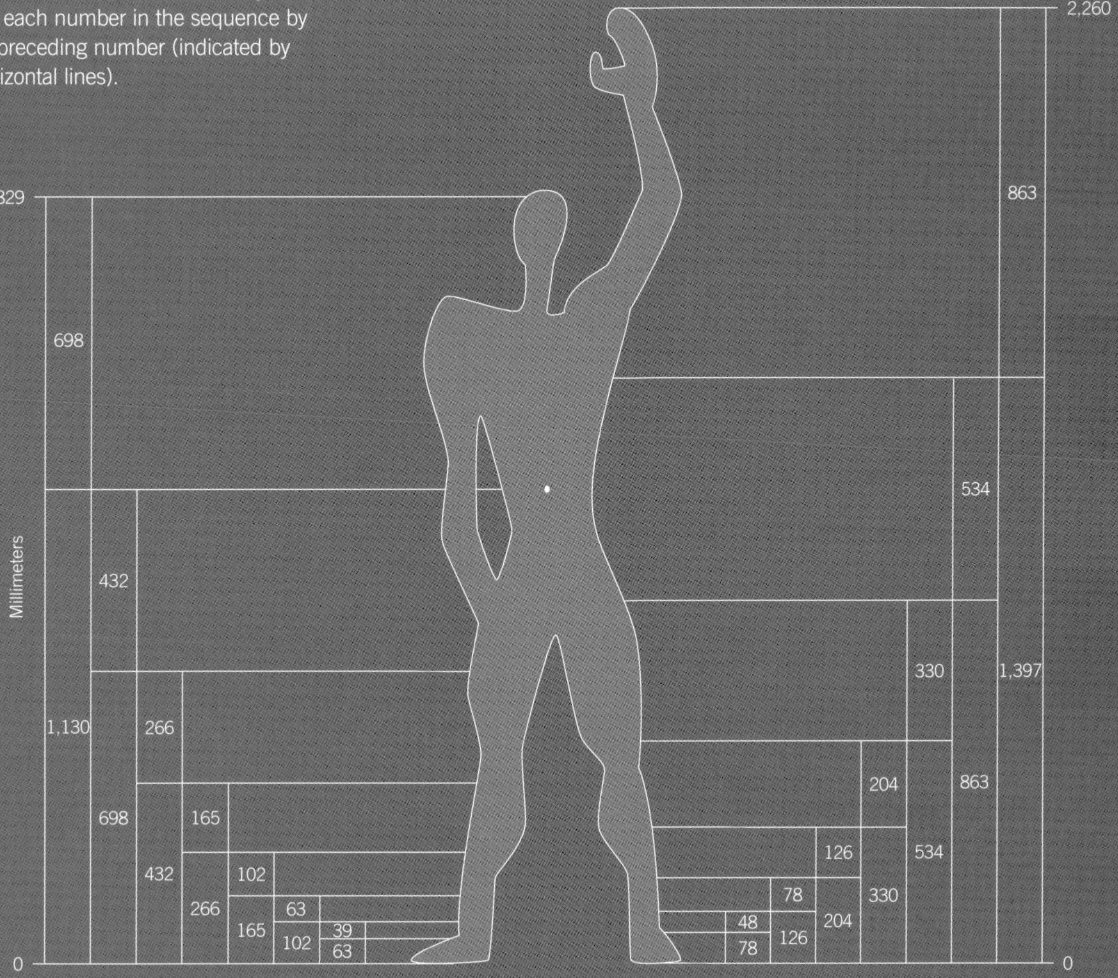

Millimeters

1,829

698

432

1,130

266

698

165

432

102

266

63

165

39

102

63

0

2,260

863

534

330

1,397

204

863

126

534

78

330

48

204

78

126

0

Figure-Ground Relationship

Elements are perceived as either figures (objects of focus) or ground (the rest of the perceptual field).

The figure-ground relationship is one of several principles referred to as *Gestalt principles of perception*. It asserts that the human perceptual system separates stimuli into either figure elements or ground elements. Figure elements are the objects of focus, and ground elements compose an undifferentiated background. This relationship can be demonstrated with both visual stimuli, such as photographs, and auditory stimuli, such as soundtracks with dialog and background music.

When the figure and ground of a composition are clear, the relationship is stable; the figure element receives more attention and is better remembered than the ground. In unstable figure-ground relationships, the relationship is ambiguous and can be interpreted in different ways; the interpretation of elements alternates between figure and ground.

The visual cues that determine which elements will be perceived as figure and which as ground are:

- The figure has a definite shape, whereas the ground is shapeless.
- The ground continues behind the figure.
- The figure seems closer with a clear location in space, whereas the ground seems farther away and has no clear location in space.
- Elements below a horizon line are more likely to be perceived as figures, whereas elements above a horizon line are more likely to be perceived as ground.
- Elements in the lower regions of a design are more likely to be perceived as figures, whereas elements in the upper regions are more likely to be perceived as ground.[2]

Clearly differentiate between figure and ground in order to focus attention and minimize perceptual confusion. Ensure that designs have stable figure-ground relationships by incorporating the appropriate visual cues listed above. Increase the probability of recall of key elements by making them figures in the composition.

See also Gutenberg Principle, Law of Prägnanz, and Top-Down Lighting Bias.

[1] The seminal work on the figure-ground relationship is "Synoplevede Figurer" [Figure and Ground] by Edgar Rubin, Gyldendalske, 1915, translated and reprinted in *Readings in Perception* by David C. Beardslee and Michael Wertheimer, D. Van Nostrand, 1958, p. 194–203.

[2] "Lower Region: A New Cue for Figure-Ground Assignment" by Shaun P. Vecera, Edward K. Vogel, and Geoffrey F. Woodman, *Journal of Experimental Psychology: General*, 2002, vol. 131(2), p. 194–205.

The Rubin vase is unstable because it can be perceived as a white vase on a black background or two black faces looking at each other on a white background.

Placing the spa name below the horizon line in the logo makes it a figure element—it will receive more attention and be better remembered than the design that places the name at the top of the logo.

Initially, there is no stable figure-ground relationship in this image. However, after a moment, the Dalmatian pops out and the figure-ground relationship stabilizes.

Placing the logo at the bottom of the page makes it a figure element—it will receive more attention and will be better remembered than the logo at the top of the page.

Fitts' Law

The time required to move to a target is a function of the target size and distance to the target.

According to Fitts' Law, the smaller and more distant a target, the longer it will take to move to a resting position over the target. In addition, the faster the required movement and the smaller the target, the greater the error rate due to a speed-accuracy tradeoff. Fitts' Law has implications for the design of controls, control layouts, and any device that facilitates movement to a target.[1]

Fitts' Law is applicable only for rapid, pointing movements, not for more continuous movements, such as writing or drawing. It has been used to predict efficiency of movement for assembly work performed under a microscope, as well as movement of a foot to a car pedal. Pointing movements typically consist of one large, quick movement toward a target (*ballistic movement*), followed by fine-adjustment movements (*homing movements*) to a resting position over (*acquiring*) the target. Homing movements are generally responsible for most of the movement time and cause most errors.[2]

Designers can decrease errors and improve usability by understanding the implications of Fitts' Law. For example, when pointing to an object on a computer screen, movement in the vertical or horizontal dimensions can be constrained, which dramatically increases the speed with which objects can be accurately acquired. This kind of constraint is commonly applied to controls such as scroll bars, but less commonly to the edges of the screen, which also act as a barrier to cursor movement; positioning a button along a screen edge or in a screen corner significantly reduces the homing movements required, resulting in fewer errors and faster acquisitions.

Consider Fitts' Law when designing systems that involve pointing. Make sure that controls are near or large, particularly when rapid movements are required and accuracy is important. Likewise, make controls more distant and smaller when they should not be frequently used, or when they will cause problems if accidentally activated. Consider strategies that constrain movements when possible to improve performance and reduce error.

See also Constraint, Errors, and Hick's Law.

[1] The seminal work on Fitts' Law is "The Information Capacity of the Human Motor System in Controlling Amplitude of Movement" by Paul M. Fitts, *Journal of Experimental Psychology*, 1954, vol. 4, p. 381–191. The Fitts' law equation is $MT = a + b \log^2 (d/s + 1)$, where MT = movement time to a target; a = 0.230 sec; b = 0.166 sec; d = distance between pointing device and target; and s = size of the target. For example, assume the distance between the center of a screen and an icon of 1" (3 cm) diameter is 6" (15 cm). The time to acquire the icon would be MT = 0.230 sec + 0.166 sec ($\log^2$ (6/1 + 1)) = 0.7 sec.

[2] See "Human Performance Times in Microscope Work" by Gary Langolf and Walton M. Hancock, *AIIE Transactions*, 1975, vol. 7(2), p. 110–117; and "Application of Fitts' Law to Foot-Pedal Design" by Colin G. Drury, *Human Factors*, 1975, vol. 17(4), p. 368–373.

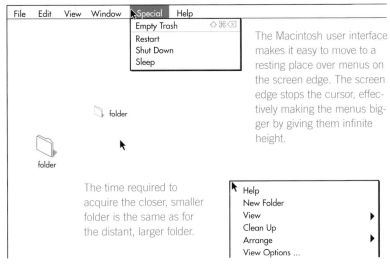

The Macintosh user interface makes it easy to move to a resting place over menus on the screen edge. The screen edge stops the cursor, effectively making the menus bigger by giving them infinite height.

The time required to acquire the closer, smaller folder is the same as for the distant, larger folder.

The Microsoft Windows user interface presents pop-up menus when you press the right mouse button. Since the distance between the cursor position and the pop-up menu is minimal, menu items are quickly acquired.

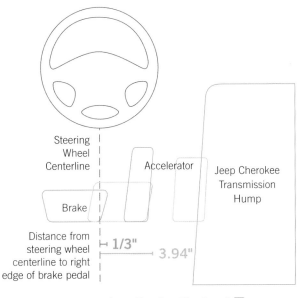

Jeep Cherokee Floorboard ▥
Ford Taurus Floorboard ▥

In the 1990s, many cases of unintended acceleration were reported in Chrysler Jeep Cherokees. Brake pedals are usually located to the right of the steering wheel centerline, as in the Ford Taurus. However, the Jeep Cherokee's large transmission hump forced the pedal positions to the left. This increased the distance between foot and brake pedal, making the latter more difficult to reach. This, combined with a violation of convention, caused Jeep Cherokee drivers to press the accelerator when they intended to press the brake pedal.

Five Hat Racks

There are five ways to organize information: category, time, location, alphabet, and continuum.[1]

The organization of information is one of the most powerful factors influencing the way people think about and interact with a design. The five hat racks principle asserts that there are a limited number of organizational strategies, regardless of the specific application: category, time, location, alphabet, and continuum.[2]

Category refers to organization by similarity or relatedness. Examples include areas of study in a college catalog, and types of retail merchandise on a Web site. Organize information by category when clusters of similarity exist within the information, or when people will naturally seek out information by category (e.g., a person desiring to purchase a stereo may seek a category for electronic appliances).

Time refers to organization by chronological sequence. Examples include historical timelines and *TV Guide* schedules. Organize information by time when presenting and comparing events over fixed durations, or when a time-based sequence is involved (e.g., a step-by-step procedure).

Location refers to organization by geographical or spatial reference. Examples include emergency exit maps and travel guides. Organize information by location when orientation and wayfinding are important or when information is meaningfully related to the geography of a place (e.g., an historic site).

Alphabet refers to organization by alphabetical sequence. Examples include dictionaries and encyclopedias. Organize information alphabetically, when information is referential, when efficient nonlinear access to specific items is required, or when no other organizing strategy is appropriate.

Continuum refers to organization by magnitude (e.g., highest to lowest, best to worst). Examples include baseball batting averages and Internet search engine results. Organize information by continuum when comparing things across a common measure.

See also Advance Organizer, Consistency, and Framing.

[1] The term *hat racks* is built on an analogy—*hats* as information and *racks* as the ways to organize information. Also known as *five ways of organizing information*.

[2] The seminal work on the five hat racks is *Information Anxiety* by Richard Saul Wurman, Bantam Books, 1990. Note that Wurman changed the hat rack title of *continuum* to *hierarchy* in a later edition of the book, which permits the acronym LATCH. The original title *continuum* is presented here, as the authors believe it to be a more accurate description of the category.

The five hat racks are applied here to the tallest structures in the world. Although the same information is presented in each case, the different organizations dramatically influence which aspects of the information are emphasized.

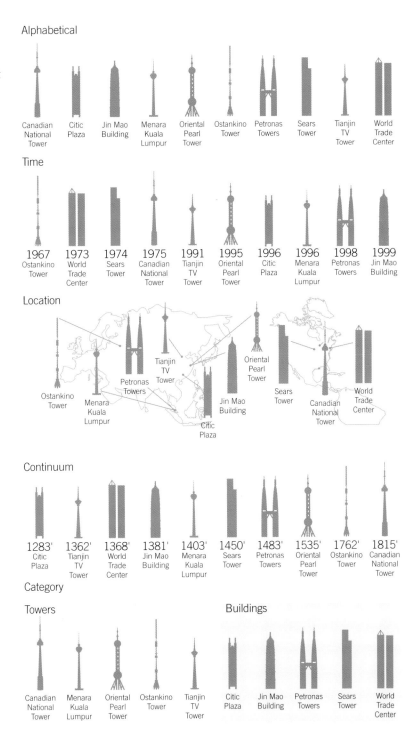

Alphabetical

Canadian National Tower · Citic Plaza · Jin Mao Building · Menara Kuala Lumpur · Oriental Pearl Tower · Ostankino Tower · Petronas Towers · Sears Tower · Tianjin TV Tower · World Trade Center

Time

1967 Ostankino Tower · 1973 World Trade Center · 1974 Sears Tower · 1975 Canadian National Tower · 1991 Tianjin TV Tower · 1995 Oriental Pearl Tower · 1996 Citic Plaza · 1996 Menara Kuala Lumpur · 1998 Petronas Towers · 1999 Jin Mao Building

Location

Ostankino Tower · Menara Kuala Lumpur · Petronas Towers · Tianjin TV Tower · Citic Plaza · Jin Mao Building · Oriental Pearl Tower · Sears Tower · Canadian National Tower · World Trade Center

Continuum

1283' Citic Plaza · 1362' Tianjin TV Tower · 1368' World Trade Center · 1381' Jin Mao Building · 1403' Menara Kuala Lumpur · 1450' Sears Tower · 1483' Petronas Towers · 1535' Oriental Pearl Tower · 1762' Ostankino Tower · 1815' Canadian National Tower

Category

Towers

Canadian National Tower · Menara Kuala Lumpur · Oriental Pearl Tower · Ostankino Tower · Tianjin TV Tower

Buildings

Citic Plaza · Jin Mao Building · Petronas Towers · Sears Tower · World Trade Center

Flexibility-Usability Tradeoff

As the flexibility of a system increases, the usability of the system decreases.

The flexibility-usability tradeoff is related to the well-known maxim, *jack of all trades, master of none*. Flexible designs can perform more functions than specialized designs, but they perform the functions less efficiently. Flexible designs are, by definition, more complex than inflexible designs, and as a result are generally more difficult to use. For example, a Swiss Army Knife has many attached tools that increase its flexibility. These tools taken together are less usable and efficient than corresponding individual tools that are more specialized but provide a flexibility of use not available from any single tool. The flexibility-usability tradeoff exists because accommodating flexibility entails satisfying a larger set of design requirements, which invariably means more compromises and complexity in the design.[1]

It is a common assumption that designs should always be made as flexible as possible. However, flexibility has real costs in terms of complexity, usability, time, and money; it generally pays dividends only when an audience cannot clearly anticipate its future needs. For example, personal computers are flexible devices that are difficult to use, relative to more specialized devices like video game players. However, the primary value of a personal computer is that it addresses uncertainty about how it can and will be used: word processing, tax preparation, email. People purchase video game players to play games, but they purchase personal computers to satisfy a variety of needs, many of which are unknown at the time of purchase.

The ability of an audience to anticipate future uses of a product is a key indicator of how they will value flexibility versus usability in design. When an audience can clearly anticipate its needs, more specialized designs that target those needs will be favored. When an audience cannot clearly define its needs, more flexible designs that enable people to address future contingencies will be favored. The degree to which an audience can or cannot define future needs should correspond to the degree of specialization or flexibility in the design. As an audience comes to understand the range of possible needs that can be satisfied, their needs become better defined and, consequently, the designs need to become more specialized. This shift from flexibility toward specialization over time is a general pattern observed in the evolution of all systems, and should be considered in the life cycle of products.

The flexibility-usability tradeoff has implications for weighing the relative importance of flexibility versus usability in a design. When an audience has a clear understanding of its needs, favor specialized designs that target those needs as efficiently as possible. When an audience has a poor understanding of its needs, favor flexible designs to address the broadest possible set of future applications. When designing multiple generations of products, consider the general shift toward specialization as audience needs become more defined.

See also 80/20 Rule, Convergence, Hierarchy of Needs, Life Cycle, Modularity, and Progressive Disclosure.

[1] See, for example, *The Invisible Computer* by Donald A. Norman, MIT Press, 1999; and "The Visible Problems of the Invisible Computer: A Skeptical Look at Information Appliances" by Andrew Odlyzko, First Monday, 1999, vol. 4 (9), http://www.firstmonday.org.

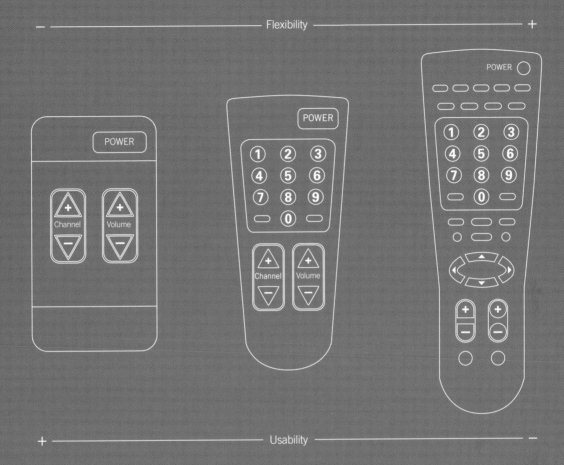

POWER

Channel   Volume

POWER

① ② ③
④ ⑤ ⑥
⑦ ⑧ ⑨
   ⓪

Channel   Volume

POWER ◯

① ② ③
④ ⑤ ⑥
⑦ ⑧ ⑨
   ⓪

Usability

There is a basic tradeoff between flexibility and usability, as demonstrated by these remote control designs. The simple remote control is the easiest to use, but not very flexible. Conversely, the universal remote control is very flexible but far more complex and difficult to use.

Forgiveness

Designs should help people avoid errors and minimize the negative consequences of errors when they do occur.

Human error is inevitable, but it need not be catastrophic. Forgiveness in design helps prevent errors before they occur, and minimizes the negative consequences of errors when they do occur. Forgiving designs provide a sense of security and stability, which in turn, fosters a willingness to learn, explore, and use the design. Common strategies for incorporating forgiveness in designs include:

Good Affordances—physical characteristics of the design that influence its correct use (e.g., uniquely shaped plug that can only be inserted into the appropriate receptacle).

Reversibility of Actions—one or more actions can be reversed if an error occurs or the intent of the person changes (e.g., undo function in software).

Safety Nets—device or process that minimizes the negative consequences of a catastrophic error or failure (e.g., pilot ejection seat in aircraft).

Confirmation—verification of intent that is required before critical actions are allowed (e.g., lock that must be opened before equipment can be activated).

Warnings—signs, prompts, or alarms used to warn of imminent danger (e.g., road signs warning of a sharp turn ahead).

Help—information that assists in basic operations, troubleshooting, and error recovery (e.g., documentation or help line).

The preferred methods of achieving forgiveness in a design are affordances, reversibility of actions, and safety nets. Designs that effectively use these strategies require minimal confirmations, warnings, and help—i.e., if the affordances are good, help is less necessary; if actions are reversible, confirmations are less necessary; if safety nets are strong, warnings are less necessary. When using confirmations, warnings, and help systems, avoid cryptic messages or icons. Ensure that messages clearly state the risk or problem, and also what actions can or should be taken. Keep in mind that too many confirmations or warnings impede the flow of interaction and increase the likelihood that the confirmation or warning will be ignored.

Create forgiving designs by using good affordances, reversibility of actions, and safety nets. If this is not possible, be sure to include confirmations, warnings, and a good help system. Be aware that the amount of help necessary to successfully interact with a design is inversely proportional to the quality of the design—if a lot of help is required, the design is poor.

See also Affordance, Confirmation, Errors, and Factor of Safety.

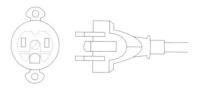

Road signs make roads more forgiving by warning drivers of impending hazards.

The Adobe Photoshop History palette enables users to flexibly undo and redo their previous actions.

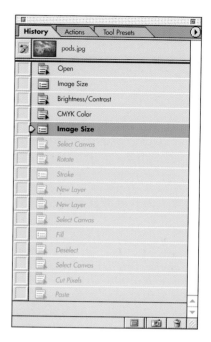

In case of a catastrophic failure, the ballistic recovery system acts as a safety net, enabling the pilot and craft to return safely to earth.

Locking and tagging equipment is a common confirmation strategy to ensure that people do not accidentally engage systems under repair.

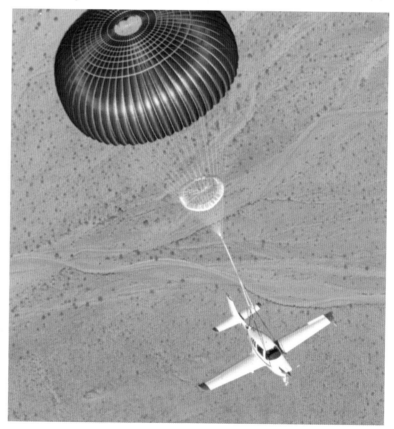

The good affordance of this plug prevents it from being inserted into the socket improperly.

Form Follows Function

Beauty in design results from purity of function.

The *form follows function* corollary is interpreted in one of two ways—as a description of beauty or a prescription for beauty. The descriptive interpretation is that beauty results from purity of function and the absence of ornamentation. The prescriptive interpretation is that aesthetic considerations in design should be secondary to functional considerations. The corollary was adopted and popularized by modernist architects in the early 20th century, and has since been adopted by designers in a variety of disciplines.[1]

The *descriptive* interpretation—i.e., that beauty results from purity of function—was originally based on the belief that form follows function in nature. However, this belief is false, since function follows form in nature if it follows anything at all. Evolution by natural selection transmits no *intention* from one generation to the next; genetic patterns are simply passed on and it is left to each organism to find use of the form that they have inherited. Despite this, functional aspects of a design are less subjective than aesthetic aspects and, therefore, functional criteria represent a more objective aesthetic than alternative approaches. The result is designs that are more timeless and enduring, but also frequently perceived by general audiences as simple and uninteresting.[2]

The *prescriptive* interpretation—i.e., that aesthetic considerations in design should be secondary to functional considerations—was likely derived from the descriptive interpretation. The use of *form follows function* as a prescription or design guideline is problematic in that it focuses the designer on the wrong question. The question should not be, "What aspects of form should be omitted or traded for function?" but rather, "What aspects of the design are critical to success?" These success criteria, not a blind allegiance to form or function, should drive design specifications and decisions. When time and resources are limited, design tradeoffs should be based on what does the least harm to the probability of success, however *success* is defined. In certain circumstances the tradeoffs will be primarily aesthetic, and in other circumstances the tradeoffs will be primarily functional.

Use the descriptive interpretation of *form follows function* as an aesthetic guide, but do not apply the prescriptive interpretation as a strict design rule. When making design decisions, focus on the relative importance of all aspects of the design—form and function—in light of the success criteria.

See also Aesthetic-Usability Effect, Exposure Effect, and Ockham's Razor.

[1] The origin of the concept is attributed to the 18th century Jesuit monk Carlo Lodoli. His theories on architecture likely influenced later designers like Horatio Greenough and Louis Sullivan who then articulated the concept in popular form. The seminal works on *form follows function* are "The Tall Office Building Artistically Considered" by Louis H. Sullivan, *Lippincott's Magazine*, March 1896; and *Form Follows Fiasco: Why Modern Architecture Hasn't Worked* by Peter Blake, Little, Brown, and Company, 1977.

[2] The tendency of general audiences to resist the *new* is a function of their familiarity with the *old*. It often takes several generations to erode population biases sufficiently such that the merits of a new design can be objectively considered.

Defining success criteria is essential to good design. For example, if the success criteria for a watch are defined in terms of speed and accuracy, the digital display is superior. If the success criteria are defined in terms of pure aesthetics, the minimalist analog display is superior (the pure function of the digital display has not yet translated to a popular aesthetic for general audiences). In all cases, the success criteria should direct design decisions and trade-offs, and should be the primary consideration in determining the specifications for a design.

Function ——————————————————————————————— Form

Perhaps no purer functional form exists than the original Humvee. Born out of military specifications, the success of the Humvee in combat led to the commercial successors—Hummer H1 and H2. Each represents a unique and compelling aesthetic that results from purity of function and minimal ornamentation.

Framing

A technique that influences decision making and judgment by manipulating the way information is presented.

Framing is the use of images, words, and context to manipulate how people think about something. Information can be presented in such a way as to emphasize the positive (e.g., *glass is half-full*) or the negative (e.g., *glass is half-empty*). The type of frame used to present information dramatically affects how people make decisions and judgments, and is consequently a powerful influencer of behavior. News media, politicians, propagandists, and advertisers all commonly use framing (knowingly or unknowingly) with great effect.[1]

In October 2002, Russian Special Forces used a sedating gas to knock out Chechen rebels who were holding over 750 hostages captive in the Moscow Theater. The gas prevented the rebels from setting off explosives and killing all of the hostages, but the gas itself caused the death of well over 100 hostages. Newspapers throughout the world reported the incident in basically one of two ways: *Gas Kills Over 100 Hostages*, or *Gas Saves Over 500 Hostages*. This event is tragic no matter how it is presented, but judgment of the Russian efforts to free the hostages is greatly influenced by the frame of its presentation. The *negative frame* emphasizes the lives lost, and presents the information in a way that suggests the Russians bungled the affair. The *positive frame* emphasizes the lives saved, and presents the information in a way that suggests the Russians cleverly salvaged a seemingly intractable situation. Similar positive and negative frames are typically used in advertising. For example, it is common to see yogurt advertised as 95 *percent fat free*, rather than *5 percent fat rich*; and tobacco legislation has been defeated more than once by framing the legislation as a matter of taxation, instead of a matter of public health.

Positive frames tend to elicit positive feelings, and result in proactive and risk-seeking behaviors. Negative frames tend to elicit negative feelings, resulting in reactive and risk-avoiding behaviors. Stress and time pressures amplify these behaviors, a phenomenon frequently exploited in high pressure sales: present a product in a positive frame, present competitors in a negative frame, and time-bound the decision to pressure the buy. However, when people are exposed to multiple conflicting frames, the framing effect is neutralized, and people think and act consistently with their own beliefs.

Use framing to elicit positive or negative feelings about a design, and to influence behaviors and decision-making. Use positive frames to move people to action (e.g., make a purchase) and negative frames to move people to inaction (e.g., prevent use of illegal drugs). To maintain a strong framing effect, make sure that frames are not conflicting. Conversely, neutralize framing effects by presenting multiple conflicting frames.

See also Expectation Effect and Exposure Effect.

[1] The seminal work on framing is "The Framing of Decisions and the Psychology of Choice" by Amos Tversky and Daniel Kahneman, *Science*, 1981, vol. 211, p. 453–458. A nice treatment of the subject is *The Psychology of Judgment and Decision Making* by Scott Plous, McGraw-Hill, 1993.

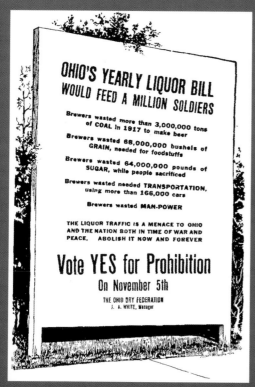

The Ohio Dry Campaign of 1918 is a case study in framing. Prohibition advocates framed the issue as either supporting prohibition of alcohol or supporting waste, poverty, crime, treason, and so on. The campaign was successful in turning public opinion, and resulted in passage of prohibition legislation in 1918. Similar framing tactics are common today. For example, abortion-rights advocates frame their position as *prochoice* and their opponents' as *antichoice*; abortion-rights critics frame their position as *prolife* and their opponents' as *anti-life* or *proabortion*.

Garbage In–Garbage Out

The quality of system output is dependent on the quality of system input.[1]

The garbage in–garbage out principle is based on the experience of early computer scientists who quickly learned that good inputs yield good results, and bad inputs yield bad results—garbage in, garbage out. The rule has been generalized over time to apply to all systems, and is commonly invoked in domains such as business, education, nutrition, and engineering, to name a few. The garbage in metaphor refers to one of two kinds of input problems: problems of type, and problems of quality.[2]

Problems of type occur when the incorrect type of input is fed into a system, such as entering a phone number into a credit card number field. Problems of type are serious because the input provided could be radically different from the input expected. This can be advantageous in that problems of type are relatively easy to detect, but problematic in that they represent the maximum form of garbage if undetected. Problems of type are generally caused by a class of errors called mistakes—incorrect actions caused by conscious actions. The primary strategies for minimizing problems of type are affordances and constraints. These strategies structure input and minimize the frequency and magnitude of garbage input.

Problems of quality occur when the correct type of input is fed into a system, but with defects, such as entering a phone number into a phone number field but entering the wrong number. Depending on the frequency and severity of these defects, problems of quality may or may not be serious. Mistyping one letter in a name may have minor consequences (e.g., search item not found); trying to request a download of fifty records but typing five thousand might lock up the system. Problems of quality are generally caused by a class of errors called slips—incorrect actions caused by unconscious, accidental actions. The primary strategies for minimizing problems of quality are previews and confirmations. These strategies allow the consequences of actions to be reviewed and verified prior to input.

The best way to avoid garbage out is to prevent garbage in. Use affordances and constraints to minimize problems of type. Use previews and confirmations to minimize problems of quality. When input integrity is critical, use validation tests to check integrity prior to input, and consider confirmation steps that require the independent verification of multiple people.

See also Errors, Feedback Loop, and Signal-to-Noise Ratio.

[1] Also known as *GIGO*.

[2] The *garbage in–garbage out* principle was first used by researchers in computer science during the 1950s.

Original Form

- Unconstrained fields increase the probability of garbage input.

Redesigned Form

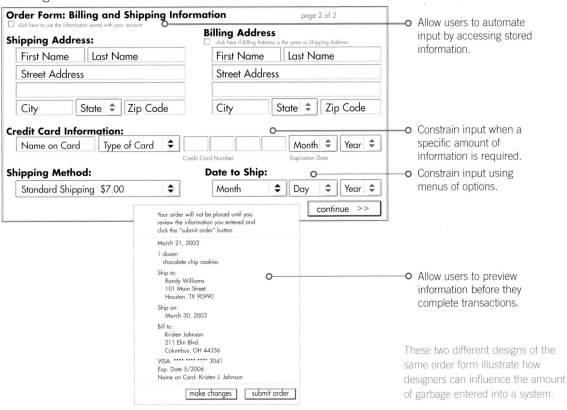

- Allow users to automate input by accessing stored information.

- Constrain input when a specific amount of information is required.

- Constrain input using menus of options.

- Allow users to preview information before they complete transactions.

These two different designs of the same order form illustrate how designers can influence the amount of garbage entered into a system.

Golden Ratio

A ratio within the elements of a form, such as height to width, approximating 0.618.[1]

The golden ratio is the ratio between two segments such that the smaller (*bc*) segment is to the larger segment (*ab*) as the larger segment (*ab*) is to the sum of the two segments (*ac*), or *bc*/*ab* = *ab*/*ac* = 0.618.[2]

The golden ratio is found throughout nature, art, and architecture. Pinecones, seashells, and the human body all exhibit the golden ratio. Piet Mondrian and Leonardo da Vinci commonly incorporated the golden ratio into their paintings. Stradivari utilized the golden ratio in the construction of his violins. The Parthenon, the Great Pyramid of Giza, Stonehenge, and the Chartres Cathedral all exhibit the golden ratio.

While many manifestations of the golden ratio in early art and architecture were likely caused by processes not involving knowledge of the golden ratio, it may be that these manifestations result from a more fundamental, subconscious preference for the aesthetic resulting from the ratio. A substantial body of research comparing individual preferences for rectangles of various proportions supports a preference based on the golden ratio. However, these findings have been challenged on the theory that preferences for the ratio in past experiments resulted from experimenter bias, methodological flaws, or other external factors.[3]

Whether the golden ratio taps into some inherent aesthetic preference or is simply an early design technique turned tradition, there is no question as to its past and continued influence on design. Consider the golden ratio when it is not at the expense of other design objectives. Geometries of a design should not be contrived to create golden ratios, but golden ratios should be explored when other aspects of the design are not compromised.[4]

See also Aesthetic-Usability Effect, Form Follows Function, Rule of Thirds, and Waist-to-Hip Ratio.

[1] Also known as *golden mean*, *golden number*, *golden section*, *golden proportion*, *divine proportion*, and *sectio aurea*.

[2] The golden ratio is irrational (never-ending decimal) and can be computed with the equation $(\sqrt{5}-1)/2$. Adding 1 to the golden ratio yields 1.618…, referred to as Phi (ϕ). The values are used interchangeably to define the golden ratio, as they represent the same basic geometric relationship. Geometric shapes derived from the golden ratio include golden ellipses, golden rectangles, and golden triangles.

[3] The seminal work on the golden ratio is Über die Frage des Golden Schnitts [On the question of the golden section] by Gustav T. Fechner, Archiv für die zeichnenden Künste [Archive for the Drawn/Graphic Arts], 1865, vol. 11, p. 100–112. A contemporary reference is "All That Glitters: A Review of Psychological Research on the Aesthetics of the Golden Section" by Christopher D. Green, *Perception*, 1995, vol. 24, p. 937–968. For a critical examination of the golden ratio thesis, see "The Cult of the Golden Ratio" in *Weird Water & Fuzzy Logic* by Martin Gardner, Prometheus Books, 1996, p. 90–96.

[4] The page spread of this book approximates a golden rectangle. The page height is 10 inches (25 cm) and the page width is 8.5 inches (22 cm). The total page-spread width (17 inches [43 cm]) divided by the page height yields a ratio of 1.7.

In each example, the ratio between the blue and red segments approximates the golden ratio. Note how the ratio corresponds with a significant feature or alteration of the form.

Examples are the Parthenon, Stradivarius Violin, Notre-Dame Cathedral, Nautilus Shell, Eames LCW Chair, Apple iPod MP3 Player, and da Vinci's Vitruvian Man.

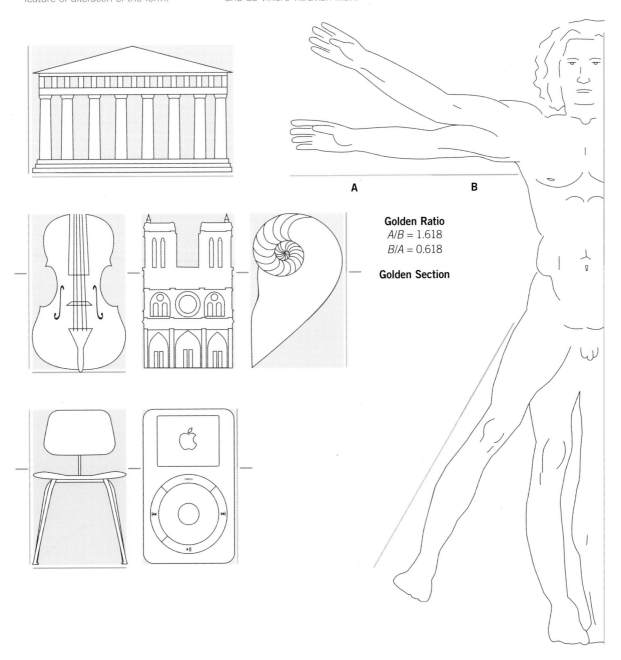

A   B

Golden Ratio
$A/B = 1.618$
$B/A = 0.618$

Golden Section

Good Continuation

Elements arranged in a straight line or a smooth curve are perceived as a group, and are interpreted as being more related than elements not on the line or curve.

Good continuation is one of several principles referred to as *Gestalt principles of perception*. It asserts that aligned elements are perceived as a single group or chunk, and are interpreted as being more related than unaligned elements. For example, speed markings on a speedometer are easily interpreted as a group because they are aligned along a linear or circular path.[1]

The principle of good continuation also explains why lines will generally be perceived as maintaining their established directions, versus branching or bending abruptly. For example, two V-shaped lines side by side appear simply as two V-shaped lines. When one V-shaped line is inverted and the other is placed above it (forming an X), the shape is interpreted as two opposing diagonal lines instead of two V-shaped lines—the less abrupt interpretation of the lines is dominant. A bar graph in which the bars are arranged in increasing or decreasing order so that the tops of the bars form a continuous line are more easily processed than bar arrangements in which the tops of the bars form a discontinuous, abrupt line.[2]

The ability to accurately perceive objects depends largely on the perceptibility of the corners and sharp curves that make up their shape. When sections of a line or shape are hidden from view, good continuation leads the eye to continue along the visible segments. If extensions of these segments intersect with minimal disruption, the elements along the line will be perceived as related. As the angle of disruption becomes more acute, the elements will be perceived as less related.[3]

Use good continuation to indicate relatedness between elements in a design. Locate elements such that their alignment corresponds to their relatedness, and locate unrelated or ambiguously related items on different alignment paths. Ensure that line extensions of related objects intersect with minimum line disruption. Arrange elements in graphs and displays such that end points of elements form continuous, rather than abrupt lines.

See also Alignment, Chunking, Five Hat Racks, and Uniform Connectedness.

[1] The seminal work on good continuation is "Untersuchungen zür Lehre von der Gestalt, II" [Laws of Organization in Perceptual Forms] by Max Wertheimer, *Psychologische Forschung*, 1923, vol. 4, p. 301–350, reprinted in *A Source Book of Gestalt Psychology* by Willis D. Ellis (ed.), Routledge & Kegan Paul, *1999*, p. 71–88. See also *Principles of Gestalt Psychology* by Kurt Koffka, Harcourt Brace, 1935.

[2] See, for example, *Elements of Graph Design* by Stephen M. Kosslyn, W. H Freeman and Company, 1994, p. 7.

[3] See, for example, "Convexity in Perceptual Completion: Beyond Good Continuation" by Zili Liu, David W. Jacobs, and Ronen Basri, *Vision Research*, 1999, vol. 39, p. 4244–4257.

Despite the gaps, the jagged line is still seen as a single object because the occlusions can be bridged with minimal disruption.

The first graph is easier to read than the second because the end points of its bars form a line that is more continuous.

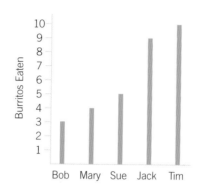

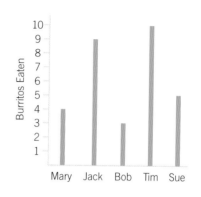

The circular alignment of the increments of this speedometer make it evident that the numbers and increments along the lines belong together.

Good continuation is commonly used in camouflage. For example, the lines on zebras continue across one another when in a herd, making it difficult for predators to target any one zebra.

Gutenberg Diagram

A diagram that describes the general pattern followed by the eyes when looking at evenly distributed, homogeneous information.[1]

The Gutenberg diagram divides a display medium into four quadrants: the *primary optical area* at the top left, the *terminal area* at the bottom right, the *strong fallow area* at the top right, and the *weak fallow area* at the bottom left. According to the diagram, Western readers naturally begin at the primary optical area and move across and down the display medium in a series of sweeps to the terminal area. Each sweep begins along an *axis of orientation*—a horizontal line created by aligned elements, text lines, or explicit segments—and proceeds in a left-to-right direction. The strong and weak fallow areas lie outside this path and receive minimal attention unless visually emphasized. The tendency to follow this path is metaphorically attributed to *reading gravity*—the left-right, top-bottom habit formed from reading.[2]

Designs that follow the diagram work in harmony with reading gravity, and return readers to a logical axis of orientation, purportedly improving reading rhythm and comprehension. For example, a layout following the Gutenberg diagram would place key elements at the top left (e.g., headline), middle (e.g., image), and bottom right (e.g., contact information). Though designs based directly or indirectly on the Gutenberg diagram are widespread, there is little empirical evidence that it contributes to improved reading rates or comprehension.

The Gutenberg diagram is likely only predictive of eye movement for heavy text information, evenly distributed and homogeneous information, and blank pages or displays. In all other cases, the weight of the elements of the design in concert with their layout and composition will direct eye movements. For example, if a newspaper has a very heavy headline and photograph in its center, the center will be the primary optical area. Familiarity with the information and medium also influences eye movements. For example, a person who regularly views information presented in a consistent way is more likely to first look at areas that are often changing (e.g., new top stories) than areas that are the same (e.g., the title of a newspaper).

Consider the Gutenberg diagram to assist in layout and composition when the elements are evenly distributed and homogeneous, or the design contains heavy use of text. Otherwise, use the weight and composition of elements to lead the eye.

See also Alignment, Entry Point, Progressive Disclosure, and Serial Position Effects.

[1] Also known as the *Gutenberg rule* and the *Z pattern of processing*.

[2] The seminal work on the Gutenberg diagram is attributed to the typographer Edmund Arnold, who is said to have developed the concept in the 1950s. See, for example, *Type & Layout: How Typography and Design Can Get Your Message Across or Get in the Way*, by Colin Wheildon, Strathmoor Press, 1995.

Reading gravity pulls the eyes from the top-left to the bottom-right of the display medium. In homogeneous displays, the Gutenberg diagram makes compositions interesting and easy to read. However, in heterogoneous displays, the Gutenberg diagram does not apply, and can constrain composition unnecessarily.

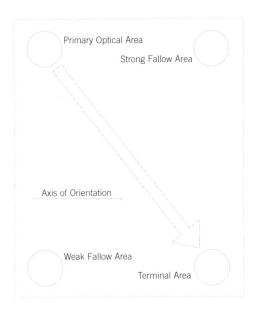

The redesign of the *Wall Street Journal* leads the eyes of readers, and does not follow the Gutenberg diagram. Additionally, recurring readers of the *Wall Street Journal* tend to go to the section they find most valuable, ignoring the other elements of the page.

The composition of these pages illustrates the application of the Gutenberg diagram. The first page is all text, and it is, therefore, safe to assume readers will begin at the top-left and stop at the bottom-right of the page. The pull quote is placed between these areas, reinforcing reading gravity. The placement of the image on the second page similarly reinforces reading gravity, which it would not do if it were positioned at the top-right or bottom-left of the page.

Hick's Law

The time it takes to make a decision increases as the number of alternatives increases.[1]

Hick's Law states that the time required to make a decision is a function of the number of available options. It is used to estimate how long it will take for people to make a decision when presented with multiple choices. For example, when a pilot has to press a particular button in response to some event, such as an alarm, Hick's Law predicts that the greater the number of alternative buttons, the longer it will take to make the decision and select the correct one. Hick's Law has implications for the design of any system or process that requires simple decisions to be made based on multiple options.[2]

All tasks consist of four basic steps: (1) identify a problem or goal, (2) assess the available options to solve the problem or achieve the goal, (3) decide on an option, and (4) implement the option. Hick's Law applies to the third step: decide on an option. However, the law does not apply to decisions that involve significant levels of searching, reading, or complex problem solving. For example, a complex task requiring reading sentences and intense concentration with three options can easily take longer than a simple stimulus-response task with six options. Therefore, Hick's Law is most applicable for simple decision-making tasks in which there is a unique response to each stimulus. For example, if A happens, then push button 1, If B happens, then push button 2. The law is decreasingly applicable as the complexity of tasks increases.[3]

Designers can improve the efficiency of a design by understanding the implications of Hick's Law. For example, the law applies to the design of software menus, control displays, wayfinding layout and signage, and emergency response training—as long as the decisions involved are simple. As the complexity of the tasks increases, the applicability of Hick's Law decreases. For example, Hick's Law does not apply to complex menus or hierarchies of options. Menu selection of this type is not a simple decision-making task since it typically involves reading sentences, searching and scanning for options, and some level of problem solving.

Consider Hick's Law when designing systems that involve decisions based on a set of options. When designing for time-critical tasks, minimize the number of options involved in a decision to reduce response times and minimize errors. When designs require complex interactions, do not rely on Hick's Law to make design decisions; rather, test designs on the target population using realistic scenarios. In training people to perform time-critical procedures, train the fewest possible responses for a given scenario. This will minimize response times, error rates, and training costs.

See also Errors, Fitts' Law, Progressive Disclosure, and Wayfinding.

[1] Also known as *Hick-Hyman Law*.

[2] The seminal work on Hick's Law is "On the Rate of Gain of Information" by W. E. Hick, *Quarterly Journal of Experimental Psychology*, 1952, vol. 4, p. 11–26; and "Stimulus information as a determinant of reaction time" by Ray Hyman, *Journal of Experimental Psychology*, 1953, vol. 45, p. 188–196.

[3] The Hick's Law equation is $RT = a + b \log_2(n)$, where RT = response time, a = the total time that is not involved with decision making, b = an empirically derived constant based on the cognitive processing time for each option (in this case ≈ 0.155 seconds for humans), n = number of equally probable alternatives. For example, assume it takes 2 seconds to detect an alarm and understand it's meaning. Further, assume that pressing one of five buttons will solve the problem caused by the alarm. The time to respond would be $RT = (2 \text{ sec}) + (0.155 \text{ sec})(\log_2(5)) = 2.36 \text{ sec}$.

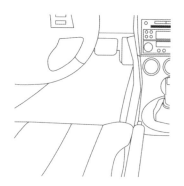

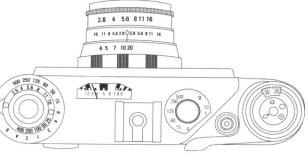

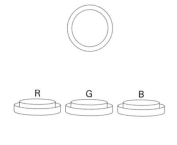

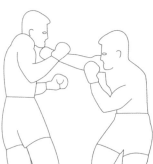

40	⊏A⊐	⊏B⊐	⊏C⊐	⊏D⊐	⊏E⊐
41	⊏A⊐	⊏B⊐	⊏C⊐	⊏D⊐	⊏E⊐
42	⊏A⊐	⊏B⊐	⊏C⊐	⊏D⊐	⊏E⊐
43	⊏A⊐	⊏B⊐	⊏C⊐	⊏D⊐	⊏E⊐
44	⊏A⊐	⊏B⊐	⊏C⊐	⊏D⊐	⊏E⊐
45	⊏A⊐	⊏B⊐	⊏C⊐	⊏D⊐	⊏E⊐
46	⊏A⊐	⊏B⊐	⊏C⊐	⊏D⊐	⊏E⊐
47	⊏A⊐	⊏B⊐	⊏C⊐	⊏D⊐	⊏E⊐
48	⊏A⊐	⊏B⊐	⊏C⊐	⊏D⊐	⊏E⊐
49	⊏A⊐	⊏B⊐	⊏C⊐	⊏D⊐	⊏E⊐
50	⊏A⊐	⊏B⊐	⊏C⊐	⊏D⊐	⊏E⊐
51	⊏A⊐	⊏B⊐	⊏C⊐	⊏D⊐	⊏E⊐

Menus

The time for a person to select an item from a simple software menu increases with the number of items. However, this may not be the case for more complex menus involving a lot of text or submenus.

Predatory Behavior

The time for a predator to target a prey increases with the number of potential prey.

Simple Tasks

The time for a person to press the correct button (R, G, or B) depending on the color of the light (red, green, or blue) increases with the number of possible colors.

Test Options

Hick's Law does not apply to tasks involving significant levels of reading and problem solving, as in taking an exam.

Device Settings

The time for a person to make simple decisions about adjustments on a device increases with the number of controls. This may not be the case for more complex decisions or combinations of settings.

Martial Arts

The time for a martial artist to block a punch increases with the number of known blocking techniques.

Braking

The time for a driver to press the brake to avoid hitting an unexpected obstacle increases if there is a clear opportunity to steer around the obstacle.

Road Signs

As long as road signs are not too dense or complex, the time for a driver to make a turn based on a particular road sign increases with the total number of road signs.

Hierarchy

Hierarchical organization is the simplest structure for visualizing and understanding complexity.

Increasing the visibility of the hierarchical relationships within a system is one of the most effective ways to increase knowledge about the system. Examples of visible hierarchies are book outlines, multi-level software menus, and classification diagrams. Perception of hierarchical relationships among elements is primarily a function of their relative left-right and top-down positions, but is also influenced by their proximity, size, and the presence of connecting lines. Superordinate elements are commonly referred to as *parent* elements, and subordinate elements as *child* elements. There are three basic ways to visually represent hierarchy: trees, nests, and stairs.[1]

Tree structures illustrate hierarchical relationships by locating child elements below or to the right of parent elements, or through the use of other strategies indicating hierarchy (e.g., size, connecting lines). Tree structures are effective for representing hierarchies of moderate complexity, but can become cumbersome for large or complex hierarchies. Tree structures grow large quickly, and become tangled when multiple parents share common child elements. Tree structures are commonly used to represent overviews or high-level maps of system organization.

Nest structures illustrate hierarchical relationships by visually containing child elements within parent elements, as in a Venn diagram. Nest structures are most effective when representing simple hierarchies. When the relationships between the different levels of the hierarchy become too dense and complex to be clearly distinguishable, nest structures become less effective. Nest structures are most commonly used to group information and functions, and to represent simple logical relationships.

Stair structures illustrate hierarchical relationships by stacking child elements below and to the right of parent elements, as in an outline. Stair structures are effective for representing complex hierarchies, but are not easily browsed, and falsely imply a sequential relationship between the stacked child elements. Interactive stair structures found in software often deal with the former problem by concealing child elements until a parent element is selected. Stair structures are commonly used to represent large system structures that change over time.[2]

Hierarchical representation is the simplest method of increasing knowledge about the structure of a system. Consider tree structures when representing high-level views of hierarchies of moderate complexity. Consider nest structures when representing natural systems, simple hierarchical relationships, and grouped information or functions. Consider stair structures when representing complex hierarchies, especially if the volatility and growth of the system represented is unpredictable. Explore ways to selectively reveal and conceal the complexity of hierarchical structures to maximize their clarity and effectiveness.[3]

See also Advance Organizer, Alignment, Five Hat Racks, Layering, and Proximity.

[1] The seminal works on hierarchy are "The Architecture of Complexity," Proceedings of the American Philosophical Society, 1962, vol. 106, p. 467–482; and The Sciences of the Artificial, MIT Press, 1969, both by Herbert A. Simon.

[2] Note that stair hierarchies in software are often referred to as tree hierarchies.

[3] Representing these structures in three-dimensional space improves little in terms of clarity and comprehensibility—though it does result in some fascinating structures to view and navigate. See, for example, "Cone Trees: Animated 3D Visualizations of Hierarchical Information" by George G. Robertson, Jock D. Mackinlay, Stuart K. Card, *Proceedings of CHI '91: Human Factors in Computing Systems*, 1991, p. 189–194.

Trees

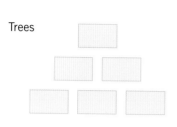

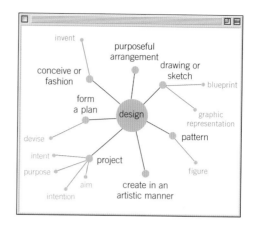

Nests

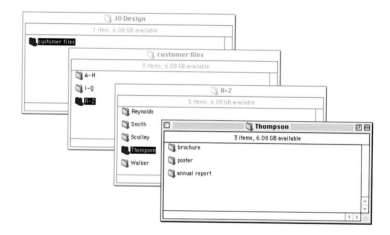

Stairs

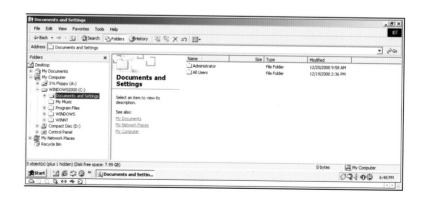

Hierarchy of Needs

In order for a design to be successful, it must meet people's basic needs before it can attempt to satisfy higher-level needs.[1]

The hierarchy of needs principle specifies that a design must serve the low-level needs (e.g., it must function), before the higher-level needs, such as creativity, can begin to be addressed. Good designs follow the hierarchy of needs principle, whereas poor designs may attempt to meet needs from the various levels without building on the lower levels of the hierarchy first. The five key levels of needs in the hierarchy are described below.[2]

Functionality needs have to do with meeting the most basic design requirements. For example, a video recorder must, at minimum, provide the capability to record, play, and rewind recorded programs. Designs at this level are perceived to be of little or no value.

Reliability needs have to do with establishing stable and consistent performance. For example, a video recorder should perform consistently and play back recorded programs at an acceptable level of quality. If the design performs erratically, or is subject to frequent failure, reliability needs are not satisfied. Designs at this level are perceived to be of low value.

Usability needs have to do with how easy and forgiving a design is to use. For example, configuring a video recorder to record programs at a later time should be easily accomplished, and the recorder should be tolerant of mistakes. If the difficulty of use is too great, or the consequences of simple errors too severe, usability needs are not satisfied. Designs at this level are perceived to be of moderate value.

Proficiency needs have to do with empowering people to do things better than they could previously. For example, a video recorder that can seek out and record programs based on keywords is a significant advance in recording capability, enabling people to do things not previously possible. Designs at this level are perceived to be of high value.

Creativity is the level in the hierarchy where all needs have been satisfied, and people begin interacting with the design in innovative ways. The design, having satisfied all other needs, is now used to create and explore areas that extend both the design and the person using the design. Designs at this level are perceived to be of the highest value, and often achieve cult-like loyalty among users.

Consider the hierarchy of needs in design, and ensure that lower-level needs are satisfied before resources are devoted to serving higher-level needs. Evaluate existing designs with respect to the hierarchy to determine where modifications should be made.

See also 80/20 Rule, Aesthetic-Usability Effect, and Form Follows Function.

[1] The *hierarchy of needs* is based on *Maslow's Hierarchy of Needs*.

[2] The seminal work on the concept of a hierarchy of needs is *Motivation and Personality* by Abraham Maslow, Addison-Wesley, 1987 [1954].

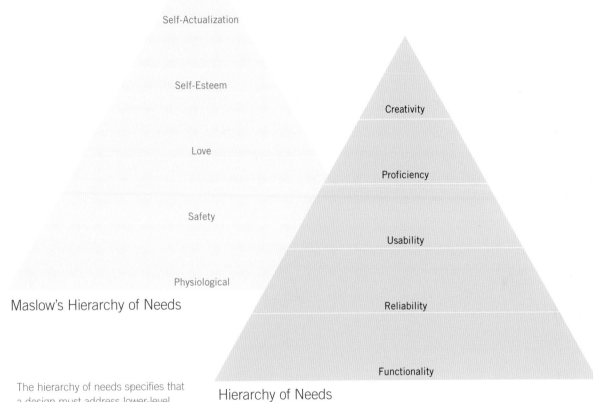

Self-Actualization

Self-Esteem

Love

Safety

Physiological

Maslow's Hierarchy of Needs

Creativity

Proficiency

Usability

Reliability

Functionality

Hierarchy of Needs

The hierarchy of needs specifies that a design must address lower-level needs before higher-level needs can be addressed. The perceived value of a design corresponds to its place in the hierarchy—i.e., higher levels in the hierarchy correspond to higher levels of perceived value. The levels of hierarchy are adapted from Maslow's Hierarchy of Needs.

Highlighting

A technique for bringing attention to an area of text or image.

Highlighting is an effective technique for bringing attention to elements of a design. If applied improperly, however, highlighting can be ineffective, and actually reduce performance in these areas. The following guidelines address the benefits and liabilities of common highlighting techniques.[1]

General
Highlight no more than 10 percent of the visible design; highlighting effects are diluted as the percentage increases. Use a small number of highlighting techniques applied consistently throughout the design.

Bold, Italics, and Underlining
Use bold, italics, and underlining for titles, labels, captions, and short word sequences when the elements need to be subtly differentiated. Bolding is generally preferred over other techniques as it adds minimal noise to the design and clearly highlights target elements. Italics add minimal noise to a design, but are less detectable and legible. Underlining adds considerable noise and compromises legibility, and should be used sparingly if at all.[2]

Typeface
Uppercase text in short word sequences is easily scanned, and thus can be advantageous when applied to labels and keywords within a busy display. Avoid using different fonts as a highlighting technique. A detectable difference between fonts is difficult to achieve without also disrupting the aesthetics of the typography.

Color
Color is a potentially effective highlighting technique, but should be used sparingly and only in concert with other highlighting techniques. Highlight using a few desaturated colors that are clearly distinct from one another.

Inversing
Inversing elements works well with text, but may not work as well with icons or shapes. It is effective at attracting attention, but adds considerable noise to the design and therefore should be used sparingly.

Blinking
Blinking—flashing an element between two states—is a powerful technique for attracting attention. Blinking should be used only to indicate highly critical information that requires an immediate response, such as an emergency status light. It is important to be able to turn off the blinking once it is acknowledged, as it compromises legibility, and distracts from other tasks.

See also Color, Legibility, and Readability.

[1] See, for example, "A Review of Human Factors Guidelines and Techniques for the Design of Graphical Human-Computer Interfaces" by Martin Maguire, *International Journal of Man-Machine Studies*, 1982, vol. 16(3), p. 237–261.

[2] A concise summary of typographic principles of this kind is found in *The Mac is Not a Typewriter* by Robin Williams, Peachpit Press, 1990. Despite the title, the book is of value to non-Macintosh owners as well.

General

"**You mean you can't take less**," said the Hatter, "**it's very easy to take more than nothing**."

"**Nobody asked your opinion**," said Alice.

"You mean you can't take **less**," said the Hatter, "it's very easy to take **more** than nothing."

"Nobody asked **your** opinion," said Alice.

Bold, Italics, and Underlining

Advice from a Caterpillar

"I can't explain **myself**, I'm afraid, sir" said Alice, "because I'm not myself, you see."

Advice from a Caterpillar

"I can't explain *myself*, I'm afraid, sir" said Alice, "because I'm not myself, you see."

<u>Advice from a Caterpillar</u>

"I can't explain <u>myself</u>, I'm afraid, sir" said Alice, "because I'm not myself, you see."

Typeface

"What is a Caucus-race?" said Alice; not that she wanted much to know, but the Dodo had paused as if it thought that somebody ought to speak, and no one else seemed inclined to say anything.

"What IS a Caucus-race?" said Alice; not that she wanted much to know, but the Dodo had paused as if it thought that SOMEBODY ought to speak, and no one else seemed inclined to say anything.

Color

Which brought them back again to the beginning of the conversation. Alice felt a little irritated at the Caterpillar's making such very short remarks, and she drew herself up and said, very gravely, "I think, you ought to tell me who you are, first."

Which brought them back again to the beginning of the conversation. Alice felt a little irritated at the Caterpillar's making such **very** short remarks, and she drew herself up and said, very gravely, "I think, you ought to tell me who **you** are, first."

Inversing

Who stole the tarts?

Who stole the tarts?

Iconic Representation

The use of pictorial images to improve the recognition and recall of signs and controls.

Iconic representation is the use of pictorial images to make actions, objects, and concepts in a display easier to find, recognize, learn, and remember. Iconic representations are used in signage, computer displays, and control panels. They can be used for identification (company logo), serve as a space-efficient alternative to text (road signs), or to draw attention to an item within an informational display (error icons appearing next to items in a list). There are four types of iconic representation: *similar*, *example*, *symbolic*, and *arbitrary*.[1]

Similar icons use images that are visually analogous to an action, object, or concept. They are most effective at representing simple actions, objects, or concepts, and less effective when the complexity increases. For example, a sign indicating a sharp curve ahead can be represented by a similar icon (e.g., curved line). A sign to reduce speed, however, is an action not easily represented by similar icons.

Example icons use images of things that exemplify or are commonly associated with an action, object, or concept. They are particularly effective at representing complex actions, objects, or concepts. For example, a sign indicating the location of an airport uses an image of an airplane, rather than an image representing an airport.

Symbolic icons use images that represent an action, object, or concept at a higher level of abstraction. They are effective when actions, objects, or concepts involve well-established and easily recognizable objects. For example, a door lock control on a car door uses an image of a padlock to indicate its function, even though the padlock looks nothing like the actual control.

Arbitrary icons use images that bear little or no relationship to the action, object, or concept—i.e., the relationship has to be learned. Generally, arbitrary icons should only be used when developing cross-cultural or industry standards that will be used for long periods of time. This gives people sufficient exposure to an icon to make it an effective communication device. For example, the icon for radiation must be learned, as nothing intrinsic to the image indicates radiation. Those who work with radiation, however, recognize the symbol all over the world.

Iconic representation reduces performance load, conserves display and control area, and makes signs and controls more understandable across cultures. Consider similar icons when representations are simple and concrete. Use example icons when representations are complex. Consider symbolic icons when representations involve well-established and recognizable symbols. Consider arbitrary icons when representations are to be used as standards. Generally, icons should be labeled and share a common visual motif (style and color) for optimal performance.

See also Chunking, Performance Load, and Picture Superiority Effect.

[1] The seminal work in iconic representation is *Symbol Sourcebook* by Henry Dreyfuss, Van Nostrand Reinhold, 1984. The four kinds of iconic representation are derived from "Icons at the Interface: Their Usefulness" by Yvonne Rogers, *Interacting With Computers*, vol. 1, p. 105–118.

Similar

Right Turn   Falling Rocks   Sharp   Stop

Example

Airport   Cut   Basketball   Restaurant

Symbolic

Electricity   Water   Unlock   Fragile

Arbitrary

Collate   Female   Radioactive   Resistor

Immersion

A state of mental focus so intense that awareness of the "real" world is lost, generally resulting in a feeling of joy and satisfaction.

When perceptual and cognitive systems are under-taxed, people become apathetic and bored. If they are over-taxed, people become stressed and frustrated. Immersion occurs when perceptual and cognitive systems are challenged at near capacity, without being exceeded. Under these conditions, the person loses a sense of the "real" world and typically experiences intense feelings of joy and satisfaction. Immersion can occur while working on a task, playing a game, reading a book, or painting a picture. Immersion is characterized by one or more of the following elements:[1]

- challenges that can be overcome
- contexts where a person can focus without significant distraction
- clearly defined goals
- immediate feedback with regards to actions and overall performance
- a loss of awareness of the worries and frustrations of everyday life
- a feeling of control over actions, activities, and the environment
- a loss of concern regarding matters of the self (e.g., awareness of hunger or thirst)
- a modified sense of time (e.g., hours can pass by in what seems like minutes).

It is not clear which of these elements must be present in what combination to create a generally immersive experience. For example, theme park rides can provide rich sensory experiences with minimal cognitive engagement and still be immersive. Conversely, complex games like chess can provide rich cognitive engagement with minimal sensory experience and also be immersive. Given the wide range of human cognitive abilities and relatively narrow range of perceptual abilities, it is generally easier to design activities and environments that achieve immersion through perceptual stimulation than through cognitive engagement. However, perceptual immersion is more difficult to sustain for long periods of time and is, therefore, usable only for relatively brief experiences. Optimal immersive experiences involve both rich sensory experiences and rich cognitive engagement.

Incorporate elements of immersion in activities and environments that seek to engage the attention of people over time—e.g., entertainment, instruction, games, and exhibits. Provide clearly defined goals and challenges that can be overcome. Design environments that minimize distractions, promote a feeling of control, and provide feedback. Emphasize stimuli that distract people from the real world, and suppress stimuli that remind them of the real world. Achieving the right balance of elements to achieve immersion is more art than science; therefore, leave ample time in the design process for experimentation and tuning.

See also Chunking, Depth of Processing, Performance Load, and Storytelling.

[1] The elements of immersion adapted from *Flow: The Psychology of Optimal Experience* by Mihaly Csikszentmihalyi, Harper Collins Publishers, 1991. See also *Narrative as Virtual Reality* by Marie-Laure Ryan, The Johns Hopkins University Press, 2000.

Personalized audio guides, lavish contexts, and interactive elements make the R.M.S. Titanic exhibit more than just another museum exhibit—it is an immersive journey through time that allows visitors to personally experience the triumphs and tragedies of the R.M.S. Titanic. The exhibit, featuring such items as a boarding pass and a scale model of the ship, engages the sight, sound, smell, and touch of visitors in the experience, all the while leaving them in control of the pace of presentation and level of interaction. A sense of time is lost, and matters of the real world fade as the tragedy slowly unfolds.

Interference Effects

A phenomenon in which mental processing is made slower and less accurate by competing mental processes.

Interference effects occur when two or more perceptual or cognitive processes are in conflict. Human perception and cognition involve many different mental systems that parse and process information independently of one another. The outputs of these systems are communicated to working memory, where they are interpreted. When the outputs are congruent, the process of interpretation occurs quickly and performance is optimal. When outputs are incongruent, interference occurs and additional processing is needed to resolve the conflict. The additional time required to resolve such conflicts has a negative impact on performance. A few examples of interference effects include:[1]

Stroop Interference—an irrelevant aspect of a stimulus triggers a mental process that interferes with processes involving a relevant aspect of the stimulus. For example, the time it takes to name the color of words is greater when the meaning and color of the words conflict.

Garner Interference—an irrelevant variation of a stimulus triggers a mental process that interferes with processes involving a relevant aspect of the stimulus. For example, the time it takes to name shapes is greater when they are presented next to shapes that change with each presentation.

Proactive Interference—existing memories interfere with learning. For example, in learning a new language, errors are often made when people try to apply the grammar of their native language to the new language.

Retroactive Interference—learning interferes with existing memories. For example, learning a new phone number can interfere with phone numbers already in memory.

Prevent interference by avoiding designs that create conflicting mental processes. Interference effects of perception (i.e., Stroop and Garner) generally result from conflicting coding combinations (e.g., a red *go* button, or green *stop* button) or from an interaction between closely positioned elements that visually interact with one another (e.g., two icons group or blend because of their shape and proximity). Minimize interference effects of learning (i.e., proactive and retroactive) by mixing the presentation modes of instruction (e.g., lecture, video, computer, activities), employing advance organizers, and incorporating periods of rest every thirty to forty-five minutes.

See also Advance Organizer, Performance Load, Errors, and Mapping.

[1] The seminal works on interference effects include "Studies of Interference in Serial Verbal Reactions" by James R. Stroop, *Journal of Experimental Psychology*, 1935, vol. 28, p. 643–662; "Stimulus Configuration in Selective Attention Tasks" by James R. Pomerantz and Wendell R. Garner, *Perception & Psychophysics*, 1973, vol. 14, p. 565–569; and "Characteristics of Word Encoding" by Delos D. Wickens, in *Coding Processes in Human Memory* edited by A. W. Melton and E. Martin, V. H. Winston, 1972, p. 191–215.

In populations that have learned that green means go and red means stop, the incongruence between the color and the label-icon results in interference.

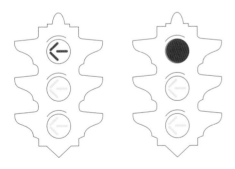

In populations that have learned that a traffic arrow always means go, the introduction of a red arrow in new traffic lights creates potentially dangerous interference.

Red   Black   White
Pink   Green   Orange
Yellow   Purple   Gray

Reading the words aloud is easier than naming their colors. The mental process for reading is more practiced and automatic and, therefore, interferes with the mental process for naming the colors.

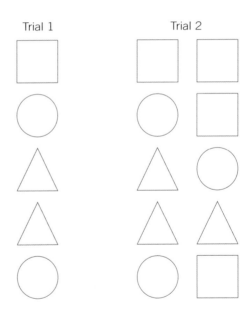

Naming the column of shapes that stands alone is easier than naming either of the columns located together. The close proximity of the columns results in the activation of mental processes for naming proximal shapes, creating interference.

Inverted Pyramid

A method of information presentation in which information is presented in descending order of importance.

The inverted pyramid refers to a method of information presentation in which critical information is presented first, and then additional elaborative information is presented in descending order of importance. In the pyramid metaphor, the broad base of the pyramid represents the most important information, while the tip of the pyramid represents the least-important information. For example, in traditional scientific writing, a historical foundation (tip of the pyramid) is presented first, followed by arguments and evidence, and then a conclusion (base of the pyramid). To invert the pyramid is to present the important information first, and the background information last. The inverted pyramid has been a standard in journalism for over one hundred years, and has found wide use in instructional design, technical writing, and Internet publishing.[1]

The inverted pyramid consists of a lead (critical information) and a body (elaborative information). The lead is a terse summary of the "what," "where," "when," "who," "why," and "how" of the information. The body consists of subsequent paragraphs or chunks of information that elaborate facts and details in descending order of importance. It is increasingly common in Internet publishing to present only the lead, and make the body available upon request (e.g., with a "more…" link).

The inverted pyramid offers a number of benefits over traditional methods of information presentation: it conveys the key aspects of the information quickly; it establishes a context in which to interpret subsequent facts; initial chunks of information are more likely to be remembered than later chunks of information; it permits efficient searching and scanning of information; and information can be easily edited for length, knowing that the least important information will always be at the end. The efficiency of the inverted pyramid is also its limiting factor. While it provides a succinct, information-dense method of information presentation, the inverted pyramid does not allow the flexibility of building suspense or creating a surprise ending, so is often perceived as uninteresting and boring.

Use the inverted pyramid when presentation efficiency is important. Develop leads that present a concise overview of the information, followed by short chunks of information of decreasing importance. If interestingness is important and has been compromised, include multiple media, interesting layouts, and interactivity to complement the information and actively engage audiences. When it is not possible to use the inverted pyramid method (e.g., in standard scientific writing), consider a compromise solution based on the principle by providing an executive summary at the beginning to present the key findings.

See also Advance Organizer, Form Follows Function, Ockham's Razor, Progressive Disclosure, and Serial Position Effects.

[1] The development of the inverted pyramid is attributed to Edwin Stanton, Abraham Lincoln's Secretary of War (1865). See, for example, *Just the Facts: How "Objectivity" Came to Define American Journalism* by David T. Z. Mindich, New York University Press, 2000.

This evening at about 9:30 P.M., at Ford's Theater, the President, while sitting in his private box with Mrs. Lincoln, Miss Harris, and Major Rathbone, was shot by an assassin who suddenly entered the box and approached the President. The assassin then leapt upon the stage, brandished a large dagger or knife, and made his escape in the rear of the theater. The pistol-ball entered the back of the President's head and penetrated nearly through the head. The wound is mortal. The President has been insensible ever since it was inflicted and is now dying.

About the same hour an assassin, whether the same or not, entered Mr. Seward's apartments, and under the pretense of having a prescription, was shown to the Secretary's sick chamber. The assassin immediately rushed to the bed, and inflicted two or three stabs on the throat and two on the face. It is hoped the wounds may not be mortal. My apprehension is that they will prove fatal. The nurse alarmed Mr. Frederick Seward, who was in an adjoining room, and hastened to the door of his father's room, when he met the assassin, who inflicted upon him one or more dangerous wounds. The recovery of Frederick Seward is doubtful.

It is not probable that the President will live throughout the night. General Grant and wife were advertised to be at the theater this evening, but he started for Burlington at six o'clock this evening. At a cabinet meeting at which General Grant was present, the subject of the state of the country, and the prospect of a speedy peace was discussed. The President was very cheerful and hopeful, and spoke very kindly of General Lee and others of the Confederacy, and of the establishment of government in Virginia. All the members of the cabinet, except Mr. Seward, are now in attendance upon the President.

I have seen Mr. Seward, but he and Frederick are both unconscious.

EDWIN M. STANTON,
Secretary of War. April 14, 1865.

This report of President Lincoln's assassination established the inverted pyramid style of writing. Its economy of style, a stark contrast to the lavish prose of the day, was developed for efficient communication by telegraph.

Iteration

A process of repeating a set of operations until a specific result is achieved.

Ordered complexity does not occur without iteration. In nature, iteration allows complex structures to form by progressively building on simpler structures. In design, iteration allows complex structures to be created by progressively exploring, testing, and tuning the design. The emergence of ordered complexity results from an accumulation of knowledge and experience that is then applied to the design. For example, a quality software user interface is developed through a series of design iterations. Each version is reviewed and tested, and the design is then iterated based on the feedback. The interface typically progresses from low fidelity to high fidelity as more is learned about the interface and how it will be used. Iteration occurs in all development cycles in two basic forms: design iteration and development iteration.[1]

Design iteration is the expected iteration that occurs when exploring, testing, and refining design concepts. Each cycle in the design process narrows the wide range of possibilities until the design conforms to the design requirements. Prototypes of increasing fidelity are used throughout the process to test concepts and identify unknown variables. Members of the target audience should be actively involved in various stages of iterations to support testing and verify design requirements. Whether tests are deemed a success or failure is irrelevant in design iteration, since both success and failure provide important information about what does and does not work. In fact, there is often more value in failure, as valuable lessons are learned about the failure points of a design. The outcome of design iteration is a detailed and well-tested specification that can be developed into a final product.[2]

Development iteration is the unexpected iteration that occurs when building a product. Unlike design iteration, development iteration is rework—i.e., unnecessary waste in the development cycle. Development iteration is costly and undesirable, and generally the result of either inadequate or incorrect design specifications, or poor planning and management in the development process. The unknowns associated with a design should ideally be eliminated during the design stage.

Plan for and employ *design* iteration. Establish clear criteria defining the degree to which design requirements must be satisfied for the design to be considered complete. One of the most effective methods of reducing development iteration is to ensure that all development members have a clear, high-level vision of the final product. This is often accomplished through well-written specifications accompanied by high-fidelity models and prototypes.

See also Development Cycle, Fibonacci Sequence, Prototyping, and Self-Similarity.

[1] A seminal contemporary work on iteration in design is *The Evolution of Useful Things* by Henry Petroski, Vintage Books, 1994. See also *Product Design and Development* by Karl T. Ulrich and Steven D. Eppinger, McGraw-Hill Higher Education, 2nd ed., 1999. See also "Positive vs. Negative Iteration in Design" by Glenn Ballard, *Proceedings of the Eighth Annual Conference of the International Group for Lean Construction*, 2000.

[2] A common problem with design iteration is the absence of a defined endpoint—i.e., each iteration refines the design, but also reveals additional opportunities for refinement, resulting in a design process that never ends. To avoid this, establish clear criteria defining the degree to which design requirements must be satisfied for the design to be considered complete.

Quality design does not occur without iteration. For example, the design of the SnoWalkers snowshoes is the result of numerous design iterations over a two-year period. The design process made ample use of prototypes, which allowed designers to improve their understanding of design requirements and product performance, and continually refine the design with each iteration.

Law of Prägnanz

A tendency to interpret ambiguous images as simple and complete, versus complex and incomplete.[1]

The Law of Prägnanz is one of several principles referred to as *Gestalt principles of perception*. It asserts that when people are presented with a set of ambiguous elements (elements that can be interpreted in different ways), they interpret the elements in the simplest way. Here, "simplest" refers to arrangements having fewer rather than more elements, having symmetrical rather than asymmetrical compositions, and generally observing the other Gestalt principles of perception.[2]

For example, a set of shapes that touches at their edges could be interpreted as either adjacent or overlapping. When the shapes are complex, the simplest interpretation is that they are adjacent like pieces in a puzzle. When the shapes are simple, the simplest interpretation is that they overlap one another. The law applies similarly to the way in which images are recalled from memory. For example, people recall the positions of countries on maps as more aligned and symmetrical than they actually are.

The tendency to perceive and recall images as simply as possible indicates that cognitive resources are being applied to translate or encode images into simpler forms. This suggests that fewer cognitive resources may be needed if images are simpler at the outset. Research supports this idea and confirms that people are better able to visually process and remember simple figures than complex figures.[3]

Therefore, minimize the number of elements in a design. Note that symmetrical compositions are perceived as simpler and more stable than asymmetrical compositions, but symmetrical compositions are also perceived to be less interesting. Favor symmetrical compositions when efficiency of use is the priority, and asymmetrical compositions when interestingness is the priority. Consider all of the Gestalt principles of perception (closure, common fate, figure-ground relationship, good continuation, proximity, similarity, and uniform connectedness).

See also Aesthetic-Usability Effect, Ockham's Razor, and Rule of Thirds.

[1] Also known as the *law of good configuration*, *law of simplicity*, *law of pregnance*, *law of precision*, and *law of good figure*.

[2] The seminal work on the Law of Prägnanz is *Principles of Gestalt Psychology* by Kurt Koffka, Harcourt Brace, 1935.

[3] See, for example, "The Status of Minimum Principle in the Theoretical Analysis of Visual Perception" by Gary Hatfield and William Epstein, *Psychological Bulletin*, 1985, vol. 97, p. 155–186.

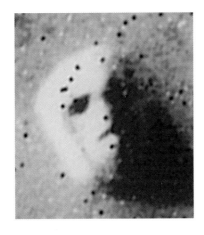
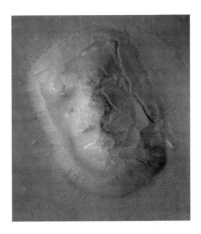

Low resolution images (left) of a rock formation on Mars led many to conclude that intelligent life once existed there. Higher-resolution images (right) taken some years later suggest a more Earth-based explanation: Humans tend to add order and meaning to patterns and formations that do not exist outside their perception.

:-)

:-(

:-|

:-O

;-)

These sets of characters are interpreted as single faces rather than multiple independent characters.

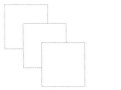

Both sets of figures are interpreted as simple overlapping shapes, rather than a more complex interpretation—e.g., two inverted "L" shapes and a square, and two triangles and a five-sided polygon.

Dazzle camouflage schemes used on war ships were designed to prevent simple interpretations of boat type and orientation, making it a difficult target for submarines. This is a rendering of the French cruiser *Gloire*.

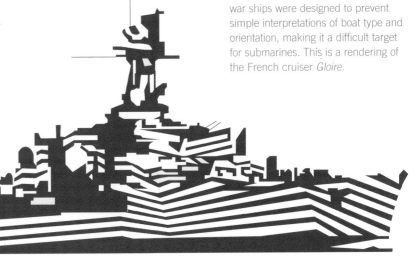

Layering

The process of organizing information into related groupings in order to manage complexity and reinforce
relationships in the information.

Layering involves organizing information into related groupings and then presenting
or making available only certain groupings at any one time. Layering is primarily used
to manage complexity, but can also be used to reinforce relationships in information.
There are two basic kinds of layering: two-dimensional and three-dimensional.[1]

Two-dimensional layering involves separating information into layers such that only
one layer of information can be viewed at a time. Two-dimensional layers can be
revealed in either a linear or nonlinear fashion. Linear layers are useful when information has a clear beginning, middle, and end (e.g., stories), and are revealed
successively like pages in a book. Nonlinear layers are useful when reinforcing
relationships between the layers. The types of nonlinear layer relationships can be
hierarchical, parallel, or web. Hierarchical layers are useful when information has
superordinate and subordinate relationships within itself (e.g., organizational chart),
and are revealed top-down or bottom-up in rigid accordance with the hierarchical
structure. Parallel layers are useful when information is based on the organization
of other information (e.g., thesaurus), and are revealed through some correspon-
dence with that organization. Web layers are useful when information has many
different kinds of relationships within itself (e.g., hypertext), and are revealed
through any number of associative linkages to other layers.

Three-dimensional layering involves separating information into layers such that
multiple layers of information can be viewed at a time. Three-dimensional layers
are revealed as either opaque or transparent planes of information that sit atop
one another (i.e., in a third dimension). Opaque layers are useful when additional
information about a particular item is desired without switching contexts (e.g., software pop-up windows). Transparent layers are useful when overlays of information
combine to illustrate concepts or highlight relationships (e.g., weather maps).[2]

Use two-dimensional layering to manage complexity and direct navigation through
information. Consider linear layers when telling stories and presenting sequences
of time-based events, and use nonlinear layers when emphasizing relationships
within the information. Use three-dimensional layering to elaborate information and
illustrate concepts without switching contexts. Consider opaque layers when presenting elaborative information, and transparent layers when illustrating concepts
or highlighting relationships in information.

See also Chunking, Five Hat Racks, and Progressive Disclosure.

[1] A similar concept is found in *Designing Business: Multiple Media, Multiple Disciplines* by Clement Mok, Adobe Press, 1996, p. 102–107 [Organizational Models].

[2] See, for example, *Envisioning Information* by Edward R. Tufte, Graphics Press, 1998, p. 53–65; 81–95 [Layering and Separation; Color and Information].

Two-Dimensional Layering

Linear

Beginning	Middle 1	Middle 2	End

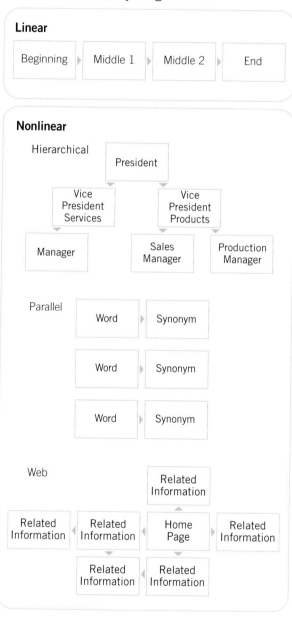

Nonlinear

Hierarchical

President

Vice President Services

Vice President Products

Manager

Sales Manager

Production Manager

Parallel

Word → Synonym

Word → Synonym

Word → Synonym

Web

Related Information

Related Information → Related Information → Home Page → Related Information

Related Information → Related Information

Three-Dimensional Layering

Opaque

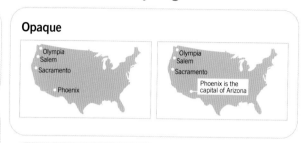

Transparent

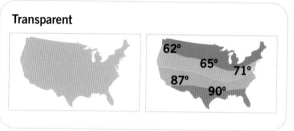

Three-dimensional layering is useful for elaboration and highlighting. Relationships and patterns on one layer of information (left) are elaborated by layers of information that pop up or overlay (right).

Two-dimensional layering is useful for presentation and navigation. Layers are revealed one at a time, like pages in a book.

Legibility

The visual clarity of text, generally based on the size, typeface, contrast, text block, and spacing of the characters used.

Confusion regarding the research on legibility is as persistent as it is pervasive. The rapid growth and advancement of modern desktop publishing, Web-based publishing, and multimedia presentation continue to compound the confusion with increasing font and layout capabilities, display and print options, and the need to effectively integrate with other media. The following guidelines address common issues regarding text legibility.[1]

Size
For printed text, standard 9- to 12-point type is considered optimal. Smaller sizes are acceptable when limited to captions and notes. Use larger type for low-resolution displays and more senior audiences.[2]

Typeface
There is no performance difference between serif and sans serif typefaces, so select based on aesthetic preference. Sentence case text should be used for text blocks. On low-resolution displays, antialiasing the text may marginally improve legibility, but primarily serves as an aesthetic enhancement of the typeface.[3]

Contrast
Use dark text on a light background or vice versa. Performance is optimal when contrast levels between text and background exceed 70 percent. Foreground/background color combinations generally do not affect legibility as long as you observe the minimum contrast level, so select based on aesthetic preference. Patterned or textured backgrounds can dramatically reduce legibility, and should be avoided.[4]

Text Blocks
There is no performance difference between justified and unjustified text, so select based on aesthetic preference. For 9- to 12-point type, a line length of 3 to 5 inches (8 cm to 13 cm) is recommended, resulting in a maximum of about 10 to 12 words per line, or 35 to 55 characters per line.[5]

Spacing
For 9- to 12-point type, set leading (spacing between text lines, measured from baseline to baseline) to the type size plus 1 to 4 points. Proportionally spaced typefaces are preferred over monospaced.

See also Iconic Representation and Readability.

[1] The seminal empirical works on legibility for print are *Bases for Effective Reading*, University of Minnesota Press, 1963; and *Legibility of Print*, Iowa State University Press, 1965, both by Miles A. Tinker. A comprehensive and elegant contemporary reference from a typographic perspective is *The Elements of Typographic Style* by Robert Bringhurst, Hartley & Marks (2nd ed.), 1997.

[2] Legibility research on low-resolution computer displays continues to yield mixed results but generally supports Tinker's original findings. However, be conservative to account for lower-resolution displays.

[3] On lower-resolution displays and for type smaller than 12 point, use sans serif typefaces without antialiasing. Serifs and antialiasing blur the characters of smaller type and, therefore, compromise legibility.

[4] Dark text on light backgrounds is preferred. High-contrast, inverse text can "visually bleed" to the background and dramatically reduce legibility. Factors other than legibility should be considered when selecting foreground/background color combinations (e.g., color blindness and fatigue), so select carefully and test atypical combinations.

[5] The speed with which text can be visually processed is greatest on long text lines (80 characters or more). However, readers prefer short text lines (35 to 55 characters). Unless visual processing speed is critical to the design task, shorter text lines are recommended. See, for example, "The Effects of Line Length and Method of Movement on Patterns of Reading from Screen," by Mary C. Dyson and Gary J. Kipping, *Visible Language*, 1998, vol. 32(2), p. 150–181.

Size

This is 9-point Trade Gothic   This is 10-point Trade Gothic   This is 12-point Trade Gothic

Typeface

Serif vs. San Serif
Serif typefaces have small "feet" at the ends of the letters.

Serif
Sans Serif

Antialiased vs. Aliased Text
Antialiased text looks smooth because of pixels added to smooth the transition between the text color and the background color. Aliased text looks jagged because it does not contain these transition pixels.

Antialiased
Aliased

Text Cases
This is sentence case
This is Title Case
this is lowercase
THIS IS UPPERCASE

Uppercase vs. Mixed Case
People recognize words by letter groups and shapes. Uppercase text is more difficult to read than sentence case and title case because the shapes of uppercase words are all rectangular.

Alice's Adventures in Wonderland
ALICE'S ADVENTURES IN WONDERLAND

Contrast

The Mad Hatter   The Mad Hatter   **The Mad Hatter**

Textblocks

Aligned Left, Ragged Right Text
Soon her eye fell on a little glass box that was lying under the table: she opened it, and found in it a very small cake, on which the words "EAT ME" were beautifully marked in currants.

Justified Text
Soon her eye fell on a little glass box that was lying under the table: she opened it, and found in it a very small cake, on which the words "EAT ME" were beautifully marked in currants.

Aligned Right, Ragged Left Text
Soon her eye fell on a little glass box that was lying under the table: she opened it, and found in it a very small cake, on which the words "EAT ME" were beautifully marked in currants.

Spacing

Leading
Leading (rhymes with sledding) is the amount of vertical space from the baseline of one line of text to the baseline of the next line of text. Below, the type size is 12 points and the leading is 18 points.

"Yes, that's it," said the Hatter with a sigh: "it's always tea-time, and we've no time to wash the things between whiles."

Baseline
Leading
Baseline

Monospaced vs. Proportionally Spaced Typefaces
In monospaced typefaces, all characters assume the same amount of horizontal space. In proportionally spaced typefaces, characters assume variable amounts of horizontal space, depending on the width of the actual character and the relationships among groups of characters.

"Off with her head!" the Queen shouted.   monospaced typeface
"Off with her head!" the Queen shouted.   proportionally spaced typeface

Life Cycle

All products progress sequentially through four stages of existence: introduction, growth, maturity, and decline.

All products progress through stages of existence that roughly correspond to birth, life, and death. For example, a new type of electronic device is envisioned and developed; its popularity grows; after a while its sales plateau; and then finally, the sales decline. Understanding the implications of each of the stages allows designers to prepare for the unique and evolving requirements of a product over its lifetime. There are four basic stages of life for all products: introduction, growth, maturity, and decline.[1]

Introduction
The introduction stage is the official birth of a product. It will at times overlap with the late testing stage of the development cycle. The design focus is to monitor early use of the design to ensure proper performance, working closely with customers to tune or patch the design as necessary.

Growth
The growth stage is the most challenging stage, where most products fail. The design focus is to scale the supply and performance of the product to meet the growing demand, and provide the level of support necessary to maintain customer satisfaction and growth. Efforts to gather requirements for the next-generation product should be underway at this stage.

Maturity
The maturity stage is the peak of the product life cycle. Product sales have begun to diminish and competition from competitors is strong. The design focus at this stage is to enhance and refine the product to maximize customer satisfaction and retention. Design and development of the next generation product should be well underway at this stage.

Decline
The decline stage is the end of the life cycle. Product sales continue to decline and core market share is at risk. The design focus is to minimize maintenance costs and develop transition strategies to migrate customers to new products. Testing of the next generation product should begin at this stage.

Consider the life cycle of a product when planning and preparing for the future. During the introduction phase, work closely with early adopters to refine and tune products. During the growth stage, focus on scaling product supply and performance. During the maturity stage, focus on customer satisfaction through performance enhancements and improved support. During decline, focus on facilitating the transition to next generation products. Note that the development cycle for the next-generation product begins during the growth stage of a current-generation product.

See also Development Cycle, Hierarchy of Needs, Iteration, and Prototyping.

[1] The seminal work on the product life cycle is "International Investment and International Trade in the Product Cycle" by Raymond Vernon, *Quarterly Journal of Economics*, 1966, vol. 80, p. 190–207. A contemporary review of the product life cycle is found in *Marketing Management* by Philip Kotler, Prentice-Hall, 11th ed., 2002.

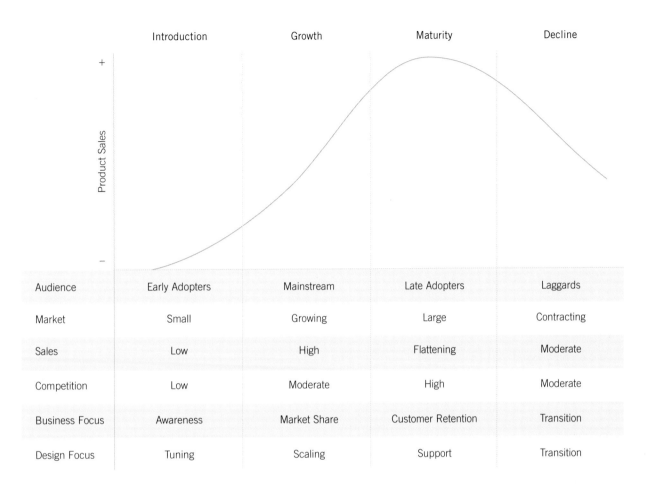

	Introduction	Growth	Maturity	Decline
Audience	Early Adopters	Mainstream	Late Adopters	Laggards
Market	Small	Growing	Large	Contracting
Sales	Low	High	Flattening	Moderate
Competition	Low	Moderate	High	Moderate
Business Focus	Awareness	Market Share	Customer Retention	Transition
Design Focus	Tuning	Scaling	Support	Transition

The needs of a product change over the course of its life cycle. It is important to understand the dynamics of these changes in order to focus business and design resources accordingly. Failure to do so shortens the life cycle of a product.

Mapping

A relationship between controls and their movements or effects. Good mapping between controls and their effects results in greater ease of use.[1]

Turn a wheel, flip a switch, or push a button, and you expect some kind of effect. When the effect corresponds to expectation, the mapping is considered to be good or natural. When the effect does not correspond to expectation, the mapping is considered to be poor. For example, an electric window control on a car door can be oriented so that raising the control switch corresponds to raising the window, and lowering the control switch lowers the window. The relationship between the control and raising or lowering the window is obvious. Compare this to an orientation of the control switch on the surface of an armrest, such that the control motion is forward and backward. The relationship between the control and the raising and lowering of the window is no longer obvious; does pushing the control switch forward correspond to raising or lowering the window?[2]

Good mapping is primarily a function of similarity of layout, behavior, or meaning. When the layout of stovetop controls corresponds to the layout of burners, this is similarity of layout; when turning a steering wheel left turns the car left, this is similarity of behavior; when an emergency shut-off button is colored red, this is similarity of meaning (e.g., most people associate red with stop). In each case, similarity makes the control-effect relationship predictable, and therefore easy to use.[3]

Position controls so that their locations and behaviors correspond to the layout and behavior of the device. Simple control-effect relationships work best. Avoid using a single control for multiple functions whenever possible; it is difficult to achieve good mappings for a one control-multiple effect relationship. In cases where this is not possible, use visually distinct modes (e.g., different colors) to indicate active functions. Be careful when relying on conventions to attach meaning to controls, as different population groups may interpret the conventions differently (e.g., in England, flipping a lightswitch *up* turns it off and flipping it *down* turns it on).

See also Affordance, Interference Effects, Proximity, and Visibility.

[1] Also known as *control-display relationship* and *stimulus-response compatibility*.

[2] The seminal work on mapping is *The Design of Everyday Things* by Donald Norman, Doubleday, 1990.

[3] For a review of these kinds of issues, see *Spatial Schemas and Abstract Thought* by Merideth Gattis (ed.), MIT Press, 2001.

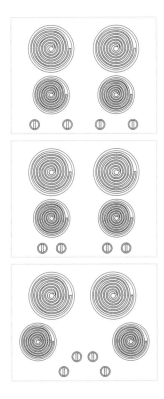

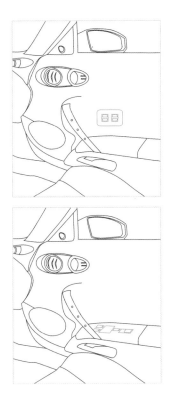

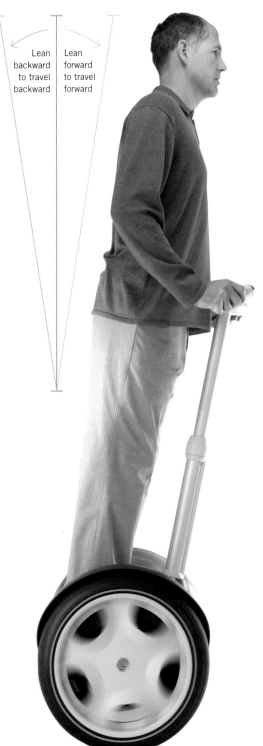

The relationship between stovetop controls and burners is ambiguous when the controls are horizontally oriented and equally spaced (poor mapping). The relationship becomes clearer when the controls are grouped with the burners, but the horizontal orientation still confuses which control goes with which burner (poor, but improved mapping). When the layout of the controls corresponds to the layout of the burners, the control-burner relationships are clear (good mapping).

The relationship between the window control and the raising and lowering of the window is obvious when it is mounted on the wall of the door (good mapping), but ambiguous when mounted on the surface of the armrest (poor mapping).

The Segway Human Transporter makes excellent use of mapping. Lean forward to go forward, and lean backward to go backward.

Mental Model

People understand and interact with systems and environments based on mental representations developed from experience.

Mental models are representations of systems and environments derived from experience. People understand and interact with systems and environments by comparing the outcomes of their mental models with the real-world systems and environments. When the outcomes correspond, a mental model is accurate and complete. When the outcomes do not correspond, the mental model is inaccurate or incomplete. With regards to design, there are two basic types of mental models: mental models of how systems work (*system models*) and mental models of how people interact with systems (*interaction models*).[1]

Designers generally have very complete and accurate system models, but often have weak interaction models—i.e., they know much about how a system works, but little about how people will interact with the system. Conversely, users of a design tend to have sparse and inaccurate system models, but through use and experience commonly attain interaction models that are more complete and accurate than those of designers. Optimal design results only when designers have an accurate and complete system model, attain an accurate and complete interaction model, and then design a system interface that reflects an efficient merging of both models.[2]

Designers can obtain accurate and complete interaction models through personal use of the system, laboratory testing (e.g., focus groups and usability testing), and direct observation of people interacting with the system, or similar systems. Use of the system by the designer will reveal obvious design problems, but will fail to reveal the problems of interaction that emerge when people are unfamiliar with the system. Laboratory testing is useful for evaluating designs in a controlled environment, but must be conducted with care, as the artificial context and expectation effects can compromise the validity of the results. Direct observation in the target environment is the preferred method for acquiring accurate information about how people interact with systems, but is costly and impractical for designs that are not yet publicly available.

Design with people's interaction models in mind. If there is a standard mental model for how something works, try to design leveraging that model. When this is not possible, (e.g., the system is new and novel), create an interaction experience that draws from common mental models as much as possible, such as the desktop metaphor for computers. However, do not contrive design just to leverage a familiar model—it is better to have people learn a new model that is clear and consistent, than to use a familiar model that does not fit. Use the systems that you design, and employ laboratory testing and field observation in order to develop accurate and complete interaction models. Above all, watch people use the design and take note of how they use it.

See also Affordance, Expectation Effects, Mapping, and Mimicry.

[1] The seminal works on mental models are *The Nature of Explanation* by Kenneth Craik, Cambridge University Press, 1943; and *Mental Models: Towards a Cognitive Science of Language, Inference, and Consciousness* by Philip N. Johnson-Laird, Cambridge University Press, 1983. For a design perspective, see "Surrogates and Mappings: Two Kinds of Conceptual Models for Interactive Devices" by Richard M. Young, and "Some Observations on Mental Models" by Donald Norman, both in *Mental Models* by D. Gentner and A. Stevens (Eds.), Lawrence Erlbaum Associates, 1983.

[2] Note that an *efficient* merging does not simply mean revealing the system model. It may mean concealing the system model from users, revealing the system model to users, or a combination therein.

Despite the measurable safety benefits of antilock brakes in controlled tests with trained drivers, research by the Highway Loss Data Institute indicates that antilock brakes have not reduced the frequency or cost of accidents in real-world driving situations.

The likely cause is that people are not using antilock brakes properly—or rather; antilock brakes are not designed properly. The interaction model for antilock brakes differs radically from the interaction model for conventional brakes.

This suggests that designers gave little consideration to the interaction models of the target audience in the design process.

Interaction Model for Conventional Brakes

On slick surfaces...
- depress the brake pedal smoothly
- pump brakes to prevent brakes from locking up
- do not steer while braking, except to counter-steer
- noise and vibration are signs that something is wrong

INCORRECT INTERACTION
slamming brakes/steering while braking
Car will take a longer time to stop and will not make the turn

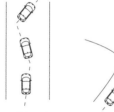

wet, slick surface   wet, slick surface

CORRECT INTERACTION
pumping brakes
Car will take a shorter time to stop and may make the turn

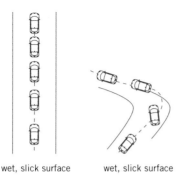

wet, slick surface   wet, slick surface

Interaction Model for ABS Brakes

On slick surfaces...
- depress the brake pedal fast and hard
- do not pump brakes
- steer while braking
- noise and vibration are signs that the system is operating properly

CORRECT INTERACTION
slamming brakes/steering while braking
Car will properly stop and make the turn

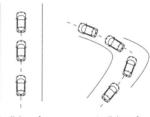

wet, slick surface   wet, slick surface

INCORRECT INTERACTION
pumping brakes
Car will take a longer time to stop and will not make the turn

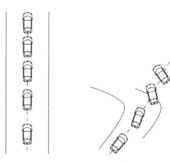

wet, slick surface   wet, slick surface

Mimicry

The act of copying properties of familiar objects, organisms, or environments in order to realize specific benefits afforded by those properties.

In nature, mimicry refers to the copying of properties of familiar objects, organisms, or environments in order to hide from or deter other organisms. For example, katydids and walking sticks mimic the leaves and branches of plants to hide from predators, and the viceroy butterfly mimics the less tasty monarch butterfly to deter predators. In design, mimicry refers to copying properties of familiar objects, organisms, or environments in order to improve the usability, likeability, or functionality of an object. There are three basic kinds of mimicry in design: surface, behavioral, and functional.[1]

Surface mimicry is defined as making a design look like something else. When a design mimics the surface aspects of a familiar object, the design implies (by its familiar appearance) the way it will function or can be used. An example is the use of computer software icons that are designed to look like folders and documents.[2]

Behavioral mimicry is defined as making a design act like something else (e.g., making a robotic dog act like a real dog). Behavioral mimicry is useful for improving likeability, but should be used with caution when mimicking complex behaviors from large repertoires. For example, mimicking behaviors like smiling generally elicit positive responses, but can give the impression of artificiality or deceit if inconsistent with other cues (e.g., a baby doll that smiles when touched—or spanked).[3]

Functional mimicry is defined as making a design work like something else. Functional mimicry is useful for solving mechanical and structural problems (e.g., mimicking the keypad of an adding machine in the design of a touch tone telephone). Significant insights and rapid progress can be achieved by mimicking existing solutions and design analogs. However, functional mimicry must be performed with caution since the physical principles governing function may not transfer from one context to another or from one scale to another (e.g., early attempts at human flight by flapping wings).[4]

Mimicry is perhaps the oldest and most efficient method for achieving major advances in design. Consider surface mimicry to improve usability, ensuring that the perception of the design corresponds to how it functions or is to be used. Consider behavioral mimicry to improve likeability, but exercise caution when mimicking complex behaviors. Consider functional mimicry to assist in solving mechanical and structural problems, but also consider transfer and scaling effects that may undermine the success of the mimicked properties.

See also Affordance, Baby-Face Bias, Convergence, Savanna Preference, and Scaling Fallacy.

[1] The history of mimicry in design likely predates the development of tools by early humans. The seminal work on mimicry in plants and animals was performed by Henry Bates and Fritz Muller in the late 1800s.

[2] See, for example, *The Design of Everyday Things* by Donald Norman, Doubleday, 1990.

[3] See, for example, *Designing Sociable Robots* by Cynthia L. Breazeal, MIT Press, 2002; and "The Lovable Cat: Mimicry Strikes Again" in *The Throwing Madonna: Essays on the Brain* by William H. Calvin, iUniverse, 2000.

[4] See, for example, *Biomimicry: Innovation Inspired by Nature* by Janine M. Benyus, William Morrow & Company, 1998; and *Cats' Paws and Catapults: Mechanical Worlds of Nature and People* by Steven Vogel, W. W. Norton & Company, 2000.

Mimicry is an effective strategy to begin exploring a design problem, but it should not be assumed that mimicked solutions are correct or best. For example, the early design of the phone keypad mimicked the keypad of adding machines. Usability testing by researchers at Bell Laboratories suggested that an inverted keypad layout was easier to master. Bell decided to abandon the mimicked solution and establish a new standard for telephones.

The Sony AIBO mimics many key canine behaviors—barking, wagging tail—leveraging the positive feelings many people have for dogs to make the design more appealing.

The Mimic Octopus is capable of both surface and behavioral mimicry, in this case changing its pattern and texture, and hiding all but two legs in order to mimic the highly poisonous Sea Snake.

Surface mimicry is common in the design of software icons and controls. Even to those unfamiliar with the software, the familiar appearance of these objects hints at their function.

Trash

Recycle Bin

Documents

Work

Document

Data.txt

Mnemonic Device

A method of reorganizing information to make the information easier to remember.

Mnemonic devices are used to reorganize information so that the information is simpler and more meaningful and, therefore, more easily remembered. They involve the use of imagery or words in specific ways to link unfamiliar information to familiar information that resides in memory. Mnemonic devices that involve imagery are strongest when they are vivid, peculiar, and exaggerated in size or quantity. Mnemonic devices that involve words are strongest when the words are familiar and clearly related. Mnemonic devices are useful for remembering names of new things, large amounts of rote information, and sequences of events or procedures. A few examples of mnemonic devices include:[1]

First-Letter—The first letter of items to be recalled are used to form the first letters in a meaningful phrase, or combined to form an acronym. For example, *Please Excuse My Dear Aunt Sally* to assist in the recall of the arithmetic order of operations: Parentheses, Exponents, Multiplication, Division, Addition, Subtraction; or *AIDS* as a simple means of referring to and remembering Acquired Immune Deficiency Syndrome.

Keyword—A word that is similar to, or a subset of, a word or phrase that is linked to a familiar bridging image to aid in recall. For example, the insurance company AFLAC makes its company name more memorable by reinforcing the similarity of the pronunciation of AFLAC and the quack of the duck. The duck in the advertising is the bridging image.

Rhyme—One or more words in a phrase are linked to other words in the phrase through rhyming schemes to aid in recall. For example, *red touches yellow kill a fellow* is a popular mnemonic to distinguish the venomous coral snake from the nonvenomous king snake.

Feature-Name—A word that is related to one or more features of something that is linked to a familiar bridging image to aid in recall. For example, the rounded shape of the Volkswagen Beetle is a key feature of its biological namesake, which serves as the bridging image.

Consider mnemonic devices when developing corporate and product identities, slogans and logos for advertising campaigns, instructional materials dealing with rote information and complex procedures, and other contexts in which ease of recall is critical to success. Use vivid and concrete imagery and words that leverage familiar and related concepts.

See also Chunking, Serial Position Effects, and von Restorff Effect.

[1] The seminal contemporary work on mnemonics is *The Art of Memory* by Frances A. Yates, University of Chicago Press, 1974.

Clever use of mnemonic devices can dramatically influence recall. These logos employ various combinations of mnemonic devices to make them more memorable.

Modularity

A method of managing system complexity that involves dividing large systems into multiple, smaller self-contained systems.

Modularity is a structural principle used to manage complexity in systems. It involves identifying functional clusters of similarity in systems, and then transforming the clusters into interdependent self-contained systems (modules). For example, the modular design of computer memory chips provides computer owners the option of increasing the memory in their computer without any requirement to do so. If the design of the computer and memory chips were not modular in this way, the only practical method of upgrading computer memory would be to buy a new computer. The option to easily and inexpensively improve a system without the requirement to do so gives modular designs an intrinsic advantage over non-modular designs.[1]

Modules should be designed to hide their internal complexity and interact with other modules through simple interfaces. The result is an overall reduction in system complexity and a decentralization of system architecture, which improves reliability, flexibility, and maintainability. Additionally, a modular design encourages innovation of modules, as well as competition regarding their design and manufacture; it creates an opportunity for third parties to compete to develop better modules.

The benefits of modular design are not without costs: modular systems are significantly more complex to design than nonmodular systems. Designers must have significant knowledge of the inner workings of a system and its environment to decompose the systems into modules, and then make those modules function together as a whole. Consequently, most modular systems that exist today did not begin that way—they have been incrementally transformed to be more modular as knowledge of the system increased.

Consider modularity when designing or modifying complex systems. Identify functional clusters of similarity in systems, and clearly define their relationships with other system elements. If feasible, create modules that conceal their complexity and communicate with other modules through simple, standard interfaces. Do not attempt complex modular designs without experienced designers and a thorough understanding of the system. However, consider the incremental modularization of existing systems, especially during maintenance and product updates.[2]

See also 80/20 Rule, Chunking, and Cost-Benefit.

[1] The seminal work on modularity is *Design Rules:* Volume I. *The Power of Modularity* by Carliss Y. Baldwin and Kim B. Clark, MIT Press, 2000.

[2] Many designers resist modularity for fear of limiting creativity. However, modules applied at the appropriate level will liberate designers from useless activity and allow them to focus creativity where it is most needed.

Personal Computer

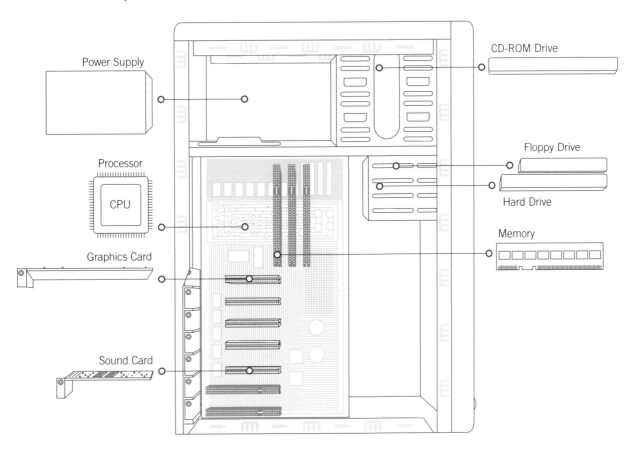

Power Supply

CD-ROM Drive

Processor

CPU

Floppy Drive

Hard Drive

Graphics Card

Memory

Sound Card

The rapid increase in availability, quality, and computing power of personal computers over the last twenty years is largely attributable to their modular designs. The key components of the computer are standard modules that use standard interfaces. This enables competition among third-party manufacturers to improve modules and reduce price, which also improves the computer and reduces its price.

Most Average Facial Appearance Effect

A tendency to prefer faces in which the eyes, nose, lips, and other features are close to the average of a population.[1]

People find faces that approximate their population average more attractive than faces that deviate from their population average. In this context, *population* refers to the group in which a person lives or was raised, and *average* refers to the arithmetic mean of the form, size, and position of the facial features. For example, when pictures of many faces within a population are combined (averaged) to form a single composite image, the composite image is similar to the facial configurations of professional models in that population.[2]

The most average facial appearance effect is likely the result of some combination of evolution, cognitive prototypes, and symmetry. Evolution by natural selection tends to select out extremes from a population over time. Therefore, it is possible that a preference for averageness has evolved as an indicator of general fitness. Cognitive prototypes are mental representations that are formed through experience. As people see the faces of other people, their mental representation of what a face is may be updated through a process similar to compositing. If this is the case, average faces pattern-match easily with cognitive prototypes, and contribute to a preference. Finally, average faces are symmetrical, and symmetry has long been viewed as an indicator of health and fitness. Asymmetric members of all species tend to have fewer offspring and live shorter lives—generally the asymmetry is the result of disease, malnutrition, or bad genes.[3]

The evolution of racial preferences among isolated ethnic groups demonstrates the influence of the most average facial appearance effect. Isolated groups form cognitive prototypes based on the faces within their population. When two of these groups first encounter one another, they invariably regard members of the unfamiliar group as strange and less attractive. The facial appearance of unfamiliar groups is perceived as less attractive because it is further from the average facial appearance of the familiar group. As the differences become more familiar, however, cognitive prototypes are updated and the definition of facial beauty changes.

The most average facial appearance for a population is an accurate benchmark of beauty for that population. There are other elements that contribute to attractiveness (e.g., smile versus scowl), but faces that are not average will not be perceived as attractive. Use composite images of faces created from randomly sampled faces of target populations to indicate local perceptions of beauty. Consider the use of digital compositing and morphing software to develop attractive faces from common faces for advertising and marketing campaigns, especially when real models are unavailable or budgetary resources are limited.

See also Attractiveness Bias, Baby-Face Bias, Mental Model, Normal Distribution, and Symmetry.

[1] Also referred to as *MAFA effect*.

[2] The seminal work on the most average facial appearance effect is "Attractive Faces are Only Average" by Judith H. Langlois and Lori A. Roggman, *Psychological Science*, 1990, vol. 1, p. 115–121.

[3] See, for example, "Developmental Stability, Disease, and Medicine" by Randy Thornhill and Anders P. Møller, *Biological Reviews*, 1997, vol. 72, p. 497–548.

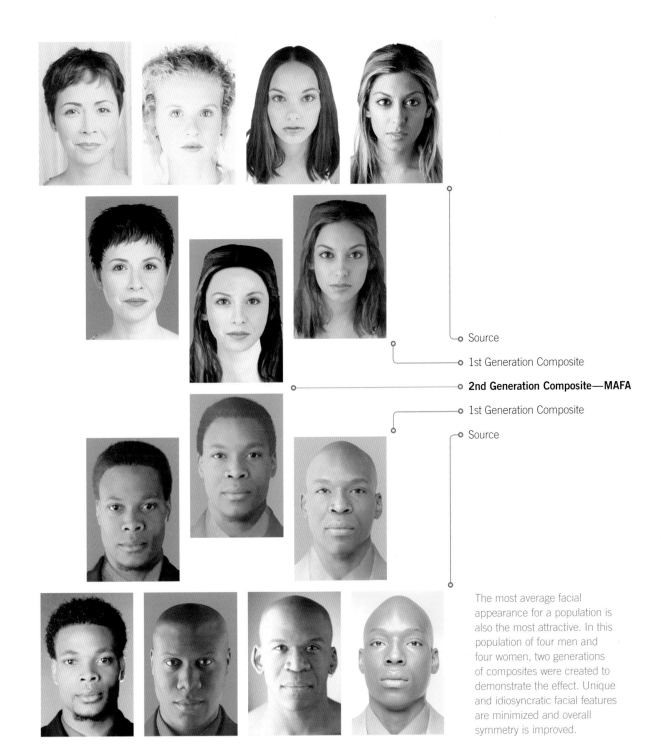

Source

1st Generation Composite

2nd Generation Composite—MAFA

1st Generation Composite

Source

The most average facial appearance for a population is also the most attractive. In this population of four men and four women, two generations of composites were created to demonstrate the effect. Unique and idiosyncratic facial features are minimized and overall symmetry is improved.

Normal Distribution

A term used to describe a set of data, that when plotted, forms the shape of a symmetrical, bell-shaped curve.[1]

Normal distributions result when many independently measured values of a variable are plotted. The resulting bell-shaped curve is symmetrical, rising from a small number of cases at both extremes to a large number of cases in the middle. Normal distributions are found everywhere—annual temperature averages, stock market fluctuations, student test scores—and are thus commonly used to determine the parameters of a design.

In a normal distribution, the average of the variable measured is also the most common. As the variable deviates from this average, its frequency diminishes in accordance with the area under the curve. However, it is a mistake to conclude that the average is the preferred design parameter because it is the most common. Generally, a range across the normal distribution must be considered in defining design parameters, since variance between the average and the rest of the population translates to the variance the design must accommodate. For example, a shoe designed for the average of a population would fit only about 68 percent of the population.

Additionally, it is important to avoid trying to create something that is average in all dimensions. A person average in one measure will not be average in other measures. The probability that a person will match the average of their population group in two measures is approximately 7 percent; this falls to less than 1 percent for eight measures. The common belief that average people exist and are the standard to which designers should design is called the "average person fallacy."[2]

Where possible, create designs that will accommodate 98 percent of the population; namely, the first to the 99th percentile. While design considerations can be expanded to accommodate a larger portion of the population, generally, the larger the audience accommodated, the greater the costs. Consideration of the target population is key. When designing specifically for a narrow portion of the population (e.g., airline seats that will accommodate 98 percent of American males), it is crucial to obtain the appropriate measurement data for this very specific group.

See also Convergence and Most Average Facial Appearance Effect.

[1] Also known as *standard normal distribution*, *Gaussian distribution*, and *bell curve*.

[2] Anthropometric data drawn from *The Measure of Man and Woman* by Alvin R. Tilley and Henry Dreyfuss Associates, The Whitney Library of Design, 1993.

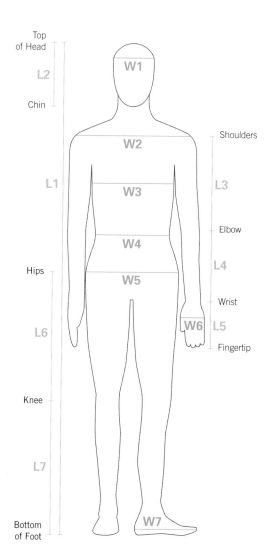

Top
of Head

L2

Chin

W1

Shoulders

W2

L1 W3 L3

Elbow

W4

L4

Hips W5

Wrist

L6 W6 L5

Fingertip

Knee

L7

Bottom
of Foot W7

	34.13% 34.13%									
	0									
	13.59%			13.59%						
2.14%		-1σ		+1σ		2.14%				
.127%							.127%			
.003% -3σ	-2σ				+2σ		.003%		
-4σ							+3σ	+4σ		
.1%	2.3%	15.9%		84.1%		97.7%	99.9%	99.997%		

	1%		50%		99%		
	male	female	male	female	male	female	
L1	62.6"	58.1"	69.1"	64.0"	75.6"	69.8"	L1
L2	6.3	7.6	8.7	8.6	9.9	9.7	L2
L3	12.5	12.5	14.4	13.2	16.2	14.8	L3
L4	10.4	9.3	11.4	10.2	12.4	11.2	L4
L5	6.6	6.0	7.5	6.9	8.4	7.8	L5
L6	15.2	13.8	16.7	15.4	18.4	16.9	L6
L7	14.7	13.3	16.6	15.1	18.0	16.4	L7
W1	5.6	5.2	6.1	5.7	6.7	6.3	W1
W2	15.8	13.5	18.3	16.1	20.6	18.0	W2
W3	10.3	8.8	12.2	10.4	14.1	12.1	W3
W4	9.2	7.4	11.4	9.0	13.6	10.7	W4
W5	11.4	11.2	14.2	14.6	16.9	16.8	W5
W6	3.7	3.2	4.1	3.6	4.6	4.1	W6
W7	9.2	8.3	10.4	9.5	11.7	11.7	W7

The measures of men and women are normally distributed. The wide range of measures across the distribution illustrates the problem of simply designing for an average group. Note that no one man or woman is represented by these measures—i.e., there is no average person in reality.

The normal distribution is represented by a symmetric bell-shaped curve. The four standard deviations represented by σ below and above the average reflect the normal percentages found in the variability around the average. Percentiles are indicated along the bottom of the curve. Note that in a normal distribution,

approximately 68 percent of the population falls within one standard deviation of the average; approximately 95 percent of the population falls within two standard deviations of the average; and approximately 99 percent of the population falls within three standard deviations of the average.

Ockham's Razor

Given a choice between functionally equivalent designs, the simplest design should be selected.[1]

Ockham's razor asserts that simplicity is preferred to complexity in design. Many variations of the principle exist, each adapted to address the particulars of a field or domain of knowledge. A few examples include:

- "Entities should not be multiplied without necessity."—William of Ockham

- "That is better and more valuable which requires fewer, other circumstances being equal."—Robert Grosseteste

- "Nature operates in the shortest way possible."—Aristotle

- "We are to admit no more causes of natural things than such as are both true and sufficient to explain their appearances."—Isaac Newton

- "Everything should be made as simple as possible, but not simpler." —Albert Einstein

Implicit in Ockham's razor is the idea that unnecessary elements decrease a design's efficiency, and increase the probability of unanticipated consequences. Unnecessary weight, whether physical, visual, or cognitive, degrades performance. Unnecessary design elements have the potential to fail or create problems. There is also an aesthetic appeal to the principle, which likens the "cutting" of unnecessary elements from a design to the removal of impurities from a solution—the design is a cleaner, purer result.

Use Ockham's razor to evaluate and select among multiple, functionally equivalent designs. Functional equivalence here refers to comparable performance of a design on common measures. For example, given two functionally equivalent displays— equal in information content and readability—select the display with the fewest visual elements. Evaluate each element within the selected design and remove as many as possible without compromising function. Finally, minimize the expression of the remaining elements as much as possible without compromising function.[2]

See also Form Follows Function, Mapping, and Signal-to-Noise Ratio.

[1] Also known as *Occam's razor*, *law of parsimony*, *law of economy*, and *principle of simplicity*. The term "Ockham's razor" references William of Ockham, a 14th century Franciscan friar and logician who purportedly made abundant use of the principle. The principle does not actually appear in any of his extant writings and, in truth, little is known about either the origin of the principle or its originator. See, for example, "The Myth of Occam's Razor" by W. M. Thorburn, *Mind*, 1918, vol. 27, p. 345–353.

[2] "Make all visual distinctions as subtle as possible, but still clear and effective. " *Visual Explanations* by Edward R. Tufte, Graphics Press, 1998, p. 73.

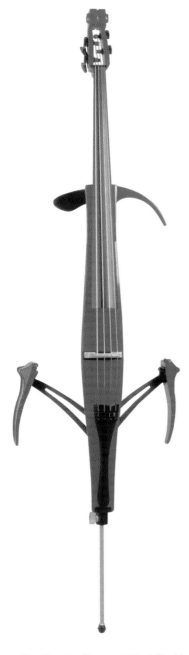

While other Internet search services were racing to add advertising and ad hoc functions to their Web sites, Google kept its design simple and efficient. The result is the best performing and easiest to use search service on the Web.

The Yamaha Compact Silent Electric Cello is a minimalist cello with only those portions touched by the player represented. Musicians can hear concert-quality cello sound through headphones while creating little external sound, or through an amplifier and speakers for public performances. The cello can also be collapsed for easy transport and storage.

The Taburet M Stacking Stool is strong, comfortable, and stackable. It is constructed from a single piece of molded wood and has no extraneous elements.

Operant Conditioning

A technique used to modify behavior by reinforcing desired behaviors, and ignoring or punishing undesired behaviors.[1]

Operant conditioning is probably the most researched and well-known technique used to modify behavior. The technique involves increasing or decreasing a particular behavior by associating the behavior with a positive or negative condition (e.g., rewards or punishments). Operant conditioning is commonly applied to animal training, instructional design, video game design, incentive programs, gambling devices, counseling, and behavioral therapy. It is also finding increased application in artificial intelligence. There are three basic operant conditioning techniques: positive reinforcement, negative reinforcement, and punishment.[2]

Positive reinforcement increases the probability of a behavior by associating the behavior with a positive condition; pulling the lever on a slot machine results in positive visual and auditory feedback, and a possible monetary reward. Negative reinforcement increases the probability of a behavior by associating the behavior with the removal of a negative condition; fastening a seat belt in a car silences an annoying buzzer. Punishment decreases the probability of a behavior by associating the behavior with a negative condition; touching a poison mushroom in a video game reduces the score. Positive and negative reinforcement should be used instead of punishment whenever possible. Punishment should be reserved for rapidly extinguishing a behavior, or it should not be used at all.

Reinforcement and punishment are administered after a behavior is performed one or more times. When there is a clear and predictive relationship between the frequency of a behavior and an outcome, behavior will be paced to do just what is required to receive reinforcement or avoid punishment. When there is not a clear and predictive relationship between the frequency of behavior and the outcome, behavior will be performed more frequently and will be more resistant to extinction (the loss of the desired behavior). An optimal behavior modification plan typically includes predictable reinforcement early in training (fixed ratio schedules) and less predictable reinforcement later in the training (variable ratio schedules).

Use operant conditioning in design contexts where behavioral change is required. Focus on positive or negative reinforcement, rather than punishment whenever possible. Use fixed ratio schedules of reinforcement early in training. As basic behaviors are mastered, switch to variable schedules of reinforcement.

See also Classical Conditioning and Shaping.

[1] Also known as *instrumental conditioning*.

[2] The seminal work on operant conditioning is *The Behavior of Organisms: An Experimental Analysis* by Burrhus F. Skinner, Appleton-Century, 1938; a nice contemporary book on the subject is *Don't Shoot the Dog: The New Art of Teaching and Training* by Karen Pryor, Bantam Doubleday Dell, 1999.

This graph shows how reinforcement strategies influence the frequency of behavior. Variable ratio schedules provide reinforcement after a variable number of correct responses. They ultimately achieve the highest frequency of behavior and are useful for maintaining behavior. Fixed ratio schedules provide reinforcement after a fixed number of correct responses. They are useful for connecting the reinforcement to the behavior during the early stages of learning.

The addictive nature of video games and gambling machines is a direct result of their application of operant conditioning.

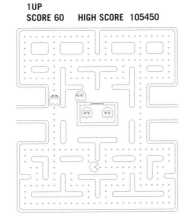

In the game Black & White, the nature of the characters evolve to become good, neutral, or evil based on how their behaviors are rewarded and punished.

Orientation Sensitivity

A phenomenon of visual processing in which certain line orientations are more quickly and easily processed and discriminated than other line orientations.

The efficiency with which people can perceive and make judgments about the orientation of lines is influenced by a number of factors. For example, the time displayed on a standard analog clock can be quickly interpreted because the numbers are positioned at 30-degree increments around the center. The 30-degree increment happens to correspond to the minimum recommended difference in line orientation required to be easily detectable; i.e., differences in line orientation of less than 30 degrees require more effort to detect. Orientation sensitivity is based on two phenomena that are observed in visual perception: oblique effect and pop-out effect.[1]

The *oblique* effect is the ability to more accurately perceive and judge line orientations that are close to vertical and horizontal, than line orientations that are oblique. For example, in tasks where people have to estimate the relative orientation of a line by any number of methods (e.g., redrawing from memory), the most accurate judgments are for horizontal and vertical lines, and the least accurate judgments are for oblique lines. The oblique effect is caused by a greater sensitivity of neurons to vertical and horizontal stimuli than to oblique stimuli. Additionally, people tend to make judgments about line orientation that are biased toward the nearest vertical or horizontal axis; lines oriented close to the vertical or horizontal axis will often be perceived or recalled as truly vertical or horizontal. Designs in which the primary elements are vertical or horizontal are also considered generally more aesthetic than designs in which primary elements are oblique.[2]

The *pop-out* effect is the tendency of certain elements in a display to pop out as figure elements, and as a result be quickly and easily detected. For example, in tasks where people have to identify a target line against a background of lines of a common orientation, the target line is easily detected when it differs from the background lines by 30 degrees or more. The pop-out effect is caused by a change in the visual stimuli sufficient to activate additional input neurons, which then help to detect differences in line orientation and patterns. The effect is strongest when combined with the oblique effect; it is easier to detect subtle differences in the orientation of a target line against a background of vertical and horizontal lines, than against a background of oblique lines.[3]

Consider orientation sensitivity in compositions requiring discrimination between different lines or textures, or decisions based on the relative position of elements. Facilitate discrimination between linear elements by making their orientation differ by more than 30 degrees. In displays requiring estimates of orientation or angle, provide visual indicators at 30-degree increments to improve accuracy in oblique regions. Use horizontal and vertical lines as visual anchors to enhance aesthetics and maximize discrimination with oblique elements.

See also Closure, Constancy, Figure-Ground Relationship, and Good Continuation.

[1] The seminal works on orientation sensitivity include "On the Judgment of Angles and Positions of Lines" by Joseph Jastrow, *American Journal of Psychology*, 1893, vol. 5, p. 214–248; and "Perception and Discrimination As a Function of Stimulus Orientation: The "Oblique Effect" in Man and Animals" by Stuart Appelle, *Psychological Bulletin*, 1972, vol. 78, p. 266-278.

[2] "An Oblique Effect in Aesthetics: Homage to Mondrian (1872–1944)" by Richard Latto, Douglas Brain, and Brian Kelly, *Perception*, 2000, vol. 29(8), p. 981–987.

[3] See, for example, "Texture Segmentation and Pop-Out from Orientation Contrast" by Christoph Nothdurft, *Vision Research*, 1991, vol. 31, p. 1073–1078.

 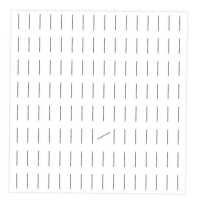 

Differences in line orientation are most easily detected when set against vertical or horizontal lines.

Standard analog clocks are easily read because numbers are separated by 30 degrees. However, the same time on a twenty-four hour clock is more difficult to read because numbers are separated by only 15 degrees.

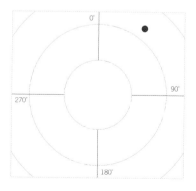 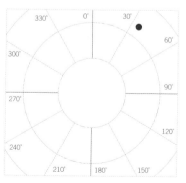

Systems that require precise estimation of orientation and position should be designed to accommodate orientation sensitivity. For example, radar-tracking displays should indicate orientation by providing markers in 30-degree increments or less. Without the markers, estimates in oblique regions of the display will be prone to error.

Performance Load

The greater the effort to accomplish a task, the less likely the task will be accomplished successfully.[1]

Performance load is the degree of mental and physical activity required to achieve a goal. If the performance load is high, performance time and errors increase, and the probability of successfully accomplishing the goal decreases. If the performance load is low, performance time and errors decrease, and the probability of successfully accomplishing the goal increases. Performance load consists of two types of loads: cognitive load and kinematic load.[2]

Cognitive load is the amount of mental activity—perception, memory, problem solving—required to accomplish a goal. For example, early computer systems required users to remember large sets of commands, and then type them into the computer in specific ways. The number of commands that had to be remembered to perform a task was the cognitive load for that task. The advent of the graphical user interface allowed users to browse sets of commands in menus, rather than recalling them from memory. This reduction in cognitive load dramatically reduced the mental effort required to use computers, and consequently enabled them to become mass-market devices. General strategies for reducing cognitive load include minimizing visual noise, chunking information that must be remembered, using memory aids to assist in recall and problem solving, and automating computation- and memory-intensive tasks.

Kinematic load is the degree of physical activity—number of steps or movements, or amount of force—required to accomplish a goal. For example, the telegraph required people to communicate letters one at a time through a series of taps on a mechanical armature. The number of taps to communicate a message was the kinematic load for that task. Samuel Morse designed Morse code to minimize kinematic load by assigning the simplest codes to the most frequently occurring letters; the letter E was expressed as *dot*, and the letter Q was expressed as the longer *dash dash dot dash*. This approach reduced the physical effort (kinematic load), dramatically reducing transmission times and error rates. General strategies for reducing kinematic load include reducing the number of steps required to complete tasks, minimizing range of motion and travel distances, and automating repetitive tasks.[3]

Design should minimize performance load to the greatest degree possible. Reduce cognitive load by eliminating unnecessary information from displays, chunking information that is to be remembered, providing memory aids to assist in complex tasks, and automating computation-intensive and memory-intensive tasks. Reduce kinematic load by reducing unnecessary steps in tasks, reducing overall motion and energy expended, and automating repetitive tasks.

See also 80/20 Rule, Chunking, Cost-Benefit, Hick's Law, Fitts' Law, Mnemonic Device, and Recognition Over Recall.

[1] Also known as the *path-of-least-resistance principle* and *principle of least effort.*

[2] The seminal works on performance load are *Cognitive Load During Problem Solving: Effects on Learning* by John Sweller, *Cognitive Science*, 1988, vol. 12, p. 257–285; "The Magical Number Seven, Plus or Minus Two: Some Limits on Our Capacity for Processing Information" by George Miller, *The Psychological Review*, 1956, vol. 63, p. 81–97; and *Human Behavior and The Principle of Least Effort* by George K. Zipf, Addison-Wesley, 1949.

[3] "Frustrations of a Pushbutton World" by Harold Thimbleby, *Encyclopedia Britannica Yearbook of Science and the Future*, 1992, p. 202–219.

Modern slot machines no longer require the pulling of a lever or the insertion of coins to play. Inserting a charge card and pressing a button is all that is required, though the lever continues to be retained as a usable ornament. This reduction in kinematic load not only makes it easier to play the slots, it makes it easier for casinos to make money.

People can easily save their favorite Internet destinations in all modern browsers. This feature replaces the more load-intensive alternatives of remembering destinations, or writing them down.

Remote keyless entry enables people to lock and unlock all doors of a vehicle at the press of a button—a dramatic reduction in kinematic load.

The use of Universal Product Codes, also known as bar codes, dramatically reduces the performance load associated with consumer transactions: products no longer need price tags, cashiers no longer need to type in prices, and inventory is automatically updated.

Performance Versus Preference

The designs that help people perform optimally are often not the same as the designs that people find most desirable.

Designers and managers often confuse the business maxim "the customer is always right" with "the user is always is right." This is a dangerous confusion, since what helps people perform well and what people like is often not the same thing. For example, the Dvorak keyboard is estimated to improve typing efficiency by more than 30 percent, but has failed to rise in popularity because people prefer the more familiar QWERTY keyboard. If you asked people if they would like to be able to type 30 percent faster with fewer errors, most would answer in the affirmative. Despite this, more than 50 years have passed since the introduction of the Dvorak keyboard, and it is still more of a novelty item than a practical alternative.[1]

This underscores an important lesson for designers: the reasons people prefer one design to another is a combination of many factors, and may have nothing to do with performance. Is the design pleasing to look at? Does it compete with long-standing designs or standards of use? Does it contribute to the well-being or self-esteem of the user? These are all factors that must be carefully balanced in the development of the design requirements. If a superbly performing design is never bought or used because people (for whatever reason) do not prefer it to alternatives, the performance benefits are moot. Conversely, if a well-liked design does not help people perform at the level required, the preference benefits are moot.

The best way to correctly balance performance and preference in design is to accurately determine the importance of performance versus preference. While surveys, interviews, and focus groups try to find out what people want or like, they are unreliable indicators of what people will actually do, especially for new or unfamiliar designs. Additionally, people are poor at discriminating between features they like, and features that actually enhance their performance; they commonly prefer designs that perform less well than available alternatives, and incorrectly believe that those designs helped them achieve the best performance.[2]

The best method of obtaining accurate performance and preference requirements is to observe people interacting with the design (or a similar design) in real contexts. When this is not feasible, test using structured tasks that approximate key aspects of the way the design will be used. It is important to obtain preference information in context while the task is being performed, and not afterward. Do not rely on reports of what people say they have done, will do, or are planning to do in the future regarding the use of a design; such reports are unreliable.

See also Aesthetic-Usability Effect, Control, Development Cycle, Flexibility-Usability Tradeoff, and Hierarchy of Needs.

[1] See, for example, "Performance Versus Preference" by Robert W. Bailey, *Proceedings of the Human Factors and Ergonomics Society 37th Annual Meeting*, 1993, p. 282–286.

[2] See, for example, "Measuring Usability: Preference vs. Performance" by Jakob Nielsen and Jonathan Levy, *Communications of the ACM*, 1994, vol. 37(4), p. 66–75.

The QWERTY layout was designed to prevent the jamming of mechanical arms on early typewriters. The Dvorak layout, by contrast, was designed to maximize typing efficiency: it grouped keys based on frequency of use, and positioned keys to promote alternating keystrokes between hands, among other refinements. The result is a 30 percent improvement in typing efficiency, and claim to most of the world records for speed typing. Despite the clear advantages of the Dvorak design, QWERTY enjoys the following of generations of people trained on the layout, which in turn drives manufacturers to continue perpetuating the standard. Dvorak wins on performance, but QWERTY wins on preference.

QWERTY Keyboard

Dvorak Keyboard

Picture Superiority Effect

Pictures are remembered better than words.[1]

It is said that a picture is worth a thousand words, and it turns out that in most cases, this is true. Pictures are generally more easily recognized and recalled than words, although memory for pictures and words together is superior to memory for words alone or pictures alone. For example, instructional materials and technical manuals that present textual information accompanied by supporting pictures enable information recall that is better than that produced by either the text or pictures alone. The picture superiority effect is commonly used in instructional design, advertising, technical writing, and other design contexts requiring easy and accurate recall of information.[2]

When information recall is measured immediately after the presentation of a series of pictures or words, recall performance for pictures and words is equal. The picture superiority effect applies only when people are asked to recall something after more than thirty seconds from the time of exposure. The picture superiority effect is strongest when the pictures represent common, concrete things versus abstract things, such as a picture of a flag versus a picture depicting the concept of freedom, and when pictures are distinct from one another, such as a mix of objects versus objects of a single type.

The picture superiority effect advantage increases further when people are casually exposed to information and the exposure time is limited. For example, an advertisement for a clock repair shop that includes a picture of a clock will be better recalled than the same advertisement without the picture. People not interested in clock repair who see the advertisement with the picture will also be better able to recall the brand if the need for clock repair service arises at a later time. The strength of the picture superiority effect diminishes as the information becomes more complex. For example, people are able to recall events from a story presented as a silent movie as well as events from the same story read as text.[3]

Use the picture superiority effect to improve the recognition and recall of key information. Use pictures and words together, and ensure that they reinforce the same information for optimal effect. Pictures and words that conflict create interference and dramatically inhibit recall. Consider the inclusion of meaningful pictures in advertising campaigns when possible, especially when the goal is to build company and product brand awareness.

See also Advance Organizer, Iconic Representation, Serial Position Effects, and von Restorff Effect.

[1] Also known as *pictorial superiority effect*.

[2] The seminal work on the picture superiority effect is "Why Are Pictures Easier to Recall than Words?" by Allan Paivio, T. B. Rogers, and Padric C. Smythe, *Psychonomic Science*, 1968, vol. 11(4), p. 137–138.

[3] See, for example, "Conditions for a Picture-Superiority Effect on Consumer Memory" by Terry L. Childers and Michael J. Houston, *Journal of Consumer Research*, 1984, vol. 11, p. 643–654.

C

Advertisements with text and pictures are more likely to be looked at and recalled than advertisements with text only. This superiority of pictures over text is even stronger when the page is quickly scanned rather than read.

Progressive Disclosure

A strategy for managing information complexity in which only necessary or requested information is displayed at any given time.

Progressive disclosure involves separating information into multiple layers and only presenting layers that are necessary or relevant. It is primarily used to prevent information overload, and is employed in computer user interfaces, instructional materials, and the design of physical spaces.[1]

Progressive disclosure keeps displays clean and uncluttered and helps people manage complexity without becoming confused, frustrated, or disoriented. For example, infrequently used controls in software interfaces are often concealed in dialog boxes that are invoked by clicking a *More* button. People who do not need to use the controls never see them. For more advanced users, the options are readily available. In either case, the design is simplified by showing only the most frequently required controls by default, and making additional controls available on request.[2]

Learning efficiency benefits greatly from the use of progressive disclosure. Information presented to a person who is not interested or ready to process it is effectively noise. Information that is gradually and progressively disclosed to a learner as they need or request it is better processed and perceived as more relevant. The number of errors is significantly reduced using this method, and consequently the amount of time and frustration spent recovering from errors is also reduced.[3]

Progressive disclosure is also used in the physical world to manage the perception of complexity and activity. For example, progressive disclosure is found in the design of entry points for modern theme park rides. Exceedingly long lines not only frustrate people in line, but also discourage new people from the ride. Theme park designers progressively disclose discrete segments of the line (sometimes supplemented with entertainment), so that no one, in or out of the line, ever sees the line in its entirety.

Use progressive disclosure to reduce information complexity, especially when people interacting with the design are novices or infrequent users. Hide infrequently used controls or information, but make them readily available through some simple operation, such as pressing a *More* button. Progressive disclosure is also an effective method for leading people though complex procedures, and should be considered when such procedures are a part of a design.

See also Chunking, Errors, Layering, and Performance Load.

[1] The seminal applied work on progressive disclosure is the user interface for the Xerox Star computer. See "The Xerox 'Star': A Retrospective" by Jeff Johnson and Teresa L. Roberts, William Verplank, David C. Smith, Charles Irby, Marian Beard, Kevin Mackey, in *Human Computer Interaction: Toward the Year 2000* by Ronald M. Baecker, Jonathan Grudin, William A. S. Buxton, Saul Greenberg, Morgan Kaufman Publishers, 1995, p. 53–70.

[2] A common mistake is to present all available information and options at once with the rationale that it reduces kinematic load. Since progressive disclosure affects only infrequently used elements and elements for which a person may not be ready, it will generally have minimal effect on kinematic load. Conversely, presenting everything at once will significantly increase cognitive load.

[3] See, for example, "Training Wheels in a User Interface" by John M. Carroll and Caroline Carrithers, *Communications of the ACM*, 1984, vol. 27(8), p. 800–806; and *The Nurnberg Funnel* by John M. Carroll, MIT Press, 1990.

Progressive disclosure is commonly used in software to conceal complexity. In this dialog box, basic search functionality is available by default. However, more complex search functionality is available upon request by clicking *More Choices*.

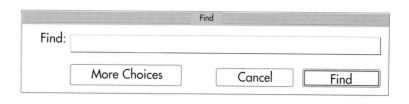

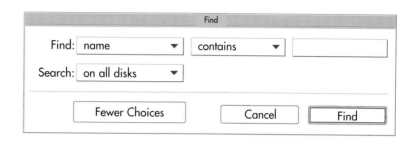

Theme park rides often have very long lines—so long that seeing the lines in their entirety would scare away many would-be visitors. Therefore, modern theme park rides progressively disclose the length of the line, so that only small segments of the line can be seen from any particular vantage point. Additional distractions are provided in the form of video screens, signage, and partial glimpses of people on the ride.

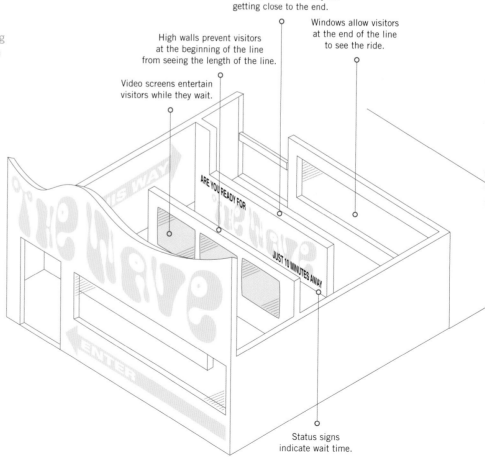

Low walls allow visitors near the end of the line to see they are getting close to the end.

Windows allow visitors at the end of the line to see the ride.

High walls prevent visitors at the beginning of the line from seeing the length of the line.

Video screens entertain visitors while they wait.

Status signs indicate wait time.

Prospect-Refuge

A tendency to prefer environments with unobstructed views (prospects) and areas of concealment and retreat (refuges).

People prefer environments where they can easily survey their surroundings and quickly hide or retreat to safety if necessary. Environments with both prospect and refuge elements are perceived as safe places to explore and dwell, and consequently are considered more aesthetic than environments without these elements. The principle is based on the evolutionary history of humans, reasoning that environments with ample prospects and refuges increased the probability of survival for pre-humans and early humans.[1]

The prospect-refuge principle suggests that people prefer the edges, rather than middles of spaces; spaces with ceilings or covers overhead; spaces with few access points (protected at the back or side); spaces that provide unobstructed views from multiple vantage points; and spaces that provide a sense of safety and concealment. The preference for these elements is heightened if the environment is perceived to be hazardous or potentially hazardous.

Environments that achieve a balance between prospects and refuges are the most preferred. In natural environments, prospects include hills, mountains, and trees near open settings. Refuges include enclosed spaces such as caves, dense vegetation, and climbable trees with dense canopies nearby. In human-created environments, prospects include deep terraces and balconies, and generous use of windows and glass doors. Refuges include alcoves with lowered ceilings and external barriers, such as gates and fences.[2]

The design goal of prospect-refuge can be summarized as the development of spaces where people can see without being seen. Consider prospect-refuge in the creation of landscapes, residences, offices, and communities. Create multiple vantage points within a space, so that the internal and external areas can be easily surveyed. Make large, open areas more appealing by using screening elements to create partial refuges with side- and back-barriers while maintaining clear lines of sight (e.g., shrubbery, partitions). Balance the use of prospect and refuge elements for optimal effect—e.g., sunken floors and ceilings that open to larger spaces enclosed by windows and glass doors.

See also Defensible Space, Savanna Preference, and Wayfinding.

[1] The seminal work on prospect-refuge theory is *The Experience of Landscape* by Jay Appleton, John Wiley & Sons, 1975.

[2] See, for example, *The Wright Space: Pattern and Meaning in Frank Lloyd Wright's Houses* by Grant Hildebrand, University of Washington Press, 1991.

This section of an imaginary café highlights many of the practical applications of the prospect-refuge principle. The entry is separated from the interior by a greeting station, and the ceiling is lowered to create a temporary refuge for waiting patrons. As the interior is accessed, the ceiling raises and the room opens up with multiple, clear lines of sight. A bar area is set against the far wall with a raised floor and lowered ceilings, creating a protected perch to view interior and exterior areas. High-backed booths and partial screens provide refuge with minimal impediment to prospect. Windows are tinted or mirrored, allowing patrons to survey the exterior without being seen. Shrubbery surrounds the exterior as a practical and symbolic barrier, preventing outsiders from getting too close.

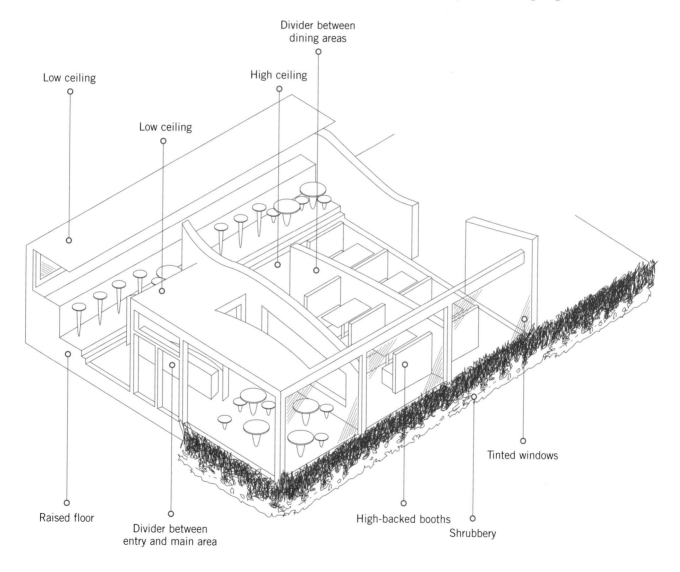

Divider between
dining areas

Low ceiling

High ceiling

Low ceiling

Raised floor

Divider between
entry and main area

High-backed booths

Shrubbery

Tinted windows

Prototyping

The use of simplified and incomplete models of a design to explore ideas, elaborate requirements, refine specifications, and test functionality.

Prototyping is the creation of simple, incomplete models or mockups of a design. It provides designers with key insights into real-world design requirements, and gives them a method to visualize, evaluate, learn, and improve design specifications prior to delivery. There are three basic kinds of prototyping: concept, throwaway, and evolutionary.[1]

Concept prototyping is useful for exploring preliminary design ideas quickly and inexpensively. For example, concept sketches and storyboards are used to develop the appearance and personality of characters in animated films well before the costly process of animation and rendering take place. This approach helps communicate the concepts to others, reveals design requirements and problems, and allows for evaluation by a target audience. A common problem with concept prototyping is the *artificial reality problem*, the plausible presentation of an implausible design. A good artist or modeler can make most any design look like it will work.

Throwaway prototyping is useful for collecting information about the functionality and performance of certain aspects of a system. For example, models of new automobile designs are used in wind tunnels to better understand and improve the aerodynamics of their form. The prototypes are discarded once the needed information is obtained. A common problem with throwaway prototyping is the assumption that the functionality will scale or integrate properly in the final design, which of course it often does not.

Evolutionary prototyping is useful when many design specifications are uncertain or changing. In evolutionary prototyping, the initial prototype is developed, evaluated, and refined continuously until it evolves into the final system. Design requirements and specifications never define a *final product*, but merely the next iteration of the design. For example, software developers invariably use evolutionary prototyping to manage the rapid and volatile changes in design requirements. A common problem with evolutionary prototyping is that designers tend to get tunnel vision, focusing on tuning existing specifications, rather than exploring design alternatives.[2]

Incorporate prototyping into the design process. Use concept prototypes to develop and evaluate preliminary ideas, and throwaway prototypes to explore and test design functionalities and performance. Schedule time for prototype evaluation and iteration. When design requirements are unclear or volatile, consider evolutionary prototyping in lieu of traditional approaches. Consider the common problems of artificial realities, scaling and integration, and tunnel vision when evaluating prototypes and design alternatives.

See also Feedback Loop, Satisficing, and Scaling Fallacy.

[1] See, for example, *Human-Computer Interaction* by Jenny Preece, et al., Addison-Wesley, 1994, p. 537–563; *The Art of Innovation* by Tom Kelley and Jonathan Littman, Doubleday, 2001; and *Serious Play: How the World's Best Companies Simulate to Innovate* by Michael Schrage, Harvard Business School Press, 1999.

[2] Evolutionary prototyping is often contrasted with incremental prototyping, which is the decomposition of a design into multiple stages that are then delivered one at a time. They are combined here because they are invariably combined in practice.

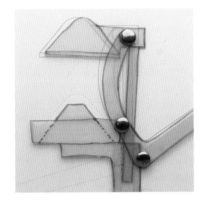

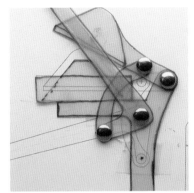

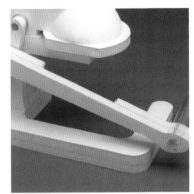

The function and elegance of the Ojex Juicer clearly demonstrate the benefits of prototyping in the design process. Simple two-dimensional prototypes were used to study mechanical motion, three-dimensional foam prototypes were used to study form and assembly, and functional breadboard models were used to study usability and working stresses.

Proximity

Elements that are close together are perceived to be more related than elements that are farther apart.

The principle of proximity is one of several principles referred to as *Gestalt principles of perception*. It asserts that elements close together are perceived as a single group or chunk, and are interpreted as being more related than elements that are farther apart. For example, a simple matrix of dots can be interpreted as consisting of multiple rows, multiple columns, or as a uniform matrix, depending on the relative horizontal and vertical proximities of the dots.[1]

The grouping resulting from proximity reduces the complexity of designs and reinforces the relatedness of the elements. Conversely, a lack of proximity results in the perception of multiple, disparate chunks, and reinforces differences among elements. Certain proximal layouts imply specific kinds of relationships, and should be considered in layout design. For example, connecting or overlapping elements are commonly interpreted as sharing one or more common attributes, whereas proximal but non-contacting elements are interpreted as related but independent.[2]

Proximity is one of the most powerful means of indicating relatedness in a design, and will generally overwhelm competing visual cues (e.g., similarity). Arrange elements such that their proximity corresponds to their relatedness. Ensure that labels and supporting information are near the elements that they describe, opting for direct labeling on graphs over legends or keys. Locate unrelated or ambiguously related items relatively far from one another.

See also Chunking, Performance Load, and Similarity.

[1] The seminal work on proximity is "Untersuchungen zür Lehre von der Gestalt, II" [Laws of Organization in Perceptual Forms] by Max Wertheimer, Psychologische Forschung, 1923, vol. 4, p. 301–350, reprinted in *A Source Book of Gestalt Psychology* by Willis D. Ellis (ed.), Routledge & Kegan Paul, 1999, p. 71–88. See also *Principles of Gestalt Psychology* by Kurt Koffka, Harcourt Brace, 1935.

[2] Euler circles and Venn diagrams (methods of illustrating the relationships between sets of things in logic and mathematics) utilize this principle.

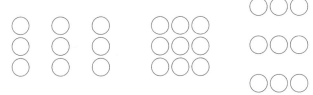

Proximity between the circles influences how they are grouped—as columns, a square group of circles, or rows.

Circles *A* and *B* are perceived as independent and sharing no attributes. Circles *C* and *D* are perceived as partially dependent and sharing some attributes. Circle *F* is perceived as dependent on Circle *E* and sharing all of its attributes.

Window controls are often placed on the center console between seats. The lack of proximity between the controls and the window makes it a poor design. A better location would be on the door itself.

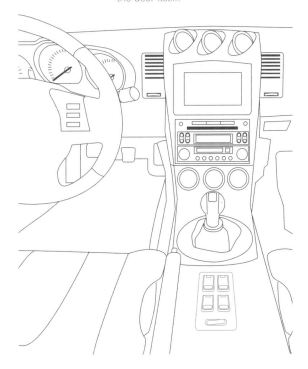

This rendering of a sign at Big Bend National Park has undoubtedly sent many hikers in unintended directions (two hikers for certain). The proximity between unrelated words (e.g., *Chisos* and *South*) lends itself to misinterpretation. Positioning the related words closer together corrects the problem.

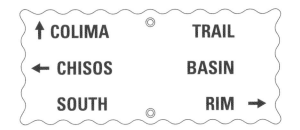

Readability

The degree to which prose can be understood, based on the complexity of words and sentences.

Readability is determined by factors such as word length, word commonality, sentence length, number of clauses in a sentence, and number of syllables in a sentence. It is an attribute that is seldom considered—either because designers are not sensitive or aware of its importance, or because of the common belief that complex information requires complex presentation. In fact, complex information requires the simplest presentation possible, so that the focus is on the information rather than the way it is presented.

For enhanced readability, omit needless words and punctuation, but be careful not to sacrifice meaning or clarity in the process. Avoid acronyms, jargon, and untranslated quotations in foreign languages. Keep sentence length appropriate for the intended audience. Generally, use active voice, but consider passive voice when the emphasis is on the message and not the messenger. When attempting to produce text for a specific reading level, use published readability formulas and software applications designed for this purpose.

A variety of readability formulas and software applications are available to assist designers in producing prose with specific readability levels. The readability rating is usually represented in the form of school levels ranging from 1st to 12th grade and college. While different tools may use slightly different approaches for calculating readability, they all generally use the same combination of core readability factors mentioned above.[1]

Use these formulas to verify that the textual components of a design are at the approximate reading level of the intended audience. However, do not write for the formulas. Readability formulas are primitive guides and should not outweigh all other considerations. For example, more sentences per paragraph may increase readability for lower-level readers, but frustrate readability for more advanced readers who are distracted by the lack of continuity. Simple language is preferred, but overly simple language obscures meaning.[2]

Consider readability when creating designs that involve prose. Express complex material in the simplest way possible. Follow guidelines for enhancing readability, and verify that the readability level approximates the level of the intended audience.[3]

See also Legibility and Ockham's Razor.

[1] Fry's Readability Graph (right) is one of many readability formulas. Other popular measures include Flesch Formula, Dale-Chall formula, Farr-Jenkins-Paterson formula, Kincaid Formula, Gunning Fog Index, and Linsear Write Index.

[2] "Use [readability formulas] as a guide after you have written, but not as a pattern before you write. Good writing must be alive; don't kill it with systems." *The Technique of Clear Writing* by Robert Gunning, McGraw-Hill, 1968.

[3] For additional writing guidelines, see *The Elements of Style* by William Strunk Jr. and E. B. White, Allyn & Bacon; 4th edition, 2000.

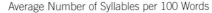

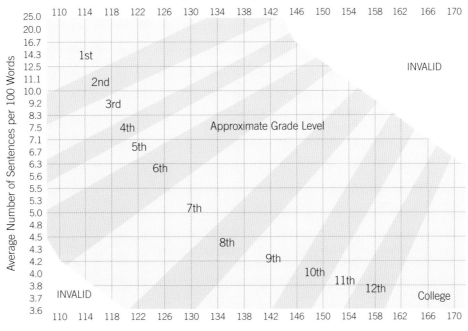

Edward Fry's Readability Graph

1. Randomly select three sample passages from a text.
2. Count 100 words starting at the beginning of these passages (count proper nouns, but not numbers).
3. Count the number of sentences in each 100-word passage, estimating the length of the last sentence to the nearest 1/10th.
4. Count the total number of syllables in each 100-word passage.
5. Calculate the average number of sentences and average number of syllables for the 100-word passage. If a great deal of variability is found, sample additional passages.
6. The area of intersection on the graph between the number of sentences and average number of syllables indicate the estimated grade level. Invalid regions indicate that a reading level could not be estimated.

Sample text written at a college reading level. In the first 100 words of this passage there are 187 syllables and almost six sentences.

Chicken pox, or varicella, is an infectious disease usually occurring in young children. Chicken pox is believed to be caused by the same herpes virus that produces shingles. Chicken pox is highly communicable and is characterized by an easily recognizable rash consisting of blisterlike lesions that appear two to three weeks after infection. Usually there are also low fever and headache. When the lesions have crusted over, the disease is believed to be no longer communicable; however, most patients simultaneously exhibit lesions at different stages of eruption. Chicken pox is usually a mild disease requiring little treatment other than medication to relieve the troublesome itching, but care must be taken so that the rash does not become infected by bacteria.

Sample text written at a 4th grade reading level. In the first 100 words of this passage there are 137 syllables and almost twelve sentences.

Not too long ago, almost everyone got chicken pox. Chicken pox is caused by a virus. This virus spreads easily. The virus spreads when an infected person coughs or sneezes. People with chicken pox get a rash on their skin. The rash is made up of clear blisters. These blisters are very itchy. It is hard not to scratch them. The blisters form scabs when they dry. Sometimes these scabs cause scars. Many people with chicken pox must stay in bed until they feel better. Until recently, almost all children in the U.S. got chicken pox between the ages of 1 and 10. In 1995, the Food and Drug Administration approved a vaccine that keeps the virus from spreading. Today, most people will never get chicken pox because of this vaccine.

Recognition Over Recall

Memory for recognizing things is better than memory for recalling things.

People are better at recognizing things they have previously experienced than recalling those things from memory. It is easier to recognize things than recall them because recognition tasks provide memory cues that facilitate searching through memory. For example, it is easier to correctly answer a multiple-choice question than a short-answer question because multiple-choice questions provide a list of possible answers; the range of search possibilities is narrowed to just the list of options. Short answer questions provide no such memory cues, so the range of search possibilities is much greater.[1]

Recognition memory is much easier to develop than recall memory. Recognition memory is attained through exposure, and does not necessarily involve any memory about origin, context, or relevance. It is simply memory that something (sight, sound, smell, touch) has been experienced before. Recall memory is attained through learning, usually involving some combination of memorization, practice, and application. Recognition memory is also retained for longer periods of time than recall memory. For example, the name of an acquaintance is often quickly forgotten, but easily recognized when heard.

The advantages of recognition over recall are often exploited in the design of interfaces for complex systems. For example, early computer systems used a command line interface, which required recall memory for hundreds of commands. The effort associated with learning the commands made computers difficult to use. The contemporary graphical user interface, which presents commands in menus, allows users to browse the possible options, and select from them accordingly. This eliminates the need to have the commands in recall memory, and greatly simplifies the usability of computers.

Decision-making is also strongly influenced by recognition. A familiar option is often selected over an unfamiliar option, even when the unfamiliar option may be the best choice. For example, in a consumer study, people participating in a taste test rated a known brand of peanut butter as superior to two unknown brands, even though one of the unknown brands was *objectively* better (determined by earlier blind taste tests). Recognition of an option is often a sufficient condition for making a choice.[2]

Minimize the need to recall information from memory whenever possible. Use readily accessible menus, decision aids, and similar devices to make available options clearly visible. Emphasize the development of recognition memory in training programs, and the development of brand awareness in advertising campaigns.

See also Exposure Effect, Serial Position Effects, and Visibility.

[1] The seminal applied work on recognition over recall is the user interface for the Xerox Star computer. See "The Xerox 'Star': A Retrospective" by Jeff Johnson and Teresa L. Roberts, William Verplank, David C. Smith, Charles Irby, Marian Beard, Kevin Mackey, in *Human Computer Interaction: Toward the Year 2000* by Ronald M. Baecker, Jonathan Grudin, William A. S. Buxton, Saul Greenberg, Morgan Kaufman Publishers, 1995, p. 53–70.

[2] Note that none of the participants had previously bought or used the known brand. See "Effects of Brand Awareness on Choice for a Common, Repeat-Purchase Product" by Wayne D. Hoyer and Steven P. Brown, *Journal of Consumer Research*, 1990, vol. 17, p. 141–148.

Early computers used command-line interfaces, which required recall memory for hundreds of commands. Graphical user interfaces eliminated the need to recall the commands by presenting them in menus. This innovation leveraged the human capacity for recognition over recall, and dramatically simplified the usability of computers.

Redundancy

The use of more elements than necessary to maintain the performance of a system in the event of failure of one or more of the elements.

System failure is the failure of a system to achieve a goal—e.g., communicate a message, maintain a structural load, or maintain operation. It is inevitable that elements within a system will fail. It is not inevitable, however, that the system as a whole fails. Redundancy is the surest method of preventing system failure. There are four kinds of redundancy: diverse, homogenous, active, and passive.[1]

Diverse redundancy is the use of multiple elements of different types (e.g., use of text, audio, and video to present the same information). Diverse redundancy is resistant to a single cause of failure, but is complex to implement and maintain. For example, high-speed trains often have diverse redundancy in their braking systems—one electric brake, one hydraulic brake, and one pneumatic brake. A single cause is unlikely to result in a cascade failure in all three braking systems.

Homogenous redundancy is the use of multiple elements of a single type (e.g., use of multiple independent strands to compose a rope). Homogenous redundancy is relatively simple to implement and maintain but is susceptible to single causes of failure—i.e., the type of cause that results in failure in one element can result in failure of other redundant elements. For example, a sharp edge that severs one strand of a rope can sever others.

Active redundancy is the application of redundant elements at all times (e.g., using multiple independent pillars to support a roof). Active redundancy guards against both system and element failure—i.e., it distributes loads across all elements such that the load on the each element and the overall system is reduced. Active redundancy also allows for element failure, repair, and substitution with minimal disruption of system performance.

Passive redundancy is the application of redundant elements only when an active element fails (e.g., using a spare tire on a vehicle in the event of a flat tire). Passive redundancy is ideal for noncritical elements, but it will result in system failure when used for elements critical to system operation. Passive redundancy is the simplest and most common kind of redundancy.

Use diverse redundancy for critical systems when the probable causes of failure cannot be anticipated. Use homogenous redundancy when the probable causes of failure can be anticipated. Use active redundancy for critical systems that must maintain stable performance in the event of element failure or extreme changes in system load. Use passive redundancy for noncritical elements within systems, or systems in which performance interruptions are tolerable. The four kinds of redundancy should be used in combination to achieve highly reliable systems.

See also Factor of Safety, Modularity, Structural Forms, and Weakest Link.

[1] See, for example, *Why Buildings Fall Down: How Structures Fail* by Matthys Levy and Mario Salvadori, W.W. Norton, 1992; and "Achieving Reliability: The Evolution of Redundancy in American Manned Spacecraft" by James E. Tomayko, *Journal of the British Interplanetary Society*, 1985, vol. 38, p. 545–552.

Parts	Purpose
1 fiberglass cow	protect the city from danger
1 canvas cape	flap in the wind
1 tower crane	provide a bovine perch
1 fabricated steel base	display cow above crane railings
4 fabricated steel hoof plates	attach cow to base
2 steel cables	attach cow to base
8 bolts	attach hoof plates to base
1 steel cross member	attach base to crane
2 fabricated double U-bolts	attach cross member to base
2 steel guy wires	attach base to crane
3 eyebolts	attach cape to cow

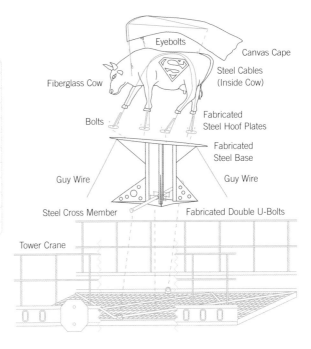

The Super Cow entry in the Houston Cow Parade 2001 had a unique design specification—it was to sit atop a thirty-story tower crane for the duration of hurricane season. Since the consequences of Super Cow taking flight in high winds could be grave, various forms of redundancy were applied to keep him attached. Despite many severe thunderstorms (wind gusts in excess of 60 MPH), Super Cow experienced no failure, damage, or unintended flights during his four-month stay on the crane.

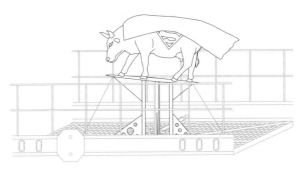

Rule of Thirds

A technique of composition in which a medium is divided into thirds, creating aesthetic positions for the primary elements of a design. [1]

The rule of thirds is a technique derived from the use of early grid systems in composition. It is applied by dividing a medium into thirds both vertically and horizontally, creating an invisible grid of nine rectangles and four intersections. The primary element within a design is then positioned on an intersection of the grid. The asymmetry of the resulting composition is interesting to look at, and generally agreed to be aesthetic.

The technique has a loyal following in design circles due to its use by the Renaissance masters and its rough relationship to the golden ratio. Although dividing a design into thirds yields a ratio different from the golden ratio (i.e., the 2/3 section = 0.666 versus golden ratio = 0.618), the users of the technique may have decided that the simplicity of its application compensated for its rough approximation.

The rule of thirds generally works well, is easy to apply, and should be considered when composing elements of a design. When the primary element is so strong as to imbalance the composition, consider centering the element rather than using the rule of thirds—especially when the strength of the primary element is reinforced by the surrounding elements or space. If the surrounding elements or space do not reinforce the primary element, use the rule of thirds and add a secondary element (known as a counterpoint) to the opposing intersection of the primary element to bring the composition to balance. In designs where there is a strong vertical or horizontal element, it is common practice to align the element along one of the grid lines of corresponding orientation.[2]

See also Alignment, Golden Ratio, and Symmetry.

[1] Also known as *golden grid rule*.

[2] A nice introduction to compositional concepts is *Design and Composition* by Nathan Goldstein, Prentice-Hall, 1997.

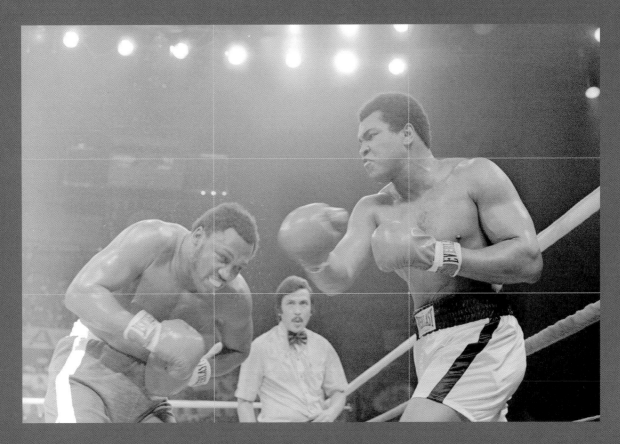

This photograph (above) from the
Muhammad Ali–Joe Frazier fight in
Manila, Philippines (1975) makes
excellent use of the rule of thirds,
placing the heads of both fighters at
opposing intersections on the grid.

This photograph (right) from the
Muhammad Ali–Sonny Liston fight in
Lewiston, Maine (1965), by contrast,
is an excellent example of when not
to use the rule of thirds—strong
primary element that is reinforced by
the surrounding space.

Satisficing

It is often preferable to settle for a satisfactory solution, rather than pursue an optimal solution.[1]

The best design decision is not always the optimal design decision. In certain circumstances, the success of a design is better served by design decisions that roughly satisfy (i.e., satisfice), rather than optimally satisfy, design requirements. For example, in seeking for the proverbial needle in a haystack, a satisficer would stop looking as soon as a needle is found; an optimizer would continue to look for all possible needles so that the sharpest needle could be determined. There are three kinds of problems for which satisficing should be considered: very complex problems, time-limited problems, and problems for which anything beyond a satisfactory solution yields diminishing returns.[2]

Complex design problems are characterized by a large number of interacting variables and a large number of unknowns. In working with such problems, a satisficer recognizes that the combination of complexity and unknowns makes an optimal solution unlikely (if not impossible). The satisficer, therefore, seeks a satisfactory solution that is just better than existing alternatives; the satisficer seeks only to incrementally improve upon the current design, rather than to achieve an optimal design.

Time-limited problems are characterized by time frames that do not permit adequate analysis or development of an optimal solution. In cases where optimality is secondary to urgency, a satisficer selects the first solution that satisfactorily meets a given design requirement. Note that satisficing should be cautiously applied in time-limited contexts, especially when the consequences of a suboptimal solution can have serious consequences.[3]

There are cases in which a satisfactory solution is better than an *optimal* solution—i.e., solutions beyond the satisfactory yield diminishing returns. Determining when satisfactory is best requires accurate knowledge of the design requirements, and accurate knowledge of the value perceptions of the users. A satisficer weighs this value perception in the development of the design specification, ensuring that optimal specifications will not consume design resources unless they are both critical to success, and accorded value by users.[4]

Consider satisficing as a means of making design decision when problems are complex with many unknowns, when problems need to be solved within a narrow time frame, and when developing design requirements and specifications. Generally, do not accept satisficed solutions that are inferior to previous or existing solutions. In time-limited contexts, consider satisficing only when the limited timelines are truly fixed, and the consequences of low-quality design and increased risk of failure are acceptable.

See also 80/20 Rule, Chunking, Cost-Benefit, and Iteration.

[1] Also known as *best is the enemy of the good principle.*

[2] The seminal works on satisficing are *Models of Man*, John Wiley & Sons, 1957; and *The Sciences of the Artificial*, MIT Press, 1969, both by Herbert A. Simon.

[3] In many time-limited contexts, the time limits are artificial (i.e., set by management), whereas the consequences of low-quality design and system failure are real. See, for example, *Crucial Decisions: Leadership in Policymaking and Crisis Management* by Irving Janis, Free Press, 1989.

[4] For example, designers at Swatch realized that watches of increasing accuracy were no longer of value to consumers—i.e., accuracy to within one minute a day was accurate enough. This "good enough" standard allowed the designers of Swatch to focus their efforts on style and cost reduction, rather than on further optimizing the timekeeping of their watches.

The *Apollo 13* Mission to the moon launched at 2:13 P.M. EST on April 11, 1970. An electrical failure occurred in the command module of the spacecraft 56 hours into the flight, causing the mission to be aborted and forcing the three-person crew to take refuge in the lunar lander. The carbon dioxide filters aboard the lunar lander were designed to support two people for two days—the planned duration of a lunar landing—and not the three people for four days needed to return the crew safely to Earth. The square carbon dioxide filters of the abandoned command module had the capacity to filter the excess carbon dioxide, but did not fit into the round filter receptacle of the lunar lander. Using materials available on the spacecraft such as plastic bags, cardboard from log books, and duct tape, NASA engineers designed a makeshift adapter for the square command module filters. The ground crew talked the astronauts through the construction process, and the adapted filters were put into service immediately thereafter. The solution was far from optimal, but it was satisfactory—it eliminated the immediate danger of carbon dioxide poisoning, and allowed ground and flight crews to focus on other critical problems. The crew of *Apollo 13* returned safely home at 1:07 P.M. EST on April 17, 1970.

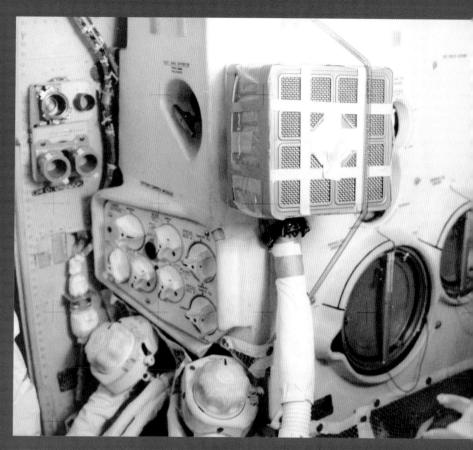

The *adapted* square carbon dioxide filter from the command module (center), and round filter receptacle of the lunar lander (lower right).

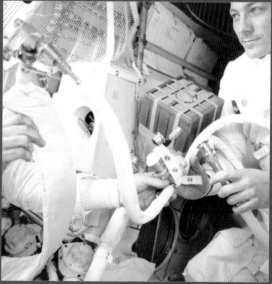

Astronaut John L. Swigert Jr., hooking up the *adapted* carbon dioxide filters.

Savanna Preference

A tendency to prefer savanna-like environments to other types of environments.[1]

People tend to prefer savanna-like environments—open areas, scattered trees, water, and uniform grassiness—to other natural environments that are simple, such as desert; dense, such as jungle; or complex, such as mountains. The preference is based on the belief that early humans who lived on savannas enjoyed a survival advantage over humans who lived in other environments. This advantage ultimately resulted in the development of a genetic disposition favoring savanna environments that manifests itself today. It may be no coincidence that the parks, resorts, and golf courses of the world all resemble savannas—they may reflect an unconscious preference for the look and feel of our ancestral, east-African home.[2]

The characteristics of savannas that people prefer include depth, openness, uniform grassy coverings, and scattered trees, as opposed to obstructed views, disordered high complexity, and rough textures. The preference is found across all age ranges and cultures, though it is strongest in children and grows weaker with age. This finding is thought to corroborate the evolutionary origin of the preference; i.e., humans are increasingly influenced by knowledge, culture, and other environments as they grow older, interfering with innate preferences.

This causal explanation has been criticized as recent evidence suggests that early humans lived in a variety of environments (e.g. closed-canopy woodlands), but evidence for the existence of the preference is strong. For example, in an experiment where people were presented with images of savannas, deciduous forests, coniferous forests, rain forests, and desert environments, lush savannas were consistently preferred over other choices as a place to live or visit. The theory that the preference is related to the savanna's perceived resource richness is supported by the finding that the least preferred environment is the arid desert landscape.[3]

People have a general landscape preference for savanna-like or parklike environments that is independent of culture. Consider the savanna preference in the design of landscapes, advertising, and any other design that involves the creation or depiction of natural environments. The preference is strongest in young children. Therefore, consider savanna-like environments in the design of settings for children's stories and play environments.

See also Archetypes, Mimicry, and Prospect-Refuge.

[1] Also known as *savanna hypothesis*.

[2] The seminal article on the savanna preference is "Development of Visual Preference for Natural Environments" by John D. Balling and John H. Falkin, *Environment and Behavior*, 1982, vol. 14, p. 5–28.

[3] See, for example, "The Biological Basis for Human Values of Nature" by Stephen R. Kellert, in *The Biophilia Hypothesis* by Stephen R. Kellert and Edward O. Wilson (editors), Island Press, 1993.

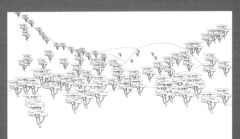

When presented with images of environments such as these, people across cultures generally prefer the environments with unobstructed views, uniform grassy coverings, and scattered trees (left), as opposed to obstructed views, high complexity, and rough textures (right). This preference is stronger in children than in adults.

Though adults generally do not share the fascination, the Teletubbies (a children's television series) mesmerize children in more than 60 countries and 35 languages. Simple stories played out by four baby-faced creatures on a lush savanna landscape equal excellent design for young children.

Scaling Fallacy

A tendency to assume that a system that works at one scale will also work at a smaller or larger scale.[1]

Much is made of the relative strength of small insects as compared to that of humans. For example, a leafcutter ant can carry about 50 times its weight; whereas an average human can only carry about half its weight. The standard reasoning goes that an ant scaled to the size of a human would retain this strength-weight advantage, giving a 200-pound ant the ability to lift 10,000 pounds. In actuality, however, an ant scaled to this size would only be able to lift about 50 pounds, assuming it could move at all. The effect of gravity at small scales is miniscule, but the effect increases exponentially with the mass of an object. This underscores the basic lesson of the scaling fallacy—systems act differently at different scales. There are two basic kinds of scaling assumptions to avoid when *growing* or *shrinking* a design: load assumptions, and interaction assumptions.[2]

Load assumptions occur when designers scale a design by some factor, and assume that the working stresses on the design scale by that same factor. For example, initial designs of the Trident 2 missile, designed to be launched from submarines, underestimated the effects of water pressure and turbulence during launch. The anticipated estimates for pressure and turbulence were based largely on the Trident 1 missile, which was much shorter and roughly half the weight of the Trident 2. When the specifications for the Trident 1 were scaled to meet the specifications for the Trident 2, the working stresses on the missile did not scale by the same factor as its physical specification. The result was multiple catastrophic failures in early tests, and a major redesign of the missile.[3]

Interaction assumptions occur when designers scale a design, and assume that the way people and other systems interact with the design will be the same at other levels of scale. For example, the design of very tall buildings involves many possible interactions that do not exist for buildings of lesser size—problems of evacuation in the case of fire, people seeking to commit suicide or base-jump off of the roof, symbolic target for terrorist attacks, to name a few. These kinds of interaction effects are usually an indirect consequence of the design, and therefore can be difficult to anticipate and manage.

The best way to avoid the scaling fallacy is to be aware of the tendency to make scaling assumptions. Therefore, raise awareness of load and interaction assumptions in the design process. Verify load assumptions through the use of careful calculations, systematic testing, and appropriate factors of safety. Minimize incorrect interaction assumptions through careful research of analogous designs, and monitoring of how the design is used once implemented.

See also Factor of Safety, Feedback Loop, Modularity, and Structural Forms.

[1] Also known as *cube law* and *law of sizes*.

[2] The seminal work on scaling is *Dialogues Concerning Two New Sciences* by Galileo Galilei, Prometheus Books [reprint], 1991.

[3] "Design Flaw Seen as Failure Cause in Trident 2 Tests" by Andrew Rosenthal, *New York Times*, August 17, 1989, p. 1.

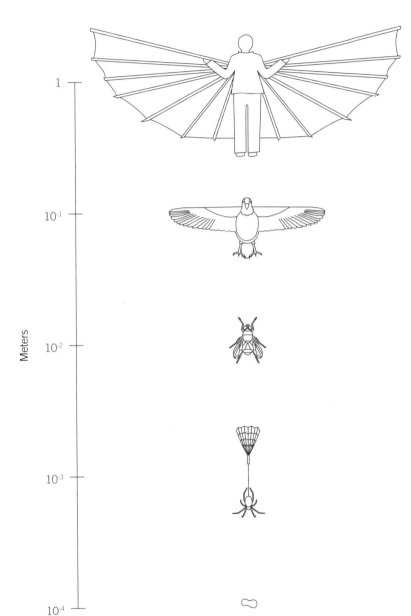

Meters

1

10^{-1}

10^{-2}

10^{-3}

10^{-4}

The scaling fallacy is nowhere more apparent than with flight. For example, at very small and very large scales, flapping to fly is not a viable strategy. At very small scales, wings are too small to effectively displace air molecules. At very large scales, the effects of gravity are too great for flapping to work—a painful lesson learned by many early pioneers of human flight. The lesson is that designs can be effective at one scale, and completely ineffective at another.

The images from small to large: aeroplankton simply float about in air; baby spiders use tiny web sails to parachute; insects flap to fly; birds flap to fly; humans flap but do not fly.

Self-Similarity

A property in which a form is made up of parts similar to the whole or to one another.

Many forms in nature exhibit self-similarity, and as a result it is commonly held to be an intrinsically aesthetic property. Natural forms tend to exhibit self-similarity at many different levels of scale, whereas human-created forms generally do not. For example, an aerial view of a coastline reveals the same basic edge pattern, whether standing at the waters edge or viewed from low-Earth orbit. Although varying levels of detail are seen, the same pattern emerges—the detail is simply a mosaic of smaller wholes.[1]

Naturally occurring self-similarity is usually the result of a basic algorithmic process called *recursion*. Recursion occurs when a system receives input, modifies it slightly, and then feeds the output back into the system as input. This recursive loop results in subtle variations in the form—perhaps smaller, skewed, or rearranged—but is still recognizable as an approximation of the basic form. For example, a person standing between two mirrors facing each other yields an infinite sequence of smaller reflections of the person in the opposing mirror. Recursion occurs with the looping of the light between the two mirrors; self-similarity is evident in the successively smaller images in the mirrors.

The ubiquity of self-similarity in nature hints at an underlying order and algorithm, and suggests ways to enhance the aesthetic (and perhaps structural) composition of human-created forms. Consider, for example, the self-similarity of form and function found in the compound arch structures of the Roman aqueducts and the flying buttresses of gothic cathedrals, structures that are beautiful in form and rarely equaled in their structural strength and longevity. The self-similarity in these structures exists at only a few levels of scale, but the resulting aesthetic and structural integrity are dramatic.

Consider self-similarity in all aspects of a design: story plots, visual displays, and structural compositions. The reuse of a single, basic form to create many levels of *metaforms* mimics nature's tendency towards parsimony and redundancy. Explore the use of basic, self-similar elements in a design to create interesting organizations at multiple levels of scale.

See also Archetypes, Ockham's Razor, Similarity, and Symmetry.

[1] The seminal work on self-similarity is *Fractal Geometry of Nature* by Benoit B. Mandelbrot, W. H. Freeman & Company, 1988.

Fractals demonstrate self-similarity on virtually every level of scale. This image of the Valley of Seahorses region of the Mandelbrot Set demonstrates the extraordinary complexity and beauty of self-similar forms.

M. C. Escher explored self-similarity and recursion in much of his work. In his *Smaller and Smaller*, a single form perfectly tiles with successively smaller self-similar forms to create a reptilian tunnel of infinite depth.

The photomosaic technique developed by Robert Silvers creates stunning meta-images from unlikely combinations of miniature images. The photomosaic of the Mona Lisa comprises 800 classic art images and demonstrates the power of self-similarity at only two levels of scale.

Serial Position Effects

A phenomenon of memory in which items presented at the beginning and end of a list are more likely to be recalled than items in the middle of a list.

Serial position effects occur when people try to recall items from a list; items at the beginning and end are better recalled than the items in the middle. The improved recall for items at the beginning of a list is called a *primacy effect*. The improved recall for items at the end of a list is called a *recency effect*.[1]

Primacy effects occur because the initial items in a list are stored in long-term memory more efficiently than items later in the list. In lists where items are rapidly presented, the primacy effect is weaker because people have less time to store the initial items in long-term memory. In lists where items are slowly presented, the primacy effect is stronger because people have more time to store the initial items in long-term memory.[2]

Recency effects occur because the last few items in a list are still in working memory, and readily available. The strength of the recency effect is unaffected by the rate of item presentation, but is dramatically affected by the passage of time and the presentation of additional information. For example, the recency effect disappears when people think about other matters for thirty seconds after the last item in the list is presented. It is important to note that the same is not true of the primacy effect, because those items have already been stored in long-term memory.[3]

For visual stimuli, items presented early in a list have the greatest influence; they are not only better recalled, but influence the interpretation of later items. For auditory stimuli, items late in a list have the greatest influence. However, if multiple presentations of information are separated in time, and a person must make a selection decision soon after the last presentation, the recency effect has the greatest influence on the decision. These effects also describe a general selection preference known as *order effects*—first and last items in a list are more likely to be selected than items in the middle (e.g., the order of presentation of candidates on a ballot).[4]

Present important items at the beginning or end of a list (versus the middle) in order to maximize recall. When the list is visual, present important items at the beginning of the list. When the list is auditory, present important items at the end. In decision-making situations, if the decision is to be made immediately after the presentation of the last item, increase the probability of an item being selected by presenting it at the end of the list; otherwise, present it at the beginning of the list.

See also Advance Organizer, Chunking, Classical Conditioning, and Operant Conditioning.

[1] The seminal work on serial position effects is *Memory: A Contribution to Experimental Psychology* by Hermann Ebbinghaus, Teachers College, Columbia University, 1885 (translated by H. A. Ruger and C. E. Bussenues, 1913).

[2] "Storage Mechanisms in Recall" by Murray Glanzer, in *The Psychology of Learning and Motivation* by G. H. Bower and J. T. Spence (eds.), 1972, Academic Press, vol. 5, p. 129–193.

[3] "Two Storage Mechanisms in Free Recall" by Murray Glanzer and Anita Cunitz, *Journal of Verbal Learning and Verbal Behavior*, 1966, vol. 5, p. 351–360.

[4] See "Forming Impressions of Personality" by Solomon E. Asch, *Journal of Abnormal and Social Psychology*, 1946, vol. 41, 258–290; and "First Guys Finish First: The Effects of Ballot Position on Election Outcomes" by Jennifer A. Steen and Jonathan GS Koppell, Presentation at the *2001 Annual Meeting of the American Political Science Association*, San Francisco, August 30–September 2, 2001.

Items at the beginning and end of a list or a sequence are easier to remember than items in the middle. If recall is attempted immediately after the presentation of the list, the primacy effect and recency effect are roughly equal in strength (word list 1). If recall is attempted more than 30 seconds after the presentation of the list, the primacy effect maintains whereas the recency effect quickly diminishes (word list 2).

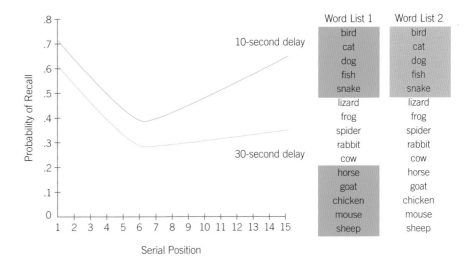

In a classic experiment, students who read the first sentence rated John more favorably than students who read the second sentence. The early words in the list had more overall influence on impressions than did later words.

John was intelligent, industrious, impulsive, critical, stubborn, and envious.

John was envious, stubborn, critical, impulsive, industrious, and intelligent.

In addition to benefits reaped from the bad design of the butterfly ballot, the Republican ticket of 2000 also benefited from an order effect—being first on the ballot is estimated to be worth between 1 percent and 4 percent of the vote.

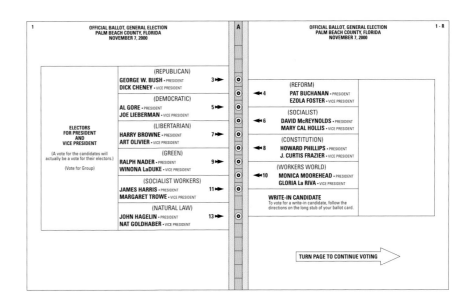

Shaping

A technique used to teach a desired behavior by reinforcing increasingly accurate approximations of the behavior.[1]

Complex behaviors can be difficult to teach. Shaping is a strategy whereby complex behaviors are broken down into smaller, simpler subbehaviors, and then taught one by one. The behaviors are reinforced (e.g., given food), and ultimately chained together to achieve a desired result. For example, to teach a mouse to press a lever, the mouse is first reinforced to move close to the lever; then reinforced only when it makes contact with the lever; and eventually only when it presses the lever.[2]

Moving   Touching   Pressing

Often, shaping occurs without awareness. For example, video games use shaping when initial game levels require simple inputs in order to "beat" the level (obtain the reinforcement), and then require increasingly difficult controller actions to master higher levels of the game. Salespeople use a form of shaping when they offer a prize to come to their location, provide food and drink to discuss the sale, and then offer a discount for making a purchase decision that day. Each action toward the goal behavior (making the sale) is reinforced.

During shaping, behaviors that have nothing to do with the desired behavior can get incidentally reinforced. For example, when training a mouse to press a lever, the mouse may incidentally press a lever with one foot in the air. The reinforcement for the lever press may also inadvertently reinforce the fact that the foot was in the air. This behavior then becomes an integrated, but unnecessary component of the desired behavior; the mouse lifts its foot whenever it presses the lever. The development of this kind of superstitious behavior is common with humans as well.

Use shaping to train complex behaviors in games, simulations, and learning environments. Shaping does not address the "hows" or "whys" of a task, and should, therefore, primarily be used to teach rote procedures and refine complex motor tasks. Shaping is being increasingly used to train complex behaviors in artificial beings, and should be considered when developing adaptive systems.[3]

See also Classical Conditioning and Operant Conditioning.

[1] Also known as *approximation conditioning* and *conditioning by successive approximations*.

[2] The seminal work on shaping is *The Behavior of Organisms: an Experimental Analysis* by B. F. Skinner, Appleton-Century, 1938. An excellent account of Skinner's early research and development is "Engineering Behavior: Project Pigeon, World War II, and the Conditioning of B. F. Skinner" by James H. Capshew, *Technology and Culture*, 1993, vol. 34, p. 835–857.

[3] See, for example, *Robot Shaping: An Experiment in Behavior Engineering* by Marco Dorigo and Marco Colombetti, MIT Press, 1997.

Project Pigeon

Project Pigeon was a classified research-and-development program during World War II. It was developed at a time when electronic guidance systems did not exist, and the only compensation for the inaccuracy of bombs was dropping them in quantity. This ingenious application of shaping would have dramatically increased the accuracy of bombs and decreased civilian casualties. Despite favorable performance tests, however, the National Defense Research Committee ended the project—it seems they couldn't get over the idea that pigeons would be guiding their bombs.

1. Pigeons were trained to peck at targets on aerial photographs. Once a certain level of proficiency was obtained, pigeons were jacketed and mounted inside tubes.

2. The pigeons in their tubes were inserted into the nosecone of the bomb. Each nosecone used three pigeons in a type of voting system, whereby the pigeon pecks of two birds in agreement would overrule the errant pigeon pecks of a single bird.

3. Sealed in the bomb, the pigeons could see through glass lenses in the nosecone.

4. Once the bomb was released, the pigeons would begin pecking at their view of the target. Their pecks shifted the glass lens off-center, which adjusted the bomb's tail surfaces and, correspondingly, its trajectory.

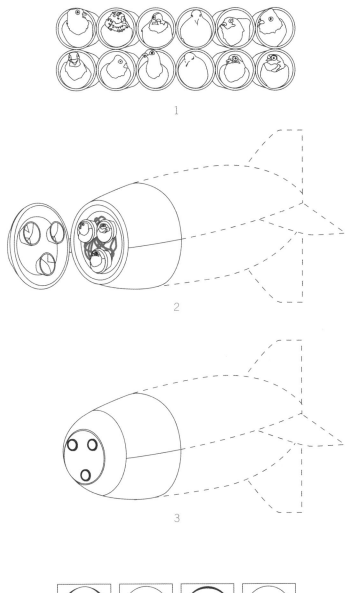

1

2

3

4

Signal-to-Noise Ratio

The ratio of relevant to irrelevant information in a display. The highest possible signal-to-noise ratio is desirable in design.

All communication involves the creation, transmission, and reception of information. During each stage of this process, the form of the information—the signal—is degraded, and extraneous information—noise—is added. Degradation reduces the amount of useful information by altering its form. Noise reduces clarity by diluting useful information with useless information. The clarity of information can be understood as the ratio of remaining signal to added noise. For example, a graph with no extraneous elements would have a high signal-to-noise ratio whereas, a graph with many extraneous elements would have a low signal-to-noise ratio. The goal of good design is to maximize signal and minimize noise, thereby producing a high signal-to-noise ratio.[1]

Maximizing *signal* means clearly communicating information with minimal degradation. Signal degradation occurs when information is presented inefficiently: unclear writing, inappropriate graphs, or ambiguous icons and labels. Signal clarity is improved through simple and concise presentation of information. Simple designs incur minimal performance loads, enabling people to better focus on the meaning of the information. Signal degradation is minimized through research and careful decision-making. For example, failing to use the correct type of graph to present a certain kind of data can fundamentally distort the meaning of the information. It is therefore important to make good design decisions at the outset, testing when necessary to verify design directions. Emphasizing key aspects of the information can also reduce signal degradation—e.g., highlighting or redundantly coding important elements in a design.

Minimizing noise means removing unnecessary elements, and minimizing the expression of necessary elements. It is important to realize that *every* unnecessary data item, graphic, line, or symbol steals attention away from relevant elements. Such unnecessary elements should be avoided or else eliminated. Necessary elements should be minimized to the degree possible without compromising function. For example, the expression of lines in grids and tables should be thinned, lightened, and possibly even removed. Every element in a design should be expressed to the extent necessary, but not beyond the extent necessary. Excess is noise.

Seek to maximize the signal-to-noise ratio in design. Increase signal by keeping designs simple, and selecting design strategies carefully. Consider enhancing key aspects of information through techniques like redundant coding and highlighting. Use well-accepted standards and guidelines when available to leverage conventions and promote consistent implementation. Minimize noise by removing unnecessary elements, and minimizing the expression of elements.

See also Alignment, Layering, Ockham's Razor, and Performance Load.

[1] The seminal works on signal-to-noise ratio in information design are "A Decision-Making Theory of Visual Detection" by Wilson P. Tanner Jr. and John A. Swets, *Psychological Review*, 1954, vol. 61, p. 401–409; and *Visual Display of Quantitative Information* by Edward R. Tufte, Graphics Press, 1983.

The signal-to-noise ratio of each of these representations on the left is improved by removing elements that do not convey information, minimizing the expression of remaining elements, and highlighting essential information.

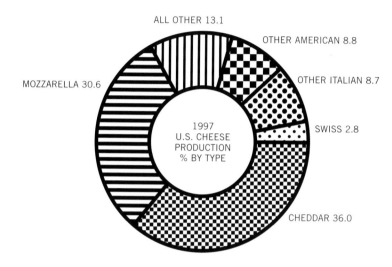

ALL OTHER 13.1
OTHER AMERICAN 8.8
MOZZARELLA 30.6
OTHER ITALIAN 8.7
SWISS 2.8
1997
U.S. CHEESE
PRODUCTION
% BY TYPE
CHEDDAR 36.0

All Other 13.1
Other American 8.8
Mozzarella 30.6
Other Italian 8.7
Swiss 2.8
1997
U.S. Cheese
Production
% by Type
Cheddar 36.0

SOYBEANS		
	PRODUCTION Billions of Bushels	HARVESTED ACREAGE Millions of Acres
1997	2.69	68.1
1998	2.74	71.3
1999	2.65	72.5
2000	2.76	72.5
2001	2.89	73.2

Soybeans

	Production Billions of Bushels	Harvested Acreage Millions of Acres
1997	2.69	68.1
1998	2.74	71.3
1999	2.65	72.5
2000	2.76	72.5
2001	2.89	73.2

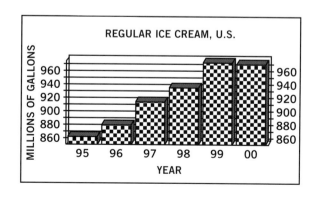

REGULAR ICE CREAM, U.S.

Regular Ice Cream, U.S.
Millions of Gallons

Similarity

Elements that are similar are perceived to be more related than elements that are dissimilar.

The principle of similarity is one of several principles referred to as *Gestalt principles of perception*. It asserts that similar elements are perceived as a single group or chunk, and are interpreted as being more related than dissimilar elements. For example, a simple matrix comprising alternating rows of dots and squares will be interpreted as a set of rows only, because the similar elements group together to form horizontal lines. A complex visual display is interpreted as having different areas and types of information depending on the similarity of color, size, and shape of its elements; similar elements are interpreted as being relevant to one another.[1]

The grouping resulting from similarity reduces complexity and reinforces the relatedness of design elements. Conversely, a lack of similarity results in the perception of multiple, disparate chunks, and reinforces differences among the elements. Certain kinds of similarity work better than others for different situations. Similarity of color results in the strongest grouping effect; it is strongest when the number of colors is small, and is decreasingly effective as the number of colors increases. Similarity of size is effective when the sizes of elements are clearly distinguishable from one another, and is an especially appropriate grouping strategy when the size of elements has additional benefits (e.g., large buttons are easier to press). Similarity of shape is the weakest grouping strategy; it is best used when the color and size of other elements is uniform, or when used in conjunction with size or color.[2]

Use similarity to indicate relatedness among elements in a design. Represent elements such that their similarity corresponds to their relatedness, and represent unrelated or ambiguously related items using different colors, sizes, and shapes. Use the fewest colors and simplest shapes possible for the strongest grouping effects, ensuring that elements are sufficiently distinct to be easily detectable.

See also Chunking, Mimicry, and Self-Similarity.

[1] The seminal work on similarity is "Untersuchungen zür Lehre von der Gestalt, II" [Laws of Organization in Perceptual Forms] by Max Wertheimer, *Psychologische Forschung*, 1923, vol. 4, p. 301–350, reprinted in *A Source Book of Gestalt Psychology* by Willis D. Ellis (ed.), Routledge & Kegan Paul, 1999, p. 71–88. See also *Principles of Gestalt Psychology* by Kurt Koffka, Harcourt Brace, 1935.

[2] Note that a significant portion of the population is color blind, limiting the strategy of using color alone. Therefore, consider using an additional grouping strategy when using color.

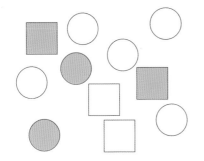
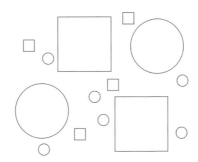
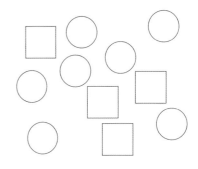

Similarity among elements influences how they are grouped—here by color, size, and shape. Note the strength of color as a grouping strategy relative to size and shape.

This remote control uses color, size, and shape to group functions. Note the relationship between the anticipated frequency of use of the buttons and their relative size and shape.

Similarity is commonly used in camouflage. For example, the mimic octopus can assume the color, pattern, and approximate form of one of its fiercest predators—the highly poisonous sole fish—as well as many other marine organisms.

Storytelling

A method of creating imagery, emotions, and understanding of events through an interaction between a storyteller and an audience.

Storytelling is uniquely human. It is the original method of passing knowledge from one generation to the next, and remains one of the most compelling methods for richly communicating knowledge. Storytelling can be oral, as in the traditional telling of a tale; visual, as in an information graph or movie; or textual, as in a poem or novel. More recently, *digital storytelling* has emerged, which involves telling a story using digital media. This might take the form of a computerized slide show, a digital video, or educational software. A storyteller can be any instrument of information presentation that engages an audience to experience a set of events.[1]

Good storytelling experiences generally require certain fundamental elements. While additional elements can be added to further augment the quality of a story or storytelling experience, they can rarely be subtracted without detriment. The fundamental elements are:

- *Setting*—The setting orients the audience, providing a sense of time and place for the story.

- *Characters*—Character identification is how the audience becomes involved in the story, and how the story becomes relevant.

- *Plot*—The plot ties events in the story together, and is the channel through which the story can flow.

- *Invisibility*—The awareness of the storyteller fades as the audience focuses on a good story. When engaged in a good movie or book, the existence of the medium is forgotten.

- *Mood*—Music, lighting, and style of prose create the emotional tone of the story.

- *Movement*—In a good story, the sequence and flow of events is clear and interesting. The storyline doesn't stall.

Use storytelling to engage an audience in a design, evoke a specific emotional response, or provide a rich context to enhance learning. When successfully employed, an audience will experience and recall the events of the story in a personal way—it becomes a part of them. This is a phenomenon unique to storytelling.

See also Framing, Immersion, and Wayfinding.

[1] The seminal work on storytelling is Aristotle's Poetics. Additional seminal references include, *The Hero with a Thousand Faces* by Joseph Campbell, Princeton University Press, 1960; and *How to Tell a Story; and Other Essays by Mark Twain*, Oxford University Press, 1996. A nice contemporary reference on visual storytelling is *Graphic Storytelling* by Will Eisner, Poorhouse Press, 1996.

Setting
Milestone events of the civil rights movement are presented with their dates and places. The memorial sits within the greater, historically relevant context of the Southern Poverty Law Center in Montgomery, Alabama.

Characters
The civil rights movement is a story of individual sacrifice toward the attainment of a greater good. Key activists and opponents are integral to the story and are listed by name.

Plot
Events are presented simply and concisely, listed in chronological order and aligned along a circular path. Progress in the civil rights movement is inferred as cause-effect relationships between events. No editorializing—just the facts.

Invisibility
The table is cantilevered to hide its structure. The black granite is minimal, providing maximum contrast with the platinum-inscribed lettering. The structure is further concealed through its interaction with water, which makes it a mirrored surface.

Mood
The table's asymmetry suggests a theme of different but equal. The mirrored surface created by the water on black granite reveals the story in union with the reflected image of the viewer. The sound of water is calming and healing.

Movement
The flow of water against gravity suggests the struggle of the civil rights movement. As the water gently pours over the edge, the struggle is overcome. Simile becomes reality as water rolls down the back wall.

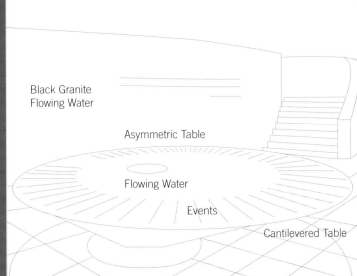

Black Granite
Flowing Water

Asymmetric Table

Flowing Water

Events

Cantilevered Table

The Civil Rights Memorial
Southern Poverty Law Center in Montgomery, Alabama

Structural Forms

There are three ways to organize materials to support a load or to contain and protect something: mass structures, frame structures, and shell structures.

Structures are assemblages of elements used to support a load or contain and protect things. In many cases, the structure supports only itself (i.e., the load is the weight of the materials), and in other cases the structure supports itself and additional loads (e.g., a crane). Whether creating a museum exhibit, large sculpture, 3-D billboard, or temporary shelter, a basic understanding of structure is essential to successful design. There are three basic types of structures: mass structures, frame structures, and shell structures.[1]

Mass structures consist of materials that are put together to form a solid structure. Their strength is a function of the weight and hardness of the materials. Examples of mass structures include dams, adobe walls, and mountains. Mass structures are robust in that small amounts of the structure can be lost with little effect on the strength of the structure, but are limited in application to relatively simple designs. Consider mass structures for barriers, walls, and small shelters—especially in primitive environments where building skills and materials are limited.

Frame structures consist of struts joined to form a framework. Their strength is a function of the strength of the elements and joints, and their organization. Often a cladding or skin is added to the frame, but this rarely adds strength to the structure. Examples of frame structures include most modern homes, bicycles, and skeletons. Frame structures are relatively light, flexible, and easy to construct. The most common frame configuration is the assembly of struts into triangles, which are then assembled to form larger structures. Consider frame structures for most large design applications.

Shell structures consist of a thin material that wraps around to contain a volume. They maintain their form and support loads without a frame or solid mass inside. Their strength is a function of their ability to distribute loads throughout the whole structure. Examples of shell structures include bottles, airplane fuselages, and domes. Shell structures are effective at resisting static forces that are applied in specific ways, but are poor at resisting dynamic forces. For example, an egg effectively resists loads that are applied to its top and bottom, but collapses quickly when the loads are applied to its sides. Shell structures are lightweight and economical with regards to material, but are complex to design and vulnerable to catastrophic failure if the structure has imperfections or is damaged. Consider shell structures for containers, small cast structures, shelters, and designs requiring very large and lightweight spans. Large shell structures should generally be reinforced by additional support elements to stabilize against buckling.[2]

See also Cost-Benefit, Factor of Safety, Modularity, and Scaling Fallacy.

[1] An excellent introduction to the dynamics of structural forms is *Why Buildings Stand Up: The Strength of Architecture* by Mario Salvadori, W. W. Norton, 1990; and *Why Buildings Fall Down: How Structures Fail* by Matthys Levy and Mario Salvadori, W. W. Norton, 1992.

[2] Note that shell structures can be reinforced to better withstand dynamic forces. For example, monolithic dome structures apply concrete over a rebar-reinforced foam shell structure. The resulting structural form is likely the most disaster-resistant structure available short of moving into a mountain.

The Geocell Rapid Deployment Flood Wall is a modular plastic grid that can be quickly assembled and filled with dirt by earthmoving equipment. The resulting mass structure forms an efficient barrier to flood waters at a fraction of the time and cost of more traditional methods (e.g., sand bag walls).

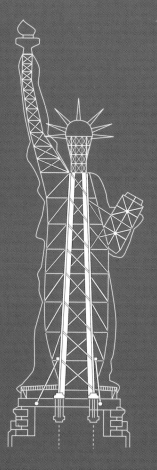

The Statue of Liberty demonstrates the flexibility and strength of frame structures. Its iron frame structure supports both itself (125 tons) and its copper cladding (100 tons). Any resemblance of the frame structure to the Eiffel Tower is more than coincidence, as the designer for both structures was Gustave Eiffel.

Icosa Shelters exploit many intrinsic benefits of shell structures: they are inexpensive, lightweight, and strong. Designed as temporary shelters for the homeless, the Icosa Shelters are easily assembled by folding sheets of precision die cut material together and sealing with tape.

Symmetry

A property of visual equivalence among elements in a form.

Symmetry has long been associated with beauty, and is a property found in virtually all forms in nature. It can be seen in the human body (e.g., two eyes, two ears, two arms and legs), as well as in animals and plants. Symmetry in natural forms is largely a function of the influence of gravity, and the kind of *averaging* of form that occurs from merging genetic information in reproduction. There are three basic types of symmetry: reflection, rotation, and translation.[1]

Reflection symmetry refers to the mirroring of an equivalent element around a central axis or *mirror line*. Reflection symmetry can occur in any orientation as long as the element is the same on both sides of the mirror line. Natural forms that grow or move across the Earth's surface have evolved to exhibit reflection symmetry. For example, a butterfly exhibits reflection symmetry in its body and wings.

Rotation symmetry refers to the rotation of equivalent elements around a common center. Rotation symmetry can occur at any angle or frequency as long as the elements share a common center. Natural forms that grow or move up or down a perpendicular to the Earth's surface have evolved to exhibit rotation symmetry. For example, a sunflower exhibits rotation symmetry in both its stem and petals.

Translation symmetry refers to the location of equivalent elements in different areas of space. Translation symmetry can occur in any direction and over any distance as long as the basic orientation of the element is maintained. Natural forms exhibit translation symmetry through reproduction—creating similar looking offspring. For example, a school of fish exhibits translation symmetry across multiple, independent organisms.[2]

Aside from their aesthetic properties, symmetric forms have other qualities that are potentially beneficial to designers. For example, symmetric forms tend to be seen as figure images rather than ground images, which means they receive more attention and be better recalled than other elements; symmetric forms are simpler than asymmetric forms, which also gives them an advantage with regards to recognition and recall; and symmetric faces are perceived as more attractive than asymmetric faces.[3]

Symmetry is the most basic and enduring aspect of beauty. Use symmetry in design to convey balance, harmony, and stability. Use simple symmetrical forms when recognition and recall are important, and more complex combinations of the different types of symmetries when aesthetics and interestingness are important.

See also Figure-Ground Relationship, Golden Ratio,
        Most Average Facial Appearance Effect, and Self-Similarity.

[1] A seminal work on symmetry in design is *Elements of Dynamic Symmetry* by Jay Hambidge, Dover Publishers, 1978.

[2] A nice source for various combinations of types of symmetries in natural and human-created forms is *Handbook of Regular Patterns* by Peter S. Stevens, MIT Press, 1984.

[3] See, for example, "The Status of Minimum Principle in the Theoretical Analysis of Visual Perception" by Gary Hatfield and William Epstein, *Psychological Bulletin*, 1985, vol. 97, p. 155–186; and "Facial Resemblance Enhances Trust" by Lisa M. DeBruine, *Proceedings of The Royal Society: Biological Sciences*, vol. 269(1498), p. 1307-1312.

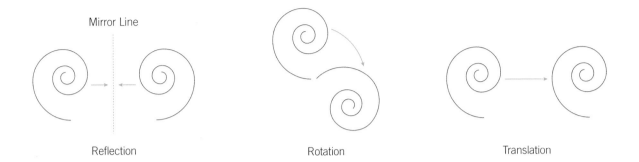

Mirror Line

Reflection   Rotation   Translation

Combinations of symmetries can
create harmonious, interesting, and
memorable designs. For example,
the Notre Dame Cathedral

incorporates multiple, complex
symmetries in its design, resulting in
a structure that is both pleasing and
interesting to the eye.

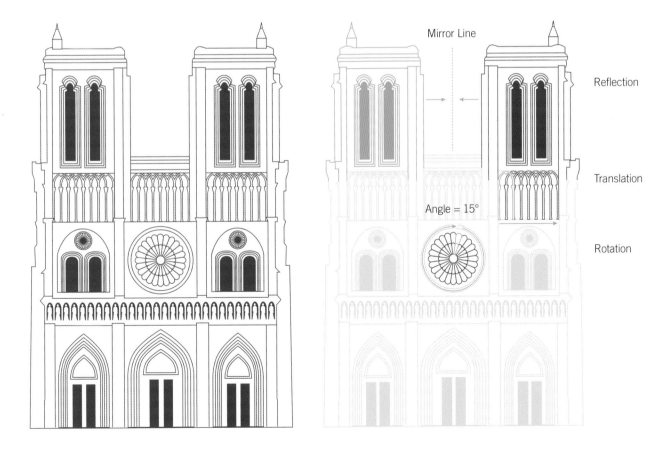

Mirror Line

Reflection

Translation

Angle = 15°

Rotation

Threat Detection

An ability to detect threatening stimuli more efficiently than nonthreatening stimuli.

People are born with automatic visual detection mechanisms for evolutionarily threatening stimuli, such as snakes. These threatening stimuli are detected more quickly than nonthreatening stimuli and are thought to have evolutionary origins; efficiently detecting threats no doubt provided a selective advantage for our human ancestors.[1]

For example, when presented with images containing threatening elements, such as spiders, and nonthreatening elements, such as flowers, people can locate the threatening elements more quickly than the non-threatening elements. The search times are not affected by the location of the threatening element or the number of distracters surrounding the element. Similarly, people can locate an angry face in a group of happy or sad faces more quickly than a happy or sad face in a group of angry faces. The ability to detect evolutionarily threatening stimuli is a function of perceptual processes that automatically scan the visual field below the level of conscious awareness. Unlike conscious processing, which is relatively slow and serial, threat detection occurs quickly and in parallel with other visual and cognitive processes.[2]

Almost anything possessing the key threat features of snakes, spiders, and angry faces can trigger the threat detection mechanism, such as the wavy line of a snake, the thin legs and large circular body of spiders, and the V-shaped eyebrows of an angry face. It is reasonable that other general predatory features (e.g., forward-looking eyes) will also trigger the threat-detection mechanism given their evolutionary relevance, but little research of this type has been conducted. In any event, the sensitivity to certain threat features explains why twigs and garden hoses often frighten young children, and why people have a general fear of insects that superficially resemble spiders (e.g., roaches). When people have conscious fears or phobias of the threatening stimuli, the threat detection ability is more sensitive, and search times for threatening stimuli are further reduced. Once attention is captured, threatening stimuli are also better at holding attention than nonthreatening stimuli.

Consider threatening stimuli to rapidly attract attention and imply threat or foreboding (e.g., designs of markers to keep people away from an area). Abstracted representations of threat features can trigger threat-detection mechanisms without the accompanying negative emotional reaction. Therefore, consider such elements to attract attention in noisy environments, such as a dense retail shelf display. Achieving a balance between maximum detectability and minimal negative affect is more art than science, and therefore should be explored with caution and verified with testing on the target audience.

See also Archetypes, Baby-Face Bias, and Mimicry.

[1] The seminal theoretical work on threat detection in humans is *The Principles of Psychology* by William James, Henry Holt and Company, 1890. While the evidence suggests innate detection mechanisms for snakes, spiders, and angry faces, it is probable that similar detection mechanisms exist for other forms of threatening stimuli.

[2] See "Emotion Drives Attention: Detecting the Snake in the Grass" by Arne Öhman, Anders Flykt, and Francisco Esteve, *Journal of Experimental Psychology: General*, September 2001, vol. 130(3), p. 466–478; and "Finding the Face in the Crowd: An Anger Superiority Effect" by Christine H. Hansen and Ranald D. Hansen, *Journal of Personality and Social Psychology*, 1988, vol. 54, p. 917–924.

In visually noisy environments, the average search time for threatening stimuli is less than for nonthreatening stimuli.

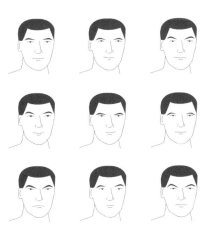

Angry faces are more quickly detected and maintain attention more effectively than neutral or happy faces.

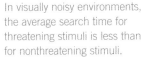

Amid the many billboards lining Houston freeways, the University of Houston billboard pops out and commands attention. The design of the advertisement is certainly clean and well composed, but its unique ability to capture and hold attention may be due to threat detection.

Three-Dimensional Projection

A tendency to see objects and patterns as three-dimensional when certain visual cues are present.

People have evolved to see things as three-dimensional whenever possible—even when the things are clearly not three-dimensional. The following visual cues are commonly used to encourage the perception of three-dimensional relationships:[1]

Interposition
When two overlapping objects are presented, the overlapped object is perceived to be farther away than the overlapping object.

Size
When two similar objects of different size are presented together, the smaller object is perceived to be farther away than the larger object. The size of familiar objects can also be used to indicate the size and depth of unfamiliar objects.

Elevation
When two objects are presented at different vertical locations, the object at the higher elevation is perceived to be farther away.[2]

Linear Perspective
When two vertical lines converge near their top ends, the converging ends of the lines are perceived to be farther away than the diverging ends.

Texture Gradient
When the texture of a surface varies in density, the areas of greater density are perceived to be farther away than areas of lesser density.

Shading
When an object has shading or shadows, the shaded areas are perceived to be the farthest away from the light source and the light areas are interpreted as being closest to the light source.

Atmospheric Perspective
When multiple objects are presented together, the objects that are bluer and blurrier are perceived to be farther away than the objects that are less blue and blurry.[3]

Consider these visual cues in the depiction of three-dimensional elements and environments. Strongest depth effects are achieved when the visual cues are used in combination; therefore, use as many of the cues as possible to achieve the strongest effect, making sure that the cues are appropriate for the context.

See also Figure-Ground Relationship and Top-Down Lighting Bias.

[1] Note that only static cues (as opposed to motion cues) are presented here. A nice review the various depth cues is found in *Sensation and Perception* by Margaret W. Matlin and Hugh J. Foley, Allyn & Bacon, 1997, p. *165–193*.

[2] An exception to this is when a strong horizontal element is present, which tends to be perceived as a *horizon line*. In this case, objects that are closer to the horizon line are perceived as farther away than objects that are distant from the horizon line.

[3] The relationship between the degree of blueness and blurriness to distance is a function of experience—i.e., people who live in a smoggy city will have a different sense of atmospheric perspective than people who live in less-polluted rural areas.

Video games make ample use of
three-dimensional projection to
represent three-dimensional
environments on two-dimensional
screens. For example, the game
Black & White uses three-dimensional
projection to create a believable
and navigable three-dimensional
world. All of the depth cues are
demonstrated in these screen shots
from the game.

Top-Down Lighting Bias

A tendency to interpret shaded or dark areas of an object as shadows resulting from a light source above the object.[1]

Humans are biased to interpret objects as being lit from a single light source from above. This bias is found across all age ranges and cultures, and likely results from humans evolving in an environment lit from above by the Sun. Had humans evolved in a solar system with more than one sun, the bias would be different.

As a result of the top-down lighting bias, dark or shaded areas are commonly interpreted as being farthest from the light source, and light areas are interpreted as being closest to the light source. Thus, objects that are light at the top and dark at the bottom are interpreted as convex, and objects that are dark at the top and light at the bottom are interpreted as concave. In each case, the apparent depth increases as the contrast between light and dark areas increases. When objects have ambiguous shading cues the brain switches back and forth between concave and convex interpretation.[2]

The top-down lighting bias can also influence the perception of the naturalness or unnaturalness of familiar objects. Objects that are depicted with top-down lighting look natural, whereas familiar objects that are depicted with bottom-up lighting look unnatural. Designers commonly exploit this effect in order to create scary or unnatural looking images. Interestingly, there is evidence that objects look most natural and are preferred when lit from the top-left, rather than from directly above. This effect is stronger for right-handed people than left-handed people, and is a common technique of artists and graphic designers. For example, in a survey of over two hundred paintings taken from the Louvre, the Prado, and the Norton Simon Museums, more than 75 percent were lit from the top left. Top-left lighting is also commonly used in the design of icons and controls in computer software interfaces.[3]

The top-down lighting bias plays a significant role in the interpretation of depth and naturalness, and can be manipulated in a variety of ways by designers. Use a single top-left light source when depicting natural-looking or functional objects or environments. Explore bottom-up light sources when depicting unnatural-looking or foreboding objects or environments. Use the level of contrast between light and dark areas to vary the appearance of depth.

See also Figure-Ground Relationship, Iconic Representation, and Three-Dimensional Projection.

[1] Also known as *top-lighting preference* and *lit-from-above assumption*.

[2] See "Perception of Shape from Shading," Nature, 1988, vol. 331, p. 163–166; and "Perceiving Shape from Shading," *Scientific American*, vol. 256, p. 76–83, both by Vilayanur S. Ramachandran.

[3] "Where Is the Sun?" by Jennifer Sun and Pietro Perona, *Nature Neuroscience*, 1998, vol. 1(3), p. 183–184.

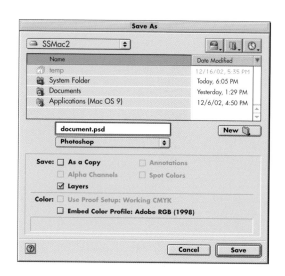

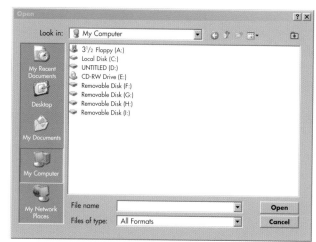

Graphical user interfaces generally use top-left lighting to imply dimensionality of windows and controls.

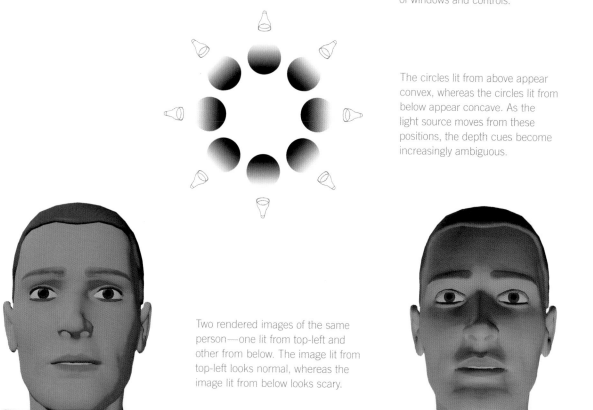

The circles lit from above appear convex, whereas the circles lit from below appear concave. As the light source moves from these positions, the depth cues become increasingly ambiguous.

Two rendered images of the same person—one lit from top-left and other from below. The image lit from top-left looks normal, whereas the image lit from below looks scary.

Uncertainty Principle

The act of measuring certain sensitive variables in a system can alter them, and confound the accuracy of the measurement.

This principle is based on Heisenberg's uncertainty principle in physics. Heisenberg's uncertainty principle states that both the position and momentum of an atomic particle cannot be known because the simple act of measuring either one of them affects the other. Similarly, the general uncertainty principle states that the act of measuring sensitive variables in any system can alter them, and confound the accuracy of the measurement. For example, a common method of measuring computer performance is event logging: each event that is performed by the computer is recorded. Event logging increases the visibility of what the computer is doing and how it is performing, but it also consumes computing resources, which interferes with the performance being measured.

The uncertainty introduced by a measure is a function of the sensitivity of variables in a system, and the invasiveness of the measure. *Sensitivity* refers to the ease with which a variable in a system is altered by the measure. *Invasiveness* refers to the amount of interference introduced by the measure. Generally, the invasiveness of the measure should be inversely related to the sensitivity of the variable measured; the more sensitive the variable, the less invasive the measure. For example, asking people what they think about a set of new product features is a highly invasive measure that can yield inaccurate results. By contrast, inconspicuously observing the way people interact with the features is a minimally invasive measure, and will yield more reliable results.

In cases where highly invasive measures are used over long periods of time, it is common for systems to become permanently altered in order to adapt to the disruption of the measure. For example, the goal of standardized testing is to measure student knowledge and predict achievement. However, the high stakes associated with these tests change the system being measured: high stress levels cause many students to perform poorly; schools focus on teaching the test to give their students an advantage; students seek training on how to become *test wise* and answer questions correctly without really knowing the answers; and so on. The validity of the testing is thus compromised, and the invasiveness of the measure fundamentally changes the focus of the system from learning to test-preparation.

Use low-invasive measures whenever possible. Avoid high-invasive measures; they yield questionable results, reduce system efficiency, and can result in the system adapting to the measures. Consider using natural system indicators of performance when possible (e.g., number of widgets produced), rather than measures that will consume resources and introduce interference (e.g., employee log of hours worked).

See also Cost-Benefit, Expectation Effects, Feedback Loop, Framing, and Signal-to-Noise Ratio.

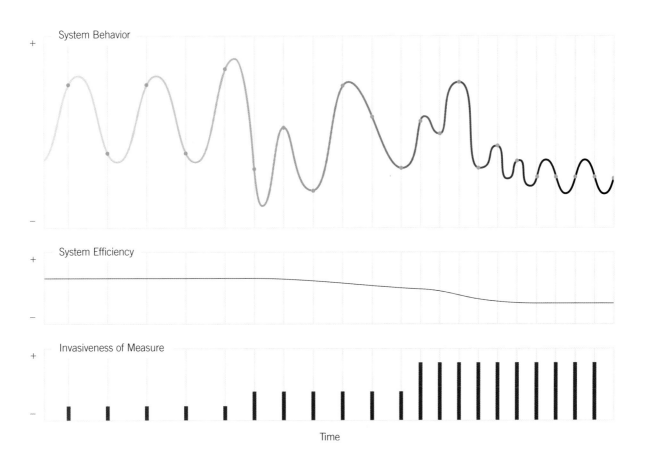

System Behavior

System Efficiency

Invasiveness of Measure

Time

There is an inverse relationship
between the invasiveness and the
accuracy of system measures.
The more invasive the techniques
to measure a phenomenon, the less
accurate the measurements. In
extreme cases, invasive measures
can so severely disrupt a system
that it will alter its goal to serve the
measure, making measurement
meaningless. System efficiency also
suffers from invasive measurement
techniques, since system resources
must be applied increasingly to
accommodate the measurement.

Uniform Connectedness

Elements that are connected by uniform visual properties, such as color, are perceived to be more related than elements that are not connected.

The principle of uniform connectedness is the most recent addition to the principles referred to as *Gestalt principles of perception*. It asserts that elements connected to one another by uniform visual properties are perceived as a single group or chunk and are interpreted as being more related than elements that are not connected. For example, a simple matrix composed of dots is perceived as columns when common regions or lines connect the dots vertically, and is perceived as rows when common regions or lines connect the dots horizontally.[1]

There are two basic strategies for applying uniform connectedness in a design: common regions and connecting lines. Common regions are formed when edges come together and bound a visual area, grouping the elements within the region. This technique is often used to group elements in software and buttons on television remote controls. Connecting lines are formed when an explicit line joins elements, grouping the connected elements. This technique is often used to connect elements that are not otherwise obviously grouped (e.g., not located closely together) or to imply a sequence.

Uniform connectedness will generally overpower the other Gestalt principles. In a design where uniform connectedness is at odds with proximity or similarity, the elements that are uniformly connected will appear more related than either the proximal or similar elements. This makes uniform connectedness especially useful when correcting poorly designed configurations that would otherwise be difficult to modify. For example, the location of controls on a control panel is generally not easily modified, but a particular set of controls can be grouped by connecting them in a common region using paint or overlays. In this case, the uniform connectedness resulting from the common region will overwhelm and correct the poor control positions.

Use uniform connectedness to visually connect or group elements in a design. Employ common regions to group text elements and clusters of control elements, and connecting lines to group individual elements and imply sequence. Consider this principle when correcting poorly designed control and display configurations.

See also Chunking, Figure-Ground Relationship, and Good Continuation.

[1] The seminal work on uniform connectedness is "Rethinking Perceptual Organization: The Role of Uniform Connectedness" by Stephen Palmer and Irvin Rock, 1994, *Psychonomic Bulletin & Review*, vol. 1, p. 29–55.

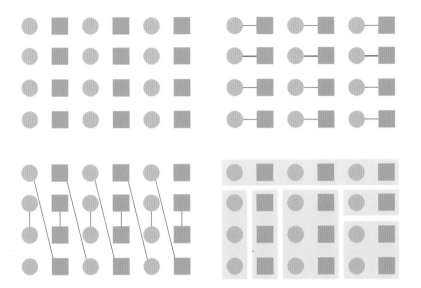

The use of common regions and connecting lines is a powerful means of grouping elements and overwhelming competing cues like proximity and similarity.

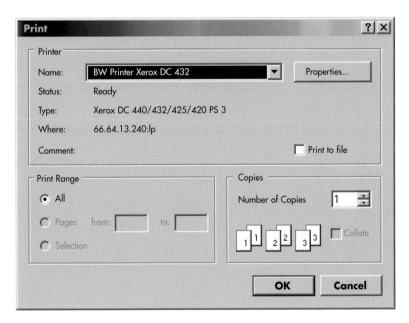

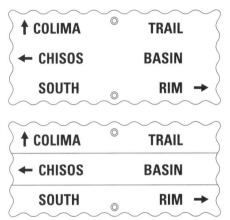

Common regions are frequently used in software interfaces to group related controls.

The proximity between unrelated words (e.g., *Chisos* and *South*) on this rendering of a sign at Big Bend National Park lends itself to misinterpretation. Grouping the related words in a common region would be a simple way to correct the sign.

Visibility

The usability of a system is improved when its status and methods of use are clearly visible.

According to the principle of visibility, systems are more usable when they clearly indicate their status, the possible actions that can be performed, and the consequences of the actions once performed. For example, a red light could be used to indicate whether or not a device is receiving power; illuminated controls could be used to indicate controls that are currently available; and distinct auditory and tactile feedback could be used to acknowledge that actions have been performed and completed. The principle of visibility is based on the fact that people are better at recognizing solutions when selecting from a set of options, than recalling solutions from memory. When it comes to the design of complex systems, the principle of visibility is perhaps the most important and most violated principle of design.[1]

To incorporate visibility into a complex system, one must consider the number of conditions, number of options per condition and number of outcomes—the combinations can be overwhelming. This leads many designers to apply a type of kitchen-sink visibility—i.e., they try to make everything visible all of the time. This approach may seem desirable, but it actually makes the relevant information and controls more difficult to access due to an overload of information.[2]

Hierarchical organization and context sensitivity are good solutions for managing complexity while preserving visibility. Hierarchical organization puts controls and information into logical categories, and then hides them within a parent control, such as a software menu. The category names remain visible, but the controls and information remain concealed until the parent control is activated. Context sensitivity reveals and conceals controls and information based on different system contexts. Relevant controls and information for a particular context are made highly visible, and irrelevant controls (e.g., unavailable functions), are minimized or hidden.

Visible controls and information serve as reminders for what is and is not possible. Design systems that clearly indicate the system status, the possible actions that can be performed, and the consequences of the actions performed. Immediately acknowledge user actions with clear feedback. Avoid kitchen-sink visibility. Make the degree of visibility of controls and information correspond to their relevance. Use hierarchical organization and context sensitivity to minimize complexity and maximize visibility.

See also Affordance, Mapping, Mental Model, Modularity, Progressive Disclosure, and Recognition Over Recall.

[1] The seminal work on visibility is *The Design of Everyday Things* by Donald Norman, Doubleday, 1990.

[2] The enormity of the number of visibility conditions is why visibility is among the most violated of the design principles—it is, quite simply, difficult to accommodate all of the possibilities of complex systems.

Three Mile Island Unit 2
Harrisburg, Pennsylvania
March 28, 1979, 4:00 A.M.

Visibility of complex systems is essential for problem solving—especially in times of stress. An analysis of key events of the TMI accident reveals a number of blind spots in the system that made understanding and solving the problems exceedingly difficult.

To further complicate matters, alarms were blaring, lights were flashing, and critical system feedback was routed to a printer that could only print 15 lines a minute—status information was more than an hour behind for much of the crisis.

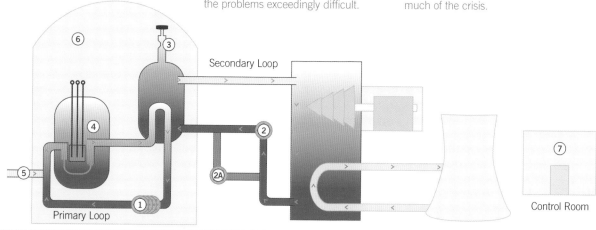

TIME	PLACE	EVENT
00:00:00	②	Coolant pumps in the secondary loop malfunction and shut down.
00:00:02		Temperature and pressure in the primary loop increase.
00:00:03	③	The pressure release valve (PORV) opens automatically to lower the pressure.
00:00:04	②A	Backup pumps automatically turn on.
	②A ⑦	**Operators do not know that the backup pumps are disconnected.**
00:00:09	④	The control rods are lowered to slow the nuclear chain reaction and reduce the temperature.
00:00:11	③ ⑦	The PORV light goes out in the control room, indicating that the PORV closed.
	③ ⑦	**Operators cannot see that the PORV is stuck open. Steam and water is released through the PORV.**
00:02:00	⑤	Emergency water is automatically injected into the primary loop to keep the water at a safe level.
00:04:30	⑤ ⑦	Instruments in the control room indicate that water level in the primary loop is rising. Operators shut down the emergency water injection.
	③ ⑦	**Operators cannot see that the water level in the primary loop is actually dropping. Steam and water continue to be released through the PORV.**
00:08:00	②A ⑦	An operator notices that the backup pumps are not working. He connects the pumps and they begin operating normally.
01:20:00	① ⑦	Pumps in the primary loop vibrate violently because of steam in the line. Two of four pumps are shut down.
01:40:00	①	The other two pumps shut down. Temperature and pressure in the primary loop continue to rise.
02:15:00	③ ④	The water level drops below the core. Radioactive gas is released through the PORV.
02:20:00	③ ⑦	An operator notices that the temperature at the PORV is high. He stops the leak by shutting a PORV backup valve.
	⑦	**Operators still cannot see that the water level in the primary loop is actually dropping.**
02:45:00		Radiation alarms sound and a site emergency is declared. The level of radioactivity in the primary loop is over 300 times the normal level.
07:30:00	③ ⑤ ⑦	Operators pump water into the primary loop, but cannot bring the pressure down. They open the backup valve to the PORV to lower pressure.
09:00:00	⑥	An explosion occurs in the containment structure.
	⑦	**Operators cannot see that an explosion occurred. They attribute the noise and instrument readings to an electrical malfunction.**
15:00:00	①	The pumps in the primary loop are reactivated. Temperatures decline and the pressure lowers. Disaster is averted—except, of course, for the leaking radiation.

von Restorff Effect

A phenomenon of memory in which noticeably different things are more likely to be recalled than common things.[1]

The von Restorff effect is the increased likelihood of remembering unique or distinctive events or objects versus those that are common. The von Restorff effect is primarily the result of the increased attention given to the distinctive items in a set, where a set may be a list of words, a number of objects, a sequence of events, or the names and faces of people. The von Restorff effect occurs when there is a *difference in context* (i.e., a stimulus is different from surrounding stimuli) or a *difference in experience* (i.e., a stimulus is different from experiences in memory).[2]

Differences in context occur when something is noticeably different from other things in the same set or context. For example, in trying to recall a list of characters such as *EZQL4PMBI*, people will have heightened recall for the *4* because it is the only number in the sequence—compare the relative difficulty of recall of the *4* to the *T* in a similar list, *EZQLTPMBI*. The difference between the *4* and the text characters makes the *4* more memorable than the *T*. Differences in context of this type explain why unique brands, distinctive packaging, and unusual advertising campaigns are used to promote brand recognition and product sales—i.e., difference attracts attention and is better remembered.

Differences in experience occur when something is noticeably different from past experience. For example, people often remember major events in their life, such as their first day of college or their first day at a new job. Differences in experience also apply to things like atypical words and faces. Unique words and faces are better remembered than typical words and faces.[3]

Take advantage of the von Restorff effect by highlighting key elements in a presentation or design (e.g., bold text). If everything is highlighted, then nothing is highlighted, so apply the technique sparingly. Since recall for the middle items in a list or sequence is weaker than items at the beginning or end of a list, consider using the von Restorff effect to boost recall for the middle items. Unusual words, sentence constructions, and images are better remembered than their more typical counterparts, and should be considered to improve interestingness and recall.

See also Highlighting, Serial Position Effects, and Threat Detection.

[1] Also known as the *isolation effect* and *novelty effect*.

[2] The seminal work on the von Restorff effect is "Analyse von Vorgangen in Spurenfeld. I. Über die Wirkung von Bereichsbildung im Spurenfeld" [Analysis of Processes in the Memory Trace: On the Effect of Region-Formation on the Memory Trace] by Hedwig von Restorff, *Psychologische Forschung*, 1933, vol. 18, p. 299–342.

[3] Unusual words with unusual spellings are found in abundance in the Harry Potter books of J. K. Rowling, and are among the frequently cited reasons for their popularity with children.

Items in the middle of a list or a sequence are harder to remember than items at the beginning or end. However, the middle items can be made more memorable if they are different from other items in the set.

Word List
milk
eggs
bread
lettuce
butter
flour
ostrich
orangutan
penguin
cheese
sugar
ice cream
oranges
apples
coffee

The unique paint schemes on certain Southwest Airlines planes are very distinct and memorable. The paint schemes differentiate Southwest Airlines from their competitors, promote vacation destinations and partners, and reinforce their reputation as a fun, people-centered airline. This is a photograph of the Shamu One, a Southwest Airlines Boeing 737.

The Chick-fil-A billboards use a combination of dimensionality and humor to attract attention and increase memorability. The billboards effectively command attention in visually noisy environments, clearly and intelligently promote the Chick-fil-A brand, and are quickly read and understood. As billboard design goes, it does not get much better.

Waist-to-Hip Ratio

A preference for a particular ratio of waist size to hip size in men and women.

The waist-to-hip ratio is a primary factor for determining attractiveness for men and women. It is calculated by dividing the circumference of the waist (narrowest portion of the midsection) by the circumference of the hips (area of greatest protrusion around the buttocks). Men prefer women with a waist-to-hip ratio between .67 and .80. Women prefer men with a waist-to-hip ratio between 0.85 and 0.95.[1]

The waist-to-hip ratio is primarily a function of testosterone and estrogen levels, and their effect on fat distribution in the body. High estrogen levels result in low waist-to-hip ratios, and high testosterone levels result in high waist-to-hip ratios. Human mate selection preferences likely evolved to favor visible indicators of these hormone levels (i.e., waist-to-hip ratios), as they are reasonably indicative of health and reproductive potential.[2]

For men, attraction is primarily a function of physical appearance. Women who are underweight or overweight are generally perceived as less attractive, but in all cases women with waist-to-hip ratios approximating 0.70 are perceived as the most attractive for their respective weight group. For women, attraction is a function of both physical appearance and financial status. Financial status is biologically important because it ensures a woman of security and status for herself and her children. However, as women become increasingly independent with resources of their own, the strength of financial status as a factor in attraction diminishes. Similarly, women of modest resources may be attracted to men of low financial status when their physical characteristics indicate strong male features like dominance and masculinity (e.g., tall stature), but men with both high waist-to-hip ratios and high financial status are perceived as the most desirable.

The waist-to-hip ratio has design implications for the depiction of the human form. When the presentation of attractive women is a key element of a design, use renderings or images of women with waist-to-hip ratios of approximately 0.70. When the presentation of attractive men is a key element of a design, use renderings or images of men with waist-to-hip ratios of approximately 0.90, strong male features, and visible indicators of wealth or status (e.g., expensive clothing).

See also Attractiveness Bias, Baby-Face Bias, and Golden Ratio.

[1] The seminal work on the waist-to-hip ratio is "Adaptive Significance of Female Physical Attractiveness: Role of Waist-to-Hip Ratio," *Journal of Personality and Social Psychology*, 1993, vol. 65, p. 293–307; and "Female Judgment of Male Attractiveness and Desirability for Relationships: Role of Waist-to-Hip Ratio and Financial Status," *Journal of Personality and Social Psychology*, 1995, vol. 69, p. 1089–1101, both by Devendra Singh.

[2] While preferences for particular features like body weight or breast size have changed over time, the preferred waist-to-hip ratios have remained stable. For example, in analyzing the measurements of *Playboy* centerfolds since the 1950s and Miss America winners since the 1920s, researchers discovered that the waist-to-hip ratios remained between 0.68 and 0.72 despite a downward trend in body weight.

When asked to select the most attractive figures from renderings of men and women of varying weights and body types, people favored *male C* and *female A*, corresponding to waist-to-hip ratios of 0.90 and 0.70, respectively.

The world famous Adel Rootstein mannequins have changed to match the ideal look and body type of men and women for over five decades (1960s - 2000s). The waist-to-hip ratios of the mannequins, however, have not changed—they have remained constant at around 0.90 for men, and 0.70 for women.

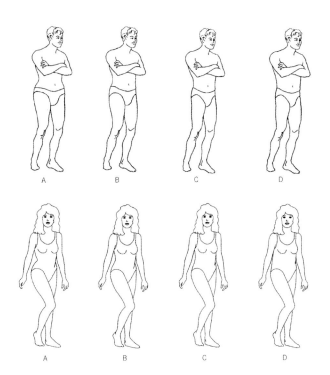

Wayfinding

The process of using spatial and environmental information to navigate to a destination.[1]

Whether navigating a college campus, the wilds of a forest, or a Web site, the basic process of wayfinding involves the same four stages: Orientation, Route Decision, Route Monitoring, and Destination Recognition.[2]

Orientation refers to determining one's location relative to nearby objects and the destination. To improve orientation, divide a space into distinct small parts, using landmarks and signage to create unique subspaces. Landmarks provide strong orientation cues, and provide locations with memorable identities. Signage is one of the easiest ways to tell a person where they are and where they can go.

Route Decision refers to choosing a route to get to the destination. To improve route decision-making, minimize the number of navigational choices, and provide signs or prompts at decision points. People prefer shorter routes to longer routes (even if the shorter route is more complex), so indicate the shortest route to a destination. Simple routes can be followed most efficiently with the use of clear narrative directions or signs. Maps provide more robust mental representations of the space, and are superior to other strategies when the space is very large, complex, or poorly designed. This is especially true in times of stress, where the wayfinding may need to be adaptive (e.g., escaping a burning building).[3]

Route Monitoring refers to monitoring the chosen route to confirm that it is leading to the destination. To improve route monitoring, connect locations with paths that have clear beginnings, middles, and ends. The paths should enable a person to easily gauge their progress along their lengths using clear lines of sight to the next location, or signage indicating relative location. In cases where paths are particularly lengthy or the traffic in them slow moving, consider augmenting the sight lines with visual lures, such as pictures, to help pull people through. *Breadcrumbs*—visual cues highlighting the path taken—can aid route monitoring, particularly when a wayfinding mistake has been made and backtracking is necessary.

Destination Recognition refers to recognizing the destination. To improve destination recognition, enclose destinations such that they form dead-ends, or use barriers to disrupt the flow of movement through the space. Give destinations clear and consistent identities.

See also Errors, Mental Model, and Progressive Disclosure.

[1] The seminal work on wayfinding is *The Image of the City* by Kevin Lynch, MIT Press, 1960.

[2] "Cognitive Maps and Spatial Behavior" by Roger M. Downs and David Stea, in *Image and Environment*, Aldine Publishing Company, 1973, p. 8–26.

[3] See, for example, "Wayfinding by Newcomers in a Complex Building" by Darrell L. Butler, April L. Acquino, Alicia A. Hissong, and Pamela A. Scott, *Human Factors*, 1993, vol. 35(1), p. 159–173.

Map Key

→ Recommended path

🅣 Aetna Tram and Rest Stop
(seasonal)

💲 ATM

⏣ Drinking fountain

✚ First aid

🎁 Gift shops

🥤 PEPSI & snacks

🍴 Restaurant

🚻 Restrooms

☎ Telephone

PITTSBURGH ZOO
& PPG AQUARIUM

3 Tropical Forest

The Safari Plaza

🚻 Safari Grille/Ice Cream

🍴 Safari Pizza/Fries

5 Bears

Elephant House

4 Cheetah Valley

Northern Shores

6 PPG Aquarium

2 African Savanna

7 Niches of the World

1 Asian Forest

8 Kids Kingdom

Savanna Stop

Safari Amphitheater

Wilderness Walkway

Beaver Lodge

The Village

Village Picnic Pavilion

🍴 Village Restaurant

Ride Tickets

Research Station

Security

Carousel

Kids Kingdom Picnic Pavilion

Garden Tent

Log Ride

Safari Cars

Safari Wheels

Information

Ride Tickets

CoGo's Sumatran Express

Bayer Science Education
Amphitheater

9 Discovery Pavilion

Education Complex

Visitor Services

Admin. offices

HIGHMARK First Aid Station

🅣 Entrance Gate

Parking Lot

N

🍴 Animal
Connections

The wayfinding design of the
Pittsburgh Zoo and PPG Aquarium is
divided into unique subspaces based
on the type of animal and environment.
Navigational choices are minimal
and destinations are clearly marked
by signage and dead ends. The visitor

map further aids wayfinding by
featuring visible and recognizable
landmarks, clear and consistent
labeling of important locations and
subspaces, and flow lines to assist
in route decisionmaking.

Weakest Link

The use of a weak element that will fail in order to protect other elements in the system from damage.

It is said that a chain is only as strong as its weakest link. This suggests that the weakest link in a chain is also the least valuable and most expendable link—a liability to the system that should be reinforced, replaced, or removed. However, the weakest element in a system can be used to protect other more important elements, essentially making the weakest link one of the most important elements in the system. For example, electrical circuits are protected by fuses, which are designed to fail so that a power surge doesn't damage the circuit. The fuse is the weakest link in the system. As such, the fuse is also the most valuable link in the system.

The weakest link in a system can function in one of two ways: it can fail and passively minimize damage, or it can fail and activate additional systems that actively minimize damage. An example of a passive design is the use of fuses in electrical circuits as described above. An example of an active design is the use of automatic sprinklers in a building. Sprinkler systems are typically activated by components that fail (e.g., liquid in a glass cell that expands to break the glass when heated), which then activate the release of the water.

Applying the weakest link principle involves several steps: identify a failure condition; identify or define the weakest link in the system for that failure condition; further weaken the weakest link and strengthen the other links as necessary to address the failure condition; and ensure that the weakest link will only fail under the appropriate, predefined failure conditions. The weakest link principle is limited in application to systems in which a particular failure condition affects multiple elements in the system. Systems with decentralized and disconnected elements cannot benefit from the principle since the links in the *chain* are not connected.

The weakest link in a system exists by design or by default—either way, it is always present. Therefore, consider the weakest link principle when designing systems in which failures affect multiple elements. Use the weakest link to shut down the system or activate other protective systems. Perform adequate testing to ensure that only specified failure conditions cause the weakest link to fail. Further weaken the weakest element and harden other elements as needed to ensure the proper failure response.

See also Factor of Safety, Modularity, and Structural Forms.

Crumple Zone   Passenger Shell   Crumple Zone

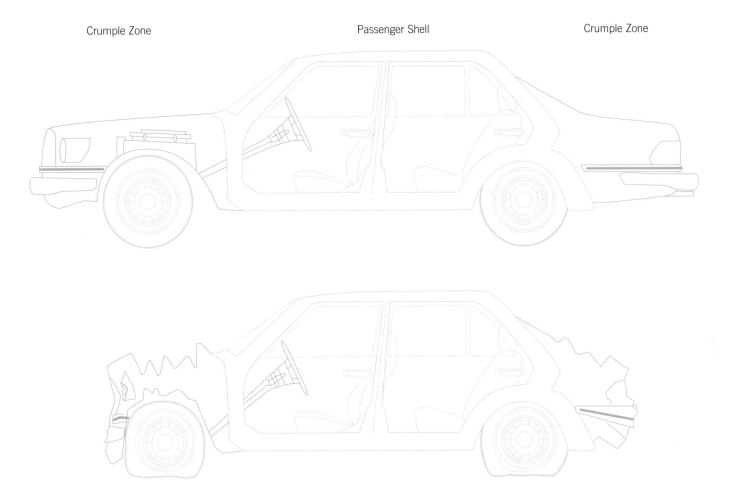

Crumple zones are one of the most significant automobile safety innovations of the 20th century. The front and rear sections of a vehicle are weakened to easily crumple in a collision, reducing the impact energy transferred to the passenger shell. The passenger shell is reinforced to better protect occupants. The total system is designed to sacrifice less important elements for the most important element in the system—the people in the vehicle.

Index

Credits

Accessibility
For more information about accessible design, please visit the Center for Universal Design at www.design.ncsu.edu/cud. Special thanks to Sally Haile for her assistance.

Aesthetic-Usability Effect
Photographs of phones courtesy of Nokia. TiVo screen shots © 2002 TiVo Inc. All rights reserved.

Affordance
Photograph of Segway courtesy of Segway, LLC. Photograph of teakettle and peeler courtesy of OXO International.

Archetypes
Images courtesy of Sue Weidemann Brill. Design concepts by Michael Brill, illustrations by Safdar Abidi. Other team members involved in the project included Dieter G. Ast, Ward H. Goodenough, Maureen Kaplan, Frederick J. Newmeyer, and Woodruff Sullivan. Michael Brill passed away unexpectedly on July 26, 2002, during the development of this book. The design community is poorer for his absence. For more information about Michael Brill's work, please visit www.bosti.com.

Attractiveness Bias
Photographs of Kennedy and Nixon © Bettman/Corbis.

Baby-Face Bias
Photograph of Teletubbies © 1996-2003 Ragdoll Ltd. Used with permission. All rights reserved.

Chunking
Screen shot of e-learning course courtesy of EduNeering, Inc.

Classical Conditioning
Poster courtesy of Texas Department of Transportation. Photograph by Rob Buck. Advertising campaign by Sherry Matthews Advocacy Marketing. For more information about Jacqueline's story and recovery progress, please visit www.helpjacqui.com.

Cognitive Dissonance
Image of AOL CD © 2002 America Online, Inc. All rights reserved.

Consistency
Photographs courtesy of Bob Evans Farms. Special thanks to Jeff Tenut of DiscoverLink for his assistance.

Constraint
The Apple iPod is a trademark of Apple Computer, Inc. All rights reserved.

Control
Macromedia Flash is a trademark of Macromedia, Inc. All rights reserved.

Depth of Processing
Screen shot of e-learning course courtesy of EduNeering, Inc.

Entry Point
Photographs of WSJ courtesy of Dow Jones & Company. Special thanks to Mario Garcia of Garcia Media for his assistance.

Exposure Effect
Posters courtesy of Ota Nepily, Studio Gappo, Brno, Czech Republic. The posters on this page and similar works are available for purchase at www.poster. wz.cz. Special thanks to Petr Kuca for his assistance.

Forgiveness
Photograph of parachuting plane courtesy of Ballistic Recovery Systems, Inc. Screenshot of history palette taken from Adobe Photoshop. Adobe Photoshop is a registered trademark of Adobe Systems, Inc. All rights reserved.

Form Follows Function
Photographs of HUMMER H2 taken by Tim Simmons Photography for Modernista!, Ltd. Photographs of HUMMER H1 taken by Stuart Hamilton Photography for Modernista!, Ltd. HUMVEE images are courtesy of General Motors Corp. and American General Corp. Photographs of HUMMER courtesy of 2002 General Motors Corporation. Used with permission of HUMMER and General Motors.

Framing
Advertisements courtesy of the Ohio State University Department of History.

Golden Ratio
The Apple iPod is a registered trademark of Apple Computer, Inc.

Gutenberg Diagram
Photographs of WSJ courtesy of Dow Jones & Company. Special thanks to Mario Garcia of Garcia Media for his assistance.

Immersion
Photographs of the R.M.S. Titanic exhibit courtesy of Clear Channel Communications.

Law of Prägnanz
Photographs of Mars' face courtesy of NASA.

Mapping
Photograph of Segway HT courtesy of Segway, LLC.

Mimicry
Photograph of Sony AIBO courtesy of Sony Electronics Inc.

Ockham's Razor
Photograph of cello courtesy of Yamaha Corporation of America. Photograph of Taburet stool courtesy of Design Within Reach.

Operant Conditioning
Rendered creatures from Black & White © Lionhead Studios.

Readability
Fry's Readability Graph reproduced with permission from The McGraw-Hill Companies.

Rule of Thirds
Photographs of Ali vs. Liston and Ali vs. Frasier © Bettman/Corbis.

Satisficing
Photographs courtesy of NASA.

Savanna Preference
Photograph of Teletubbies © 1996-2003 Ragdoll Ltd. Used with permission. All rights reserved.

Self-Similarity
M.C. Escher's *Smaller and Smaller* © 2002 Cordon Art–Baarn, Holland. All rights reserved. Photomosaic by Robert Silvers/Runaway Technology Inc. For more information about the work of Robert Silvers, please visit www.photomosaic.com.

Storytelling
Photographs of Civil Rights Memorial courtesy of Southern Poverty Law Center. Photographs by John O'Hagan. Designed by Maya Lin.

Structural Forms
Photographs of RDFW courtesy of Geocell Systems. Pod photograph courtesy of Sanford Ponder, Icosa Village, Inc.

Threat Detection
Photograph of billboard courtesy of University of Houston. Photograph by Pam Francis Photography.

Three-Dimensional Projection
Screenshots of Black & White © Lionhead Studios.

Top-Down Lighting Bias
Rendered man images courtesy of Gerry Manacsa.

von Restorff Effect
Photographs of billboards courtesy of Chick-fil-A, Inc. Photographs of Shamu One courtesy of Southwest Airlines and SeaWorld–San Antonio. Photograph by Bob French.

Waist-to-Hip Ratio
Photograph of mannequins courtesy of Adel Rootstein, Inc. Drawn images reproduced with permission from Devendra Singh.

Wayfinding
Map courtesy of Pittsburgh Zoo and PPG Aquarium. Illustration by David Klug.

Acknowledgments

The authors would like to thank a number of people and organizations that contributed to this work. First, we would like to thank the many contributors whose works are featured, and ask that readers review the credits section to learn more about these very talented individuals and companies. Second, we would like to thank the wonderful people at Rockport Publishers for their encouragement, support, and professionalism. Finally, we would like to thank a number of individuals on a personal level for their support and involvement in the development of this book. These include Wendy Adair, Peggy Adams, Sue Weidemann Brill, Robert Delamontagne, Kristin Ellison, Mario Garcia, Chris Jensen, Melanie Jones, Petr Kuca, Janet Lea, David Learned, Gerry Manacsa, Jacqueline Saburido, Michael Schaner, Paul Selvaggio, Robert Silvers, Devendra Singh, Jeff Tenut, Carole Thomson, and Aaron Warren.

About the Authors

William Lidwell is a partner and chief research and development officer at the Applied Management Sciences Institute. Kritina Holden is a lead usability engineer at BMC Software. Jill Butler is the founder and president of Stuff Creators Design Studio. The authors live in Houston, Texas.